Dedicated to my wife Gloria

Preface to the Second Edition

This year marks the twenty-fifth anniversary of the American College of Surgeons' Advanced Trauma Life Support Course for physicians. The course is now widely taught around the world. The principles of trauma care delineated in Part I. of this book are derived from the ATLS course.

The response to the first edition of *Body Trauma* was remarkable. With over twenty thousand copies in print, I sensed that the need for this sort of information was only partly met. Fortunately, Lynn Price at Behler Publications agreed with me. New material in this edition includes a discussion of shock states and new approaches to the very sick trauma patient. The latter includes unique ways to improve survival, such as damage control exploratory surgery. I'm often asked about the course of treatment so we've added a typical trauma case at the end of the book.

People continue to get injured by accident and by design. Trauma is still an epidemic. The government is still doing too little to make expert trauma care a nationally available resource. Medical malpractice lawsuits, the early retirement of surgeons, and the training of an inadequate number of general surgeons makes the future of trauma care uncertain. Still, your characters will get hurt and suffer.

You need to know how to get the injuries to sound right on the page.

Foreword

Conflict is the core of all fiction. Without conflict there is no story. When obstacles prevent a character from attaining his or her goals, there is conflict. It is also necessary that the consequences of not attaining the goal be profoundly significant for the character. The threat of death or severe bodily injury is among the most serious and dreadful obstacles a character must face, and therefore creates conflict and tension.

Death is an important part of most fiction. This includes all genres, not just murder mysteries (which are always one of the top-selling genres). But it is not always necessary to kill a character to have conflict. A character sustaining a severe injury can often be more compelling than a dead person when the injury is used wisely and with accurate details. Whereas my book *Cause of Death* in the Writer's Digest Books Howdunit Series discusses death and dying, this book provides vital information on nonfatal wounds and trauma.

If a hunter accidentally shoots himself, can he walk out of the woods to safety, or does he crawl, slowly bleeding to death? How long can he survive, and how much pain and anguish does he experience? Survivors of a plane wreck, a child hit by a car, an old lady attacked by dogs, a ranger struck by lightning, or a farmer crushed beneath his tractor could create great tension and conflict in a story.

In this book, Dr. David Page expertly guides you through such scenarios, shows you how to use proper medical terminology, gives surgical "tips" along the way, and discusses emergency care, all presented in a manner geared specifically for you, the writer. Adding accurate details to such scenes makes the story come to life and draws the reader into the world you have created.

In addition to being an accomplished writer, David Page is also a surgeon and an expert on trauma. Dave is a good friend of mine, and what he won't tell you is that in addition to being a surgeon with a busy practice, he also teaches medical students and surgical residents and has won several Citations for Excellence in Teaching from Tufts University School of Medicine.

This reference book is a must for all writers. Keep it at your desk. You'll use it over and over.

Keith Wilson, M.D.

Acknowledgments

No single mind writes a book. This Second Edition is bolstered by help offered from many sources. I wish to thank my colleagues at Baystate Medical Center, Tufts University School of Medicine's Western Campus in Springfield, Massachusetts. I am especially grateful to Richard B. Wait, MD, PhD, Chairman of the Department of Surgery, for providing me with an opportunity to pursue my second love, teaching surgery, while tolerating my writing distractions. Over the years I've also received encouragement and support from my colleague at Baystate and dear friend, Nicholas P. W. Coe, MD FACS, who is a fine writer as well as a master surgeon.

Thanks to my manuscript readers Linda and Michael Anelli and Bill Yorzyk.

My gratitude goes out to the Stonecoast MFA faculty of the University of Southern Maine. Thanks to former Stonecoast faculty members who have taught me the craft: Dennis Lehane, Tom Perotta, Michael Kimball, and Walter Wetherell. And special thanks to these current faculty members: James Patrick Kelly, Ann Hood, Brad Barkley, Mike White, and David Anthony Durham.

To the home team: David and Amy, Cari and David G. and sweet little Emily Jade. And Kendra and Kayla. And to Gloria, again, because you are my first love.

This Second Edition of *Body Trauma* came to fruition because of the foresight, diligence, and creativity of Behler's Acquisitions Editor Lynn Price who I cannot thank enough. Lynn, you made it happen.

Table of Contents

Introduction

Part I: An Overview of Trauma

Part II: Specific Traumatic Injuries By Organ System

Part III: Unique Traumatic Injuries

Introduction

In literature, as in life, sooner or later everyone becomes injured — accidentally or as a consequence of malice — somewhere in the story. The writer must force characters to face conflict. And that includes creating injuries. Every writer needs to understand how to create authentic traumatic injuries as well as how to deal with their consequences.

The focus of this book is on violent injuries that do not result in death.

Every writer confronted with the dilemma of how severely to hurt a character must understand the consequences of the physical havoc created. Injuries should be realistic, reflect the character of the person inflicting the insult, and be tailored to the needs of the plot. More sophisticated than in the past, today's readers have become avid, critical consumers of media violence. Hence, your story's accidents and injuries and the convalescence they cause must ring true.

As you write what is referred to in this book as an "injury scenario", you must hold the tuning fork of authenticity to your ear. You'll learn to review pertinent anatomy, assess the world of your story — what's there to serve as a weapon and who's present in the scene to use it — and decide what mayhem your tale needs. These are the elements of a trauma prescription.

Whether the genre is mystery-murder, horror, romance, or any of the varieties of mainstream thrillers, or if your story is character-driven, the writer's art hinges on accurately depicting human suffering. Ernest Hemingway insisted it is what the writer leaves out that counts most. The late Gary Provost, in a similar vein, taught his writing students: Less is more. Richard Cohen, in *Writer's Mind*, instructs: Fiction writing should imply there is a great deal more than what has been written.

If using less material is the goal of good writing, why learn so much about inflicting injuries?

In "The Snows of Kilimanjaro," Hemingway never describes the gangrenous leg that plays a central role in the story. He alludes to the offensive smell and the progression of gangrene and even reflects on how it began with an element of neglect on Harry's part. At no point is there an explicit description of the rotting leg.

In Ian Hamilton's biography entitled *In Search of J.D. Salinger*, he describes the author of *The Catcher in the Rye* as he becomes progressively urbane, increasingly accomplished at his craft. Following the publication of Salinger's "A Perfect Day for Bananafish," Hamilton states, "Thanks to *The New Yorker*, he was beginning to learn the pleasures of reader manipulation, of having a sophisticated readership that had been trained in the enjoyment of inconsequential sorrow. He was learning how to leave things out, to flatter and deceive."

In his critique of my first novel manuscript, Dennis Lehane stated, "The authorial voice you want to aspire to is quiet and clean. It's confident. It knows that if it whispers, the reader will lean in to hear, but if it shouts, the reader will leave the room to escape the noise. This is never more true as when it applies to violence and horror."

Herein lies the paradox of fiction writing: You must understand what to include and what to leave out. In order to leave something out of a scene, you need to understand all of the elements that could (but shouldn't) be included.

Authenticity emerges from personal experience, struggle, and then understanding. Certainly, Hemingway had seen his share of war wounds. But most writers have little experience with traumatic injuries. This book describes in detail what you must learn about body impact and the spectrum of potential injuries in order to select what details to include in your scene. Once you understand what's there and how it gets maimed, you'll feel the pain and know what aspects of the injury to describe. The reader's visual imagery is enhanced by the inclusion of the right details. By learning a lot about a particular injury, you may select the most visual elements and write a sparse, fast-paced action scene.

Rather than being anecdotal, this book describes the process of how to create a dramatic injury scene. Included are suggestions on how to incorporate the more complicated material into your story.

No writer can describe, allude to, or choose to ignore something that she doesn't understand. And you can bet the treasury that before the chubby cherub chortles, someone in *your* story is going to get hurt. If it's *your* traumatic scene, you'd better know exactly how it happens.

Body Trauma provides an organized menu of injuries and a suggested method of approach to guide you through the process of creating authentic misery. Using the various examples presented in conjunction with *master injury lists* (a menu of specific injuries) for each body system, you may construct innovative insults and terrible wounds to fit the specific demands of your plot. Not just a mere laundry list of clinical mutilations, this book describes how to create novel impacts, bodily disruptions and agonizing tissue trauma. By identifying where the impact occurs and what it does to the body, you can properly weave the length of the disability into the drama. This is called the *time line* of the injury.

If imaginable, any injury is possible. By using the ideas presented in this book, you'll learn how to finesse the details.

Body Trauma is divided into three distinct parts in order to organize and highlight for easy use what is at times complex material.

Part I provides an overview of trauma as well as some basic concepts about the body. Principles are explained regarding tissue impacts, mechanisms of injury and how the trauma victim is handled in different locations both in and out of the hospital.

Part II is an intense discussion of major trauma, organized by body area. It includes detailed information about head and neck, chest, abdominal and limb trauma. This section represents virtually all types of major injury seen in a busy emergency room by trauma surgeons.

Part III includes unique injuries according to their cause rather than by body region. Some of these forms of damage are quite horrible. Examples from classic and contemporary literature are included in Parts II and III to demonstrate how accomplished authors handled body insults.

At the end of the book there is a discussion of what occurs when an injured person dies and the issue of organ donation arises. Sitting on the cutting edge of high-tech medical care, organ transplantation programs struggle with a national shortage of organs suitable for donation. All seriously injured victims should be considered as potential organ donors. And although not our primary concern in this book, a discussion of the process of making this cherished gift closes our discussion about broken bodies. It's an important topic for fiction writers.

So often in contemporary fiction, as in the movies, our suspension of disbelief is stretched to near rupture by violent body insults sequenced with an implausibly swift recovery. On the other hand, it seems many writers have an intuitive sense of what is biologically correct, and this book is intended to augment that instinct. Not only will you learn how to write your injury scenarios by using this book, but by the end of the book, you should also have become a sophisticated first responder to the injured.

Just as fiction is part of real life, trauma is a glaring real-life epidemic awaiting its place in your fiction. The dilemma for the writer lies in *what* injury to fit into the world of the story.

Most of medicine is common sense. Have fun with the material, and don't panic at the med-speak.

Writing your trauma scene may be the only time *you* can be the doctor. Early in my surgical career, I performed my share of trauma surgery, and many of my personal experiences have insinuated themselves into these pages. My professional life includes a busy surgical practice as well as teaching surgical residents and medical students. As part of my teaching preparation over the years, I have used multiple editions of the American College of Surgeons Committee on Trauma's *Advanced Trauma Life Support For Doctors (ATLS) Student Course*

Manual. I wish to give special thanks to the ACS Committee on Trauma and the Seventh Edition of the Manual; I have used this precious resource for portions of this book.

PART I

An Overview of Trauma

ONE

CONCEPTS AND TERMINOLOGY IN TRAUMA CARE

Injuries occur for a reason.

Before entering the world of trauma, you need to know a few basic terms. If you understand simple mechanisms of injury causation, this part of modern medicine and its funny-sounding verbiage will be easier to grasp. For your story to sound authentic, you need to know what you're talking about.

Trauma refers to the physical wounds and innumerable body insults that result from direct or indirect contact with something in the environment. In the chaotic history of medicine, surgeons became the specialists who assumed the task of managing traumatic wounds, treating terrible numbers of war casualties from the numerous conflicts that seeded every century. With time, weaponry became more sophisticated, more destructive. Nonetheless, even the rock hatchets, spears, darts and arrows of primitive humans were deadly, and the injuries horrible.

Warriors wear scars with pride, and one wonders if physical conflict is our species' norm. In humankind's history, it seems quite possible that intentional wounding has been more frequent than the occurrence of unanticipated trauma. A cursory examination of man's warring history reveals repeated, massive conflicts in which large numbers of warriors became wounded. Many died. But many survived their injuries to fight again. Scientists refer to an animal's (including man's) response to confrontation as the "fight or flight" reaction, the choice presumably determined by recognition of the odds. Man has a poor track record of avoiding the odds of sustaining traumatic injuries.

Traumatic events can thus be *accidental* or *intentional*. Some injuries are more repugnant precisely because the assault is premeditated, an attack designed to hurt another person. But even so-called accidents may be more a matter of inattention and risk taking than of pure chance.

For the writer, the introduction of any form of body damage into a sordid tale increases suspense and introduces an element of uncertainty. Plot possibilities emerge from the doubt born of disaster and from the character's back-story—for example, the compulsion to practice risky behavior. On the other hand, some folks are so preoccupied with problems of daily living they become distracted and are therefore *accident-prone*. In this book, we look at accidents as well as injuries that result from being in a hostile environment.

Why Do Accidents Occur?

For a moment, let's consider real *accidents*. This term implies a traumatic episode occurred that could not have been anticipated and therefore is not the consequence of an expected series of events. The accident produced an unexpected outcome because it occurred suddenly, created alarm, and resulted in injury.

A true accident can't be avoided. Why do accidents occur? Two reasons why accidental events occur are sudden, unexpected changes in:

1. A person
2. The environment

Consider the elements of a typical automobile accident. Available data indicates that most accidents occur on the weekend and at night. Young people who consume alcohol are involved in the majority of car crashes. The *person components* that result in so-called "accidental" automobile mishaps include:

- Inebriation or drug abuse
- Distraction by others in the car
- Excessive speed
- Risky maneuvers, such as passing or bumper hugging
- Falling asleep at the wheel
- Anger, rage, depression, anxiety that cause preoccupation and failure to pay attention to driving chores
- Inadequate driver training
- Visual or motor skill impairment, as in some elderly drivers

Environmental factors also contribute to car crashes and may include one or a combination of the following:

- Poor road construction
- Poor road conditions, e.g., rain, snow, ice or fog
- Excessive traffic
- Lack of familiarity with road
- Abusive drivers, e.g., risky passing behavior or startling another driver with high beams

Defective car parts, such as brakes, windshield wipers, or engine components, may compound these factors. Also, an impact may involve a poorly designed car. Failure to wear a seat belt and failure or absence of an air bag makes the impact all the more dangerous.

Therefore, an accident may be viewed in general terms as an unexpected event that occurs because of the linkage of a series of related factors:

- Distraction (inattention to the task at hand)
- Lack of training with specific equipment
- Lack of motor skills (inferior innate talent)
- Cavalier attitude toward dangerous equipment
- Ignorance about potential dangers with specific equipment
- Poorly maintained equipment
- Effect of aging or disease on person's mobility, reasoning ability and perception

The terms described next are used in the assessment and care of the trauma patient.

Assault includes both physical and verbal attacks on another person. A character's interpersonal relationships and background will contribute to which element is most often employed in relationships. Verbal abuse may be more subtle, frightening and chronic than outright fisticuffs.

Domestic violence, including *elder abuse, child abuse, spouse abuse,* and *rape,* involves the most violent of crimes and produces many of the most despicable injuries. These will be covered in detail in Part III.

Self-mutilation is a fascinating topic that implies a purposeful alteration in self-image. We'll merely nudge this topic in our discussion. What happens to self-image? Why tattoos? Scars?

Mortality refers to death. The mortality rate in a given circumstance means how many people died. It's the death rate for a specific medical procedure or life event.

Morbidity, on the other hand, refers to injury. It's the meat of this book. The accidental event itself has a morbidity rate, as does the surgery performed to fix the broken body. Each event has a potentially poor outcome—things that can go wrong because of uncontrolled trauma or despite controlled surgery.

Some things just happen.

Emergency Management

The events that surround the management of major accidents are divided into the sequential events that are part of trauma care.

Extrication: This is the removal of the victim from the scene. It may involve using the "jaws of life" to get someone out of a car wreck, removing a victim from a mountaintop or a deep ravine or bringing a child up from a well shaft.

Transportation of the patient: Three methods of transportation are available for trauma victims and are dependent upon the distance from site of injury to the nearest available appropriate acute care facility.

1. Ambulance—up to about 50 miles

2. Helicopter—about 50 to 100 miles
3. Fixed wing aircraft—about 100 to 300+ miles

Helicopters and fixed wing aircraft provide rapid transport for victims who are only marginally stable and who must reach expert trauma care for specialty surgical care.

Resuscitation equipment is available in all transport vehicles. The most important principle in patient transport is to deliver the victim quickly and safely to the nearest appropriate hospital. A contingency plan for foul weather is needed.

Dead victims don't enter the Emergency Medical System (EMS) but must be taken to the proper facility as directed by the coroner or medical examiner.

Transfer of Patients: This refers to the transfer of a patient from one trauma center to another of a more sophisticated level (see "Levels of Trauma Care" on page 14). Criteria for considering early transport of the injured victim are summarized in Figure 1. An example of a transfer sheet is included in Figure 2.

The trauma victim's *illness severity* is calculated from vital signs, specific lab tests and other variables. Each patient is assigned what is called the *revised trauma score*. It gives an estimate of survival potential and consists of:

- Respiratory status
- Cardiac status (blood pressure, pulse, etc.)
- Glasgow Coma Score (see Chapter Five)

Not only does this derived number permit the trauma surgeon to predict outcome, it also gives an estimate of the patient's potential for developing major complications.

A paramedic, doctor, or layperson caring for a trauma victim must recognize where in the following sequence they have entered the continuum of trauma management:

- Assess the extent and type of injuries
- Stabilize the victim/patient
- Prepare for definitive treatment or transfer to another hospital

In the paramedic's case, the initial transportation is to the closest local hospital or to a regional trauma center, depending on the circumstances. If a smaller hospital doesn't have surgeons who are able to care for these patients either through close monitoring in the intensive care unit or by operating on them, then the patient must be transferred.

Figure 1 – High-Risk Criteria for
Consideration of Early Transfer

(These guidelines are not intended to be hospital-specific.)

Central Nervous System
- Head injury
  —Penetrating injury or open fracture (with or without cerebrospinal fluid leak)
  —Depressed skull facture
  —Glasgow Coma Scale (GCS) <14 or GCS deterioration
  —Lateralizing signs
- Spinal cord injury
  —Spinal column injury or major vertebral injury

Chest
- Major chest wall injury
- Wide mediastinum or other signs suggesting great vessel injury
- Cardiac injury
- Patients who may require prolonged ventilation

Pelvis
- Unstable pelvic ring disruption
- Unstable pelvic fracture with shock or other evidence of continuing hemorrhage
- Open pelvic injury

Major Extremity Injuries
- Fracture/dislocation with loss of distal pulses
- Open long-bone fractures
- Extremity ischemia

Multiple-System Injury
- Head injury combined with face, chest, abdominal or pelvic injury
- Burns with associated injuries
- Multiple long-bone fractures
- Injury to more than two body regions

Comorbid Factors
- Age >55 years
- Children
- Cardiac or respiratory disease
- Insulin-dependent diabetes, morbid obesity
- Pregnancy
- Immunosuppression

Secondary Deterioration (late Sequelae)
- Mechanical ventilation required
- Sepsis
- Single or multiple organ system failure (deterioration in central nervous, cardiac, pulmonary, hepatic, renal or coagulation systems)
- Major tissue necrosis

Making a decision to transfer a patient occurs as the doctor quickly assesses the patient in the ER trauma room. It's not just a matter of the surgeon's time. It's also a question of the local capabilities and limitations. Will the care of one complicated patient consume most of a limited ICU staff's time?

If the decision is made to transfer a patient, no further work-up (tests such as a CT scan, ultrasound, etc.) should be performed. The goal is to get the patient into the hands of surgeons who can immediately institute the proper care. Delay results in increased mortality. If your doctor character hesitates, fumbles the ball, or acts out of his own ego needs, the victim may die or incur serious disabilities. Your doctor must decide whether an operation should be performed at the smaller hospital prior to transfer to a trauma center to assure the patient's safety.

You may be surprised to learn that some rather serious blunt and penetrating traumatic injuries are managed without surgery. Here's the catch. Let's say your fictional doctor is watching a trauma patient, (instead of transferring the patient to a medical center) monitoring his vital signs and re-checking his clinical examination to determine if the patient is stable or deteriorating. If she's going to do this, she must have the surgical skills and an available operating room - not to mention a full capability blood bank, ICU and other ancillary support personnel - at her disposal if the patient "crashes" (plunges into shock). Your fictional surgeon can't admit, assess, and watch her patient in hopes of a good outcome unless she's ready to perform emergency surgery if "observation" doesn't work.

If someone else died in the accident, the mechanism of injury was probably such that your patient harbors obvious or occult life-threatening injuries as well. Alcohol and drugs may alter a victim's level of consciousness. But the surgeon must assume until proven otherwise that the patient has a significant head injury. A head CT scan must be performed to rule out intracranial bleeding if certain "lateralizing" signs (neurological findings on examination that result from a so-called space occupying lesion, blood clot, for example, in the brain) are present.

The severity of the injury is assessed in the field by a paramedic before the trauma surgeon becomes involved. Field assessment of the degree of injury is determined by the following four factors:

1. Abnormal body functions such as low blood pressure and fast pulse that describe shock or abnormal respirations and neurological findings that suggest a severe head injury
2. Obvious disruption of the victim's anatomy, e.g., traumatic amputation, impalement, gaping chest or belly wound
3. The mechanism of injury—blunt or penetrating, the caliber of the gun, speed of the motorcycle, length of the knife, distance of the fall, etc.
4. Associated illnesses, such as diabetes, hypertension, heart failure, chronic lung disease, or kidney failure

Once the paramedic identifies major life-threatening injuries, he institutes emergency care before moving the victim. The pattern of identifying and treating trauma emergencies is ritualized to avoid mistakes.

Prehospital protocols refer to specific instructions given to paramedics and EMTs as part of their training to assure reproducible and safe care for all trauma victims. These kinds of treatment plans are also available for a variety of medical conditions seen "in the field". The goals of all emergency care protocols are:

- To provide lifesaving care in the field
- To provide comfort to victim
- To transport victim to the appropriate hospital in a timely fashion

The elements of prehospital "cookbook" emergency care plans are taught in a defined order to be followed by every emergency responder in exactly the same way. The concept is to eliminate freelancing and creative thinking in the management of life-threatening emergencies. Anyone who has been responsible for another human who was in the act of dying knows the intense fear that surrounds providing acute care. It's easy to forget what to do for the victim.

Figure 2 – Example of a Transfer Form

A. Patient's name _____
   Address _____
   Age_____ Sex_____ Weight_____
   Next of kin_____
   Address_____
   Phone number (_____) _____

B. History of current injury:
   Time and date of injury:
   Mechanism of injury:
   History of previous conditions, injuries and medications:

C. Condition on admission:
   Blood Pressure_____Pulse_____Temperature_____
   Respiratory rate_____

D. Initial diagnostic impressions:

E. Diagnostic studies:
   1. Laboratory
      a. Complete blood cell count
      b. Urinalysis
      c. Electrolytes
      d. Arterial blood gases
   2. Electrocardiogram
   3. Radiological studies

F. Treatment rendered to patient:
   1. Medications given with amount and time:
   2. Intravenous (IV) fluids with type and amount
   3. Other

G. Status of patient when transferred:

H. Management during transport:

I. Name of physician referring patient:_____
   Phone number (_____) _____

J. Name of physician and hospital receiving patient:

   _____
   _____

Thus, the basic resuscitation scheme used by all EMTs, paramedics, nurses, and physicians is *ABCDE*. This translates into looking for and solving the following acute problems, which, if not reversed, may result in a life-ending tragedy.

- *A* is for *airway*. Assure nothing is blocking free flow of air in the mouth and trachea.
- *B* is for *breathing*. Make certain air exchange is actually occurring.
- *C* is for *circulation*. The heart is beating, pulses are present, and bleeding is stopped.
- *D* is for *disability*. Check the nervous system. Is the victim verbally responding? Are eyes open? Arms moving? Legs?
- *E* is for *exposure*. Take off the victim's clothes, if necessary, and check for other hidden life-threatening injuries.

Triage refers to the sorting out of trauma victims according to the severity of their injuries. This process occurs in the field, in the trauma room, and in the setting of mass casualties. It's crucial to know that half of all trauma victims who will eventually die never reach a hospital. Two-thirds of those who die in spite of acute medical care will expire within the first four hours.

Your "first responder" character should know who to let die at the scene—unless you are purposely creating conflict by having him make the wrong decision or involving him in a dispute with someone else at the scene about triage priorities.

Why do trauma victims die after reaching the hospital? The reasons include:

- Delayed transportation to a trauma care facility
- Improper triage in the field with missed vital injuries
- Inadequate or delayed resuscitation

The paramedic must consider four situations when performing triage in the field:

1. Who to ignore because they are going to make it without attention (minor lacerations, abrasions, etc.)
2. Whom to let die at the scene because no amount of care will reverse their overwhelming injuries (massive head injuries, profound shock from blood loss, etc.)
3. Who has life-threatening injuries that must be reversed immediately at the accident scene (obstructed airway; major ongoing bleeding requiring pressure dressings; head or neck injuries, requiring stabilization, urgent evacuation and hospital treatment; etc.)
4. Who needs care for major injuries that are not life threatening (broken bones, bleeding, uncertain internal injuries, etc.)

Sadly, the sickest victim isn't always the one you pay most attention to when sorting injuries. It's a numbers game and it's tough.

Finally, before a trauma patient is transferred to another facility, it is the original doctor's responsibility to communicate doctor-to-doctor to the receiving surgeon at the Level One medical center. There is no place in a well-executed transfer for relying on ER notes or asking a nurse to call the other hospital. The receiving surgeon will want to know specifics about the patient's status in order to consider what will be needed in terms of interventions when the patient arrives, as well as if there has been a change in the patient's status during transport. The doctor who had the original contact must provide this information.

Levels of Trauma Care

Now we'll discuss in detail the different levels of trauma care available throughout the U.S. and the way various hospitals mesh together to form a regional trauma care system. There are four recognized levels of trauma care expertise—all of which are vital for a smoothly run national system of trauma care delivery.

Level I trauma centers are major urban medical centers, with all surgical specialties available, including a neurosurgeon, plastic surgeon, urologist, cardiac surgeon, orthopedic surgeon, ophthalmologist, ENT surgeon, pediatric surgeon, and hand surgeon. A trauma surgeon is on call in-house (surgical resident) at all times, while intensivists work in multi-specialty critical care units (ICU). There exists an excellent blood bank, laboratory facility and support systems, such as rehabilitation, social services and religious support.

Level II trauma centers are urban community hospitals with most surgical specialties represented. They handle ninety-five percent of all traumas. Level II centers have board-certified general surgeons with trauma experience and many, but not all, support services. More complex cases are referred to Level I centers.

Level III trauma centers are usually rural hospitals. Surgeons aren't on call twenty-four hours a day specifically for trauma, but they are readily available. Most other surgical specialties are available as well. Less complicated cases—for example, patients with single system trauma—may be handled at these facilities.

Level IV trauma centers are rural hospitals or clinics with minimal resources, but they are the only care available for some trauma patients. There may not be a doctor present, so paramedical personnel play a vital role in resuscitating and transporting trauma victims.

The transport of the victim to a big-city Level I super-specialty medical center characterizes a continuum of expertise and opportunity.

Every link in the national trauma system is vital for the effective running of the program. But some victims suffer from only one injury.

Single system trauma involves only one organ system in the impact event. For example, head trauma by itself causes a majority of traumatic deaths and many long-term disabilities. A fractured leg is also single system trauma but carries little potential for prolonged disability and rehabilitation.

Multiple system trauma is seen in auto accidents, falls, and other extreme accidental impacts where deceleration affects any organ that is poorly anchored and not well protected. That is, the aortic arch, spleen, kidney, or intestine may continue to move after the body halts abruptly with collision or contact with the ground. In addition to multiple fractures, internal organs are often torn or ruptured, creating a variety of clinical problems for the surgeon. And because so many impacts occur as different force vectors are applied, it isn't surprising that, at times, injuries go undetected.

Missed injuries just happen. Think about the trauma center setting and the chaotic way victims of serious trauma come into the hospital. It's difficult to know exactly how the accident occurred. At first, there's little information about the event. A number of factors contribute to the failure to diagnose certain conditions:

- Fatigue—late at night, the surgeon has already put in a full day and another awaits and there are no residents to help.
- Poor history—occasionally what happened at the accident scene isn't transmitted to the treating doctors. Also, the history is often given by a belligerent patient who may be further confused by substance abuse, shock, concussion, etc.
- Severe, life-threatening injuries—these injuries may preoccupy the surgeon's initial interaction with the victim.
- Ventilator intubation—patient can't indicate the site of pain.
- Paralysis—patient can't localize pain.
- Examining doctor's inexperience—a physical finding may be missed or misinterpreted, or an x-ray may be misread.
- Breakdown in usual evaluation routine—doctor becomes distracted and omits parts of the physical exam or does not perform an essential x-ray.

While surgeons in the past have been reluctant to acknowledge that injuries were periodically missed, most trauma surgeons in the last few years have elected to "look the issue straight in the eye" rather than attribute omitted diagnoses to the inexperience of new surgeons. All surgeons miss something at some point in their careers.

In one study of trauma victims who underwent autopsy, the incidence of missed diagnosis was thirty-four percent! It is felt that available data suggests only about five percent of missed diagnoses caused death while an additional twenty-three percent of concealed injuries contributed to death. Half of all missed x-ray diagnoses in a Cook County (Chicago) study involved trauma patients. A lot of these patients were victims of inner city war.

Perhaps that sad fact is fitting as, historically, advancements in trauma care have been concentrated in times of conflict. War has educated doctors through the centuries and continued in the modern era to dictate how trauma surgeons care for civilian patients. A brief overview of developments that accompanied modern wars:

- American Civil War—use of antiseptics, amputation, and horse ambulances in the field
- World War I—improved wound care, delayed closure of infected wounds to avoid abscess formation; blood loss related to shock, with intravenous salt solution used to replace lost volume; field ambulances with motors
- World War II—blood transfusions used, rapid evacuation (about two hours), surgical units placed closer to the front lines, colostomy used for traumatic colon injuries
- Korean War—vascular surgery developed for repair of arteries, use of helicopters (evacuation time less than an hour), MASH units developed, kidney failure understood and dialysis developed
- Vietnam War—rapid helicopter evacuation (twenty to thirty minutes from field to hospital); massive IV fluid replacement for shock; realization that respiratory failure is secondary to shock and understanding of resuscitation, leading to new treatment strategies for what became modern critical care medicine

War wounds became better understood through these epic struggles as scientists began to study injury models as well as the effect of various ballistics on tissue. The U.S. Army had special teams in the field evaluating traumatic wounds during the Vietnam era and had research programs involving the study of projectile injuries in animal subjects. Surgical care improved as tissue insults became better understood.

Destructive Impacts

Different types of forces act on human flesh to cause damage and may act simultaneously or concurrently in the same victim. There are four forces that produce destructive impacts in a specific manner.

Impact-Producing Forces

High-velocity versus low-velocity projectiles: Rather than mass, it is the speed (and "tumbling") of a projectile that determines the extent of the damage.

Crush injuries: Soft tissue is squeezed between deep bony structures and whatever is pressing against the skin. The Oklahoma City federal building collapse witnessed many crush injuries. First, damage caused by the direct injury to crushed tissues occurs, followed by the release of toxic inflammatory substances from the area of the crush. "Washed out" into the blood stream when the victim is resuscitated, these toxins may cause lung and kidney failure.

Shear forces: One type of tissue shears against the tissue next to it, often because the first tissue decelerates or stops suddenly and another adjacent tissue keeps in motion. If solid, the organ rips and bleeds, and if hollow, like the bowel, for example, the organ tears and perforates, releasing irritating body fluid.

Cavitation: This may be instantaneous and temporary, or permanent. A temporary cavity forms when tissue is compressed by an external force, creating a hole or tear in the tissue that then re-closes when the force stops. As will be discussed in a moment, the best example is a gunshot wound that leaves a bullet track.

Automobile Accidents

Now, we'll examine the forces that may cause injuries to a person inside an automobile during impact. Serious injury occurs when an object or another body strikes a part of the body. The fascinating part is the variable end results. Why variable? Because the differences in the force applied and the individual's anatomy are just enough to create an unpredictable and, at times, bizarre array of injuries.

Automobile accidents are so common that the mechanisms of injury deserve special mention. In addition to any torque or spinning motions created by the collision of one car with another or with a roadside object, there are three types of impact: frontal, rear, and side.

A *frontal* or *rear impact* stops the car, but the occupants continue to move forward. The driver strikes the steering wheel; the passenger strikes the dash or windshield. Rear impacts snap the neck. Both traumatic events are more severe if the occupants aren't wearing seat belts or if the car doesn't have air bags or neck protection. These devices are designed to blunt the effects of moving inertia, to "cushion" the kinetic energy of the people in the car. Injuries may include:

- Flexion-extension injury to the neck
- Blunt chest trauma

- Compression of intra-abdominal organs with possible rupture
- Blunt facial trauma with fractured facial bones and lacerations, and scalp lacerations
- Skull fracture, brain contusion, laceration, intracranial hemorrhage

Lateral, or side, impact may cause any of the above injuries as well as spinal fractures caused by rotation and compression of the torso or pelvis upon direct contact. Arm and leg fractures may also occur from lateral force. If the car rolls over, anything can happen.

Injury may be related to the restraining device, particularly the seat belt. Let it be said loud and clear that restraints prevent a vastly larger number of injuries than they cause. Three-point seat belts must be used with air bags, as the latter are useless in lateral and rear impacts. Besides, when the air bag deflates, which is immediately after impact, any secondary hits will only be reduced by the seat belt.

Lap seat belts used alone may result in trapped bowel and intestinal rupture as well as flexion spinal cord injury. The use of diagonal belts only may cause neck and chest trauma. Thus, both are needed to protect the automobile occupant from serious harm during impact.

For a moment, consider the basic principles of physics that determine what happens during impact. Newton's first law of motion states that an object will remain in motion in a straight line until acted upon by some external agent or force. The passenger of a car experiences impact when the car stops because his body is in motion as well. Not until the seat belt, air bag or dashboard intervenes does the driver's forward momentum cease. Which restraint or auto part is impacted partially determines the type and degree of injury.

The idea of *acceleration* is that of changing velocity. A body may be induced to move faster or slower or change direction. It accelerates or decelerates. To do so the body must acquire kinetic energy or energy on the run, moving energy, and when that body stops suddenly, all of that kinetic energy must be transferred to something else. If that something else is your character's body, he gets seriously hurt.

Other Destructive Impacts

Falls can be disastrous because of the *acceleration of gravity*, the increase in velocity of a falling body because of its pull by Earth's gravitational forces. Each second during a free fall, the velocity of the falling body increases by thirty-two feet per second. What your character strikes also partially defines the traumatic injury. The results of a fall are determined by:

- The distance of the fall—a fall from a standing position to a tumble into the Grand Canyon.

- The body part first struck when contact with the ground is made—neck, head, arm, etc.
- The nature of the impact point—water, gravel, concrete, grass, shrubs, etc.

Any of the minor or major injuries described in Part II may be the consequence of a fall, and there can be surprises in the degree of trauma resulting from different tumbles. A slip on the ice may result in a ruptured spleen, as I discovered recently in a young patient. And a fall from a cliff may cause only scratches and bruises.

Gunshot wounds are just as unpredictable. The following discussion focuses more on what happens to human flesh because of the peculiarities of ballistics and body structure.

As you can see in Figure 3, bullets don't leave simple wounds. It is the velocity of the bullet that primarily determines the nature and extent of the wound, although this isn't the only factor, as a .45 caliber slug traveling at 850 feet per second will cause more damage than a .22 caliber bullet at 1000 feet per second. Part of the damage is due to the soft lead projectile, which disintegrates and disperses all of its kinetic energy in the flesh. A faster copper jacket bullet may pass through a body structure without causing much harm because a lot of its energy is still in motion after the exit wound. Add a few bone fragments to a disintegrating bullet and now you've got secondary missiles, which cause more damage.

Shock waves are transmitted to the surrounding tissues and cause damage far away from the missile track. Also, the bullet path is not initially narrow, but rather, *cavitation* occurs. This sudden expansion and then collapse of the tissues may suck clothing and other debris into the wound. The entry wound may appear to be small because the skin's normal elasticity partially closes it. These wounds often require extensive surgical debridement, or cleaning, to clear the track of dirt and dead tissue.

Shotgun wounds are quite different from gunshot impacts. Multiple pellets cause a literal chewing up of a specific area, with less body penetration than a single bullet. Massive damage to skin, soft tissue, and vital structures close to the surface occurs. This is particularly true of the heavier duck and goose loads (numbers 2 and 4, BBs).

Figure 3 – Bullet Cavitation

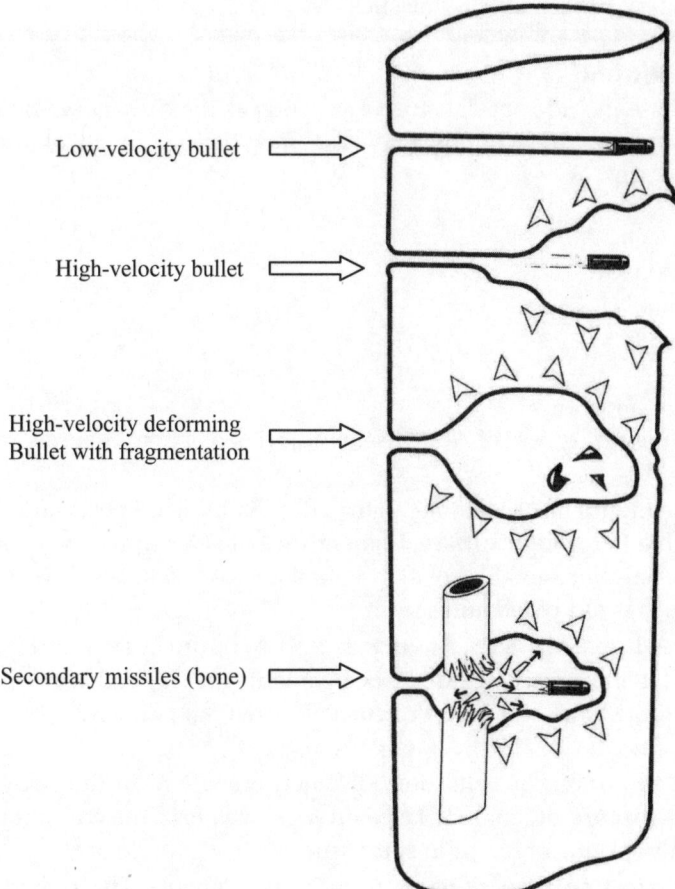

Low-velocity bullet ⟹

High-velocity bullet ⟹

High-velocity deforming
Bullet with fragmentation ⟹

Secondary missiles (bone) ⟹

Wounds in a Trauma Victim

Any tissue in a trauma victim may be injured, and a host of terms are used to describe these injuries. First, we'll describe those injuries that do not involve bone.

Important Facts About a Bullet and the Wound It Causes

- Weight and diameter (caliber) of projectile
- Muzzle velocity

- Design of bullet jacket
- Point of impact (skull, leg, buttocks, etc.)
- Pathway through body (specific tissues encountered)
- Secondary bone fragment missiles

Soft Tissue Wounds

Not only do these include special structures, such as the ears, nose, eyes and genitalia, soft tissue wounds may also include any or all of the following structures:

- Skin
- Fat
- Muscle
- Tendons
- Ligaments
- Nerves
- Arteries and veins

These common types of soft tissue injuries vary in degree of severity:

Abrasion: A superficial "scabbing" injury, like skinning a knee, caused by contact with a flat, rough surface. Sometimes called a "strawberry", it results in a partial-thickness loss of skin with some bleeding and "crust" formation, which is old blood and serum.

Contusion: A bruise or deeper injury caused by a direct strike. Skin, subcutaneous fat and muscle, tendons, or ligaments are trapped between the surface and the bone and become crushed. Swelling, pain and loss of function are common.

Hematoma: A pocket, or collection, of blood anywhere in the body. Caused by the rupture of small or large arteries or veins. The collection may be within a specific organ or in soft tissue, such as muscle or fat.

Avulsion: The tearing away of tissue from its attachments. This may be partial or complete and includes muscle tears, fingernail avulsions or the ripping away of skin from underlying tissue, a so-called "degloving" injury—skin torn away like removing a pair of gloves.

Why does one person suffer major tissue avulsion from direct trauma while another individual develops only an irritating abrasion? Why do some tissues lacerate while others resist trauma? A couple of factors determine how seriously a trauma victim may be injured:

- The elasticity of the impacted tissue—can it stretch or deform and resume its original configuration?
- The speed at which the tissue is loaded—is the arm smacked with a baseball bat at sixty miles per hour or a .44 magnum bullet at 900 feet per second? The tissue can't "escape" the bullet, and therefore

disrupts, whereas with the bat, it is compressed and then assumes its original shape. Load a joint suddenly and the ligaments and tendons tear (ruptured ligaments or torn cartilage) instead of stretch (strain).

Fractures and Dislocations

The force required to break a bone or disrupt a joint may be *direct* or *indirect*. An example of the latter is a fall on an outstretched hand causing dislocation or fracture of the shoulder. Direct force from a fall causes a variety of fractures and dislocations.

A *fracture* is a break in a bone. It may be partial or complete. Different patterns are seen and include:

- Compound fracture—bone fragment projects through the skin causing an open wound.
- Comminuted fracture—several small fragments of broken bone in wound rather than one "clean" break.
- Greenstick fracture—seen in children, a "buckle", or partial break of the cortex of an immature bone.
- Oblique, spiral, transverse fractures—result from different forces exerted on the bone.

A special case occurs with *skull fractures*, which may be *depressed* when the bony table of the skull is pushed below the plane of the normal surrounding bone. Treatment involves elevating the fragment(s) surgically. An *undisplaced* skull fracture may be left alone. Similarly, fractures of the long bones of the arms and legs in good alignment may be splinted or pinned without manipulation or realignment.

Pelvic fractures may be innocent or life threatening. The "rings of bone", or rami, may break in one place, may become disrupted on both sides, or may fracture in two or more locations on the same side. The larger bones of the pelvic bowl may also break with enough impact, and often serious visceral (organ) injuries accompany these pelvic fracture(s). These include ruptured bladder, rectum, or major blood vessels. The most serious problem associated with pelvic fractures is massive, uncontrolled hemorrhage. Torn pelvic veins traveling through bone are controlled by pushing sterile thumbtacks into the sacral bone to compress the bleeding vessels.

Dislocations are seen most often in joints with the most freedom of motion. These include the shoulder, elbow, fingers, knee, and ankle. The hip joint may dislocate, but it requires a major impact. By definition, a dislocation occurs when all or a portion of a joint surface moves out of alignment and is no longer in contact with its "mating" surface. Specific maneuvers are needed to reduce a dislocation. After a period of time, muscle spasm around the joint will prevent easy reduction.

Spinal fractures are discussed in Chapter Six.

The Control of Hemorrhage

First responders are required to staunch the flow of blood as part of resuscitating an injured trauma victim. Several techniques are useful and may be employed according to the body area that is bleeding. In order of decreasing effectiveness, they are:

- Direct pressure over the bleeding tissue
- A pressure wrapping of an extremity, especially if a large surface area is involved
- Packing a bleeding cavity
- Applying a tourniquet above the bleeding point on an extremity

If a pressure bandage becomes soaked with blood, it is often advisable to leave it in place, as beneath the gauze, the body is depositing clotting factors in an attempt to stop the bleeding. People with clotting disorders, such as hemophilia, will hemorrhage from minor abrasions and lacerations as well as from major trauma. Also, patients on blood thinners, or anticoagulants, such as Warfarin or Coumadin, will bleed more from minor trauma. These patients would include people with prosthetic heart valves, those who have had a stroke, those with blood clots in the legs, and those recovering from certain operations that carry high risk of phlebitis.

Finally, a *medical disaster* is defined as an unexpected event resulting in multiple simple and complex injuries to a large number of people with destruction of property and disruption of the daily routines of society.

Thus, a *traumatic impact* is the result of an energy transfer from an object or body to another body. Either a moving object (a missile of some sort) strikes the body or the moving body hits something.

Either way, tissue suffers.

Shock States

Shock is defined as a clinical condition in which there is inadequate blood supply to vital tissues. This state of under-perfusion results in the body's cells receiving inadequate amounts of oxygen and nutrients. We're excluding the use of the term "shock" to describe psychological stress. Shock involving the cardiovascular system may occur for several reasons. The classification of shock that will be described later shows you how complicated patients may be, particularly when they may have the same signs and symptoms for different shock states.

First, how do you recognize that someone is in shock? Let's take each measurable component of shock and review it separately. Obviously, these findings are combined in a shock patient. The sicker the patient, the more abnormal the components will be:

1. *Tachycardia* - this means a rapid heart beat; it may be absent in some shock patients; the pulse rate may drop to an abnormally slow rate in severe (advanced) shock called *bradycardia*
2. *Tachypnea* - a rapid respiratory rate driven by the accumulation of lactic acid
3. *Poor skin perfusion* - as skin arteries constrict the skin becomes "pale, cold, and clammy" as the "fight or flight" reaction kicks in; of course it may be seen in hypothermia without shock
4. *Mental changes* - confusion to loss of consciousness may occur as the brain receives less and less blood as the shock state advances
5. *Reduced urine output* - as the kidneys receive less blood, they conserve body fluid volume by excreting less urine; this is a very sensitive sign of shock regardless of the cause
6. *Chest pain* - either from a heart attack as the prime cause of the shock state, or secondarily from poor heart muscle perfusion of the coronaries because of a different shock state
7. *Heart rhythm changes* - too fast, too slow, and arrhythmias characterized by abnormal EKG complexes; some of these rhythm changes may lead to ventricular tachycardia, which results in a "machine gun" fast heart rate that is inefficient in pumping blood.
8. *Systolic blood pressure drop* - less than 110 mm hg in an adult, less than 100 mm hg in a school child, and less than 80-90 mm hg in an infant or preschooler respectively

There are a number of ways to classify shock. The easiest is based on the most important defect in the cardiovascular system. By that term, I mean the pump (heart), the hydraulic fluid (blood, plasma, body compartment salt and water component), and the vessels themselves (arteries, veins and capillaries). That's the system. The fourth category is based on compression of some part of the system (obstructive shock).

Hypovolemic ("hydraulic fluid") Shock

The causes of low blood volume and the reduction of other body fluids are numerous and frequently seen by surgeons. This is the most common form of "surgical" shock. *Hemorrhagic shock* is one form. The specific causes include:
1. Trauma (blunt and penetrating) causing disruption of major blood vessels, such as the thoracic (chest) aorta, liver, spleen, and intestinal blood supply
2. Bleeding after surgery (missed or re-bleeding points)
3. Massive body fluid losses after a major burn (>30% second degree or >10% third degree burn)
4. Inadequate replacement of IV fluids during surgery

5. Severe dehydration from vomiting, diarrhea, etc.

Cardiogenic ("pump failure") Shock

This form of shock may be associated with chest pain, dizziness and heart failure. When the pump fails you must think of a number of possible causes:

1. Heart attack (myocardial infarction) with coronary artery "plugging" with clot on top of arteriosclerotic narrowing and loss of heart muscle (ischemia)
2. Malfunctioning valves from bacterial growths for example, endocarditis
3. Inflammation of the heart sac (pericarditis)
4. Heart arrhythmias or disrupted rhythms that make the heart "spin its wheels"
5. Pulmonary embolus or blood clot blocking the outflow veins of the heart, usually from a clot breaking off from the leg or thigh veins

Neurogenic ("distributive") Shock

In this kind of shock, the volume is preserved for the most part and there's little wrong with the heart. But the arteries and/or veins dilate, becoming larger because of alterations in the nervous system input controlling the blood vessels. Thus, the vascular system is "too big for its britches." There's relatively too little blood to fill the now expanded arteries or veins and the blood pressure plunges. Causes include:

1. A high spinal cord injury
2. Spinal anesthesia
3. An anaphylactic reaction or allergic response causing "anaphylactic shock"

Obstructive ("heart compression") Shock

The neck veins may become distended in obstructive shock. Other specific findings such as one-sided chest pain, shortness of breath, and muffled heart sounds (cardiac tamponade) may help make the diagnosis. A history of chest trauma will also lead you to this diagnosis. Therefore, the two most common causes of this type of shock are:

1. Tension pneumothorax (lung collapse under pressure)
2. Cardiac tamponade (heart sac fluid or blood compressing the heart)

Septic ("infected/inflammation") Shock

Infections such as acute perforated appendicitis, colitis, perforated ulcers, or acute inflammation of the pancreas with or without infection, are examples of clinical conditions that may result in septic shock. What's unique about septic shock is that it shares many if not all of the components of the other shock states. Septic shock causes "leaky membranes" and fluid loss, the heart may not contract as forcefully (myocardial depression), and the vessels relax and dilate and contribute to the mismatch between container size (blood vessels) and volume. Treatment is directed toward surgical drainage of abscesses and intravenous antibiotics.

Invasive monitoring of the shock patient is beyond the scope of this book. However, you should be aware of the three most commonly used advanced techniques for tracking the course of a patient in shock. These involve placing catheters (plastic tubes) into veins, arteries, and the heart.

1. Central venous pressure (CVP) - placed either under the collarbone or in the neck to access the subclavian and internal jugular veins respectively; with normal heart function, the CVP line allows monitoring of right heart pressures and serves as a guide to IV fluid replacement: high pressures mean the tank is full, low pressures mean give fluids; if the heart is failing the CVP will rise regardless of the fluids status.

2. Arterial line - usually placed in the radial artery at the wrist (with the palm facing up), the "A-line" permits direct blood pressure readings on a continuous basis as well as a visual of the waveform on the monitor next to the bed.

3. Swan-Ganz catheter - a balloon-tipped special long catheter that doctors "float" into the pulmonary artery; it proves both direct numbers of how much blood the heart is ejecting and the heart pressures, as well as derived fancy numbers the computer spits out; these numbers allow the ICU staff (where most of these special lines are placed - CVPs are inserted on floor patients regularly, too) to sort out the type of shock and how to treat it.

The Treatment of Shock

Regardless of the type of shock the following steps are taken:

1. Establish an airway and make certain the patient is breathing well - monitor oxygen saturations with "finger" monitor; give facemask oxygen.

2. If the patient isn't breathing adequately - intubate and ventilate.

3. Start two large bore IVs and administrate normal saline or Lactated Ringers IV fluid; if bleeding is involved, cross match and type and give blood (check blood count).
4. Insert a Foley catheter into the bladder to monitor urine output.
5. Check blood pressure, pulse, temp and respiratory rate.
6. For complicated patients arterial blood gases, a serum lactate level, cultures of any fluid thought to be infected (including x-ray guided drainage or sampling of internal "collections" (abscesses).

Specific treatments aim at the major deficit. But, there's a lot of overlap. These treatments include blood for the hemorrhaging patient; cardiac drugs IV for the patient in cardiogenic shock, vasoconstricting drugs for patients in neurogenic shock, chest tube decompression of a tension pneumothorax, and blood thinners (anticoagulation) for a pulmonary embolus. A really sick ICU patient may require all of these at the same time. Of these treatments, intravenous fluid replacement is the most important and the first and most commonly employed.

TWO

CARE OF THE TRAUMA VICTIM IN THE FIELD

In the field, there are no formal white sheets, no forgiving first bandages, no comforting EKG beeps. In the field, there are no IV poles laden with bags of lactated Ringer's, no authoritative antiseptic odor, no crisp uniform, and no barking intercoms. In the field, no knowledgeable people stand with you to confirm the correctness of your decisions. Not a single x-ray box winks approvingly, not one overhead page announces another professional is nearby to help.

In the field, there is only terror.

Take the viewpoint of a *first responder*. By that, I mean the first person to arrive on the accident scene following a traumatic event. The interval between the accident and the arrival of the first responder may be minutes or hours. Blood and body parts may lie strewn about the accident scene while the more insidious effects of the impact on vital functions (e.g., shock) worsen before your eyes. Deterioration of the victim's condition may continue despite your best efforts. Or the situation may become stable. That's the hell of it. You never know.

In 1994, on a flight from Hong Kong, a woman suffered a collapsed lung (pneumothorax) from a motorbike accident that occurred on her way to the airport. Professor Angus Wallace of Nottingham, England, operated in the back of the plane using a urinary catheter mounted on a piece of coat hanger dipped in brandy, a bottle of Evian water, and a few first aid odds and ends. He placed a makeshift chest tube, and the lung expanded. Undoubtedly, so did the professor's free air miles with British Airways. The woman survived. She received the ultimate in field treatment. Now you see that the field can be anywhere.

This is an example of what can be done if you understand the principles of the problem. It's a grand example of how a writer may take the elements of the story's world and create novel injuries and treatments. Wasn't Stallone the first actor, as John Rambo, to suture himself on screen?

Sometimes it doesn't matter if the first responder is an EMT—an Emergency Medical Technician with basic or advanced training—or a paramedic, police officer, physician's assistant, nurse, or physician. Yes, physician. With medical training so specialty-oriented of late, not all doctors are properly trained in acute care. Most effective in this setting is the skilled person who knows how to assess injury priorities, sort out victims (triage) and start treatment.

The starkness of the accident scene and the immediacy of broken bodies provoke fear in everyone. Experienced doctors often react with trepidation at the accident scene. In that one instant, the first responder must master her emotions *and* deal with the disaster in front of her.

In Chapter One, you learned about the ABCs of resuscitation. The simplicity of this recall system seemed obvious, so casual that perhaps you skimmed over it. You may have assumed that of all the material tossed at you so far, certainly the ABCs of acute care are the easiest to remember.

How could anyone forget the alphabet?

With an incontinent trauma victim lying in a ditch gasping for air, blood dripping from his smashed face, his life ebbing before you, you forget to *breathe*. Your world spins into a blur of doubt.

Of course, not every medical emergency is a life-and-death deal. But some startling impacts can scare the hell out of you. In this chapter, we'll discuss a unified approach to common injuries. We'll learn what happens to folks with the unique problems discussed in Parts II and III *before* they arrive in the emergency room.

Many trauma victims would not live long enough to be treated in the hospital without competent initial care in the field by expert paramedical personnel. Let's assume a paramedic's viewpoint. The victim is best served in the field by an individual like a paramedic because of her level of acute care experience.

The beginning of the alphabet serves all first responders well by reminding us of lifesaving priorities in urgent care. Saving a life isn't an act of genius. Not much in medicine requires the sort of intellect required to design and direct manned space flight. Clinical care requires the application of basic principles that work—over and over again. That's what emergency care in the field's all about.

Stick to the basics. Or, if you choose, have your character miss the critical diagnosis. Because, while the doctor in your tale may look like a hero when he diagnoses bacteria-laden growths on someone's heart valves by merely examining the patient's fingernails, it's important for your paramedics to go through the proper steps in assisting a victim in the field to make the thing ring true. If it's important to the plot to have an injury missed, go ahead.

You'll recall from Chapter One that missed injuries are an unfortunate but real part of trauma care. The likelihood of not documenting every traumatic injury in the wilderness is quite possible. Stuff happens.

Again, you need to know how to get it right before you can accurately toy with making it "wrong" to complement your story. Acute care resuscitation in the field begins with this "alphabet" mnemonic:

- *A* is for *airway*.
- *B* is for *breathing*.
- *C* is for *circulation*.
- *D* is for *disability* (interruptions of neurological function).
- *E* is for *exposure*.

Managing the Airway in the Field

In the field, where resources are limited, the problem of asphyxia can quickly become dire. Two dilemmas confront the first responder:

1. Can I establish an adequate airway with the resources on hand?
2. Does this victim have a broken neck?

To begin with, ask yourself: Is this victim breathing adequately? This means (1) is there an open airway? And (2) is the victim actually breathing and exchanging air? If the airway is blocked, there are two easy ways to open it:

1. *Chin lift* — place your fingers under the front of the jaw, and, with your thumb behind the lower teeth, lift up gently without moving the neck. This is the best way to open the airway, particularly in someone who may have a broken neck.
2. *Jaw thrust* — place your fingers under the angle of the jaw and pull forward. Because the tongue is often what's blocking air exchange ("swallowed tongue") and is attached to the jaw, this move and the chin lift work to clear the passage.

What causes upper airway obstruction? Look to the story environment for the answer. Location and activity determine why blockage to the character's breathing may become a real possibility. Usually it's from:

- The tongue "falling back" in the throat in a victim who is drunk, drugged, diabetic, debilitated or otherwise suffering from decreased awareness
- Grass, sticks, stones, shells, frog, etc., from a river, pond, reservoir, lake or ocean in a case of near drowning
- Chunks of food in a restaurant, the so-called "café coronary"
- Swelling of tissues around the airway from an allergic or anaphylactic reaction to medication, seafood, bee sting, etc.
- Swelling from attempted strangulation
- Swelling from attempted suicide by hanging
- What do victims with blocked airways look like? They're not all the same. It depends on the cause. Here are a few visual clues:

- Victim is awake and anxious with noisy breathing (called stridor, it's a "crowing" sound), but the chest is moving. It's *partial* obstruction.
- Victim is becoming cyanotic—turning blue—with little chest movement and may be "bucking" to breathe but can't exchange air. It's a *completely* blocked airway.
- Victim is frantic, can't talk, is becoming panicky and flushed, then blue, with complete blockage from foreign matter or broken larynx (voice box).
- Victim is unconscious when you arrive.
- Victim is wheezing ("musical" high-pitched noisy breathing), typically in asthmatics with partial closure of lower airways (called bronchospasm).

Let's assume for the moment your character arrives on the scene and doesn't have a rescue kit; there's no tube available to place in the victim's throat. Later, in the hospital, the victim may be intubated and placed on a ventilator, but not usually in the field. Your character may carry one of those curved plastic airways in his pack. It's called an *oropharyngeal airway*.

To use it, the tongue is depressed with a spoon, hunting knife, or branch and the airway is slipped past the tongue to keep the throat open. Care should be taken to not push the tongue farther back, making the obstruction worse. Another way to insert the plastic airway is to point the tip at the roof of the mouth, inserting it upside down. Then, when it's far enough back in the throat, rotate it 180 degrees. The victim breathes around it.

If the victim's airway seems all right when the initial assessment is performed, it's time to decide if the victim needs help breathing. Adequate ventilation may be confirmed in the field if the victim is exchanging good tidal volumes of air heard with a stethoscope. If the victim is not experiencing "air hunger," you should see the chest moving with each breath, and the victim shouldn't be gasping. But if adequate ventilation is in question, a number of helpful maneuvers may be followed next:

- Provide an oxygen source—mask or nasal tongs
- Mouth-to-mouth respiration
- Ambu bag ventilation

Whatever you do, keep in mind the possibility of a fractured neck. Both the chin lift and jaw thrust must be done without yanking the neck back (hyperextension). Both techniques carry the potential risk of converting a victim with a broken neck without spinal cord damage into a cord disrupted, incontinent quadriplegic. At all times: Do no harm.

It's not always as simple as lifting the jaw. Airway obstruction may result from a major facial smash, and whether it's from a fall off of Mount Sheercliff or from an unrestrained windshield/face impact, the problems are the same. First, if the head is smashed, the neck may be broken. Second, how do you find the throat if the nose is mush and the mouth is missing? Bruises, blood clots and disrupted tissue may conceal the nose and mouth orifices.

No openings in the face? No air bubbles?

The neck!

Sure, your character must cut open the windpipe in the neck. Not a tracheotomy, the procedure is a little easier (but not much!) and still requires a cut into the upper airway. A character with courage, a sharp knife and a tube of some sort can relieve life-threatening airway obstruction when the mouth and nose are compromised.

You have your hero feel the upper notch of the larynx (Adam's apple) and slide the finger down the cartilage until the second notch, a depression, actually, is felt. That's where your character cuts horizontally across the neck skin and muscles, right through a tough membrane into the windpipe. The procedure is called a *cricothyrotomy*. A blast of air spews bloody froth all over your character when the trachea is entered, unless, of course, your wimpy character reaches the deep membrane with a Swiss Army knife and hesitates, fearful of slicing a jugular, unable to complete the job.

A Breath of Life

If the victim's chest isn't moving when the airway is cleared, or if he's unconscious, you've got to breathe for him. *B* is for breathing. What's needed is a portable respirator with a good tidal volume (the amount of air exchanged in the lungs with each breath), a ventilator that's immediately available, reliable and with an extended energy source. It means your character must perform mouth-to-mouth or mouth-to-tube respiration. A lot of issues arise in this era of infectious diseases, especially hepatitis and AIDS. Of course, we've still got the old favorites such as tuberculosis. The argument about a person's duty to risk self-harm in the emergent setting becomes distressingly philosophical if the victim is seriously injured and you're the only life-preserving agent in sight.

Conflict? You bet.

Most hotels, recreational facilities and other public places have first aid kits, and some have more advanced equipment including an Ambu bag and facemask. If available, this setup can be used to ventilate the victim. One person can hold the mask over the face *and* pump the bag, but it's quite difficult. Two helpers can share the task with more efficiency. Oxygen, if available, may be attached to the bag system.

Maintain Circulation

Circulation is best preserved by stopping blood loss as well as by giving the victim fluids by mouth. Most folks don't carry IV equipment with them. Force-feeding liquids may not be as dramatic as IV resuscitation, but in the field, it's all you've got. You may also elevate the victim's legs. This serves to auto-transfuse the person's own blood from the periphery of the body to the central heart-lung core where it's needed. This works for mild to moderate bleeding.

The best way to stop bleeding is by applying direct pressure to the hemorrhaging point. With an understanding of the distribution of arteries and veins in the body, you can apply pressure effectively in a number of settings. Bleeding can occur in the following ways:

- From the head — face and scalp
- From the neck — anterior wounds (where the jugulars and carotids live) are more dangerous than posterior
- From the chest wall or into the chest (hidden cause of shock)
- From the abdominal wall or hidden in the belly — again, shock?
- From the flank or back
- Deep inside the pelvis
- From the arms and legs

Hemorrhage from flat surfaces such as the chest wall, flank, belly, back or scalp responds to direct pressure held for several minutes. If small arteries or veins are responsible, the bleeding will stop with pressure alone. Of course, the wounds will eventually require further treatment. Big arteries can be controlled with direct pressure in an emergency, but definitive surgical care is needed to identify and ligate (tie with a suture) the offending "pumpers" or active arterial bleeders. At times, the really big arteries must be reconstructed.

Bleeding from the extremities, scalp, and some neck wounds can be controlled with pressure dressings — a lump of gauze pads placed over the bleeding point and wrapped tightly with gauze strips. If there's a cavity with tissue loss and bleeding from the defect, sterile gauzes can be stuffed into the hole and wrapped up, or pressure may be applied manually.

Tourniquets are seldom used. But if needed, a tourniquet is placed just above the bleeding point. Anything such as a rope, length of cloth, belt, etc., may be used to apply enough circumferential squeeze pressure to stop the hemorrhage. The problem with a tourniquet is the risk of leaving it on for an excessively long time. How long? The question begs how long tissue below the tourniquet can tolerate having virtually no blood supply. If it's a matter of stopping a life-threatening hemorrhage or creating potential damage, the person in the field must decide what to do. A tourniquet can be released periodically. But usually direct pressure is the best policy.

In the next chapter, we'll discuss hemorrhage in more detail, but for the moment, anyone looking at a pool of blood out there in no-man's land must have a sense of what volume of blood has been lost. A quick assessment of the victim will give you a general idea about the seriousness of the bleed. A useful guideline goes like this:

- If there's no change in the level of consciousness, breathing or pulse, and if the victim is just a little thirsty, the hemorrhage volume is about a unit of blood or less. Have the victim drink liquids and go on with life.
- If the victim is lethargic or comatose, cold or clammy, with a racing or difficult-to-find pulse and gasping for breath, the victim has probably bled over 40 percent of her total blood volume. This is a life-threatening picture, and IV fluid replacement and transfusions are essential. In this scenario, two to three quarts of blood have been lost; it doesn't matter how or where. Field treatment alone isn't going to do it for this poor soul. Transport to medical case ASAP.
- Between there two extremes are lesser degrees of hemorrhage — losses of two to four pints of blood. These victims present with a rapid pulse, rapid breathing and a look of anxiety. Although serious, they do well after transfer to a hospital where transfusions are administered.

Control of bleeding is relatively easy because the source is usually obvious, and pressure suffices for emergency treatment. Follow-up depends on how much blood is lost. Major hemorrhage requires hospitalization, intravenous fluid administration, and, often, transfusion.

Disability: Can the Victim Talk and Move?

The basis for a quick evaluation of the victim's brain and spinal cord function is observation of the best verbal and eye movement responses to questions and the presence of limb movement. Detailed in Chapter Five as the Glasgow Coma Scale, this assessment involves determining whether the victim can answer questions or is in a coma, whether the victim can open his eyes and look at the examiner, and whether the victim can move his arms and legs.

Not only is this information important as the first assessment, it must be recorded in case the examination data change. For example, if an alert trauma victim slips into a coma, the change in level of consciousness may signal a major intracranial bleed (subdural or epidural hematoma). Similarly, a person with a neck or back injury who is able to move the arms and legs may, with time, becomes paralyzed. In both scenarios, if your character is out in the wilderness, there's trouble in the wind. Brain and spinal cord injuries can progress. Prognosis may depend on whether the victim is stuck in the field or is immediately transported to medical care.

Make certain your description of the victim's initial condition is clear and that the course of any deterioration is vivid and concise. Tension mounts because of the uncertainty that characterizes the interplay between improvement and deterioration in neurological trauma.

Expose the Victim

Imagine multiple victims of a drive-by attack lying on the pavement in shock, several with obvious gunshot wounds from an assault weapon. One woman lies in shock with no visible injuries—unless you take off her glove and examine her hand.

Why?

Figure 4 demonstrates the random nature of some impacts. Other serious trauma such as impalement may be quirky and occult. Such trauma may only become evident after thorough examination of the victim. More than once, a gaggle of young doctors have stared at a trauma victim lying on a stretcher with no obvious reason to be near death. Only when they flip the victim over do they discover the tiny stiletto wound between the patient's ribs.

ABCDE. It's the beginning of acute care in the field. If it's done improperly, the victim may die or suffer unnecessary disability.

Once life-threatening problems are cared for, the next step is to address specific impacts and evaluate them with respect to transport to a hospital.

Special Problems in the Field
Extraction with Head and Neck Trauma

In-line traction on the head and neck is mandatory during any movement of the victim from the accident scene, onto a backboard or stretcher or out of a building, vehicle or wilderness cranny. But get the victim away from a dangerous situation as quickly as possible while controlling the neck and the airway. Scalp wounds bleed profusely and look worse than they are. Compress head and neck bleeding with sterile bandages, and transport the victim to a trauma center. Always remember: a skull fracture or brain damage may be associated with a scalp laceration.

Figure 4 – Erratic Internal Bullet Track

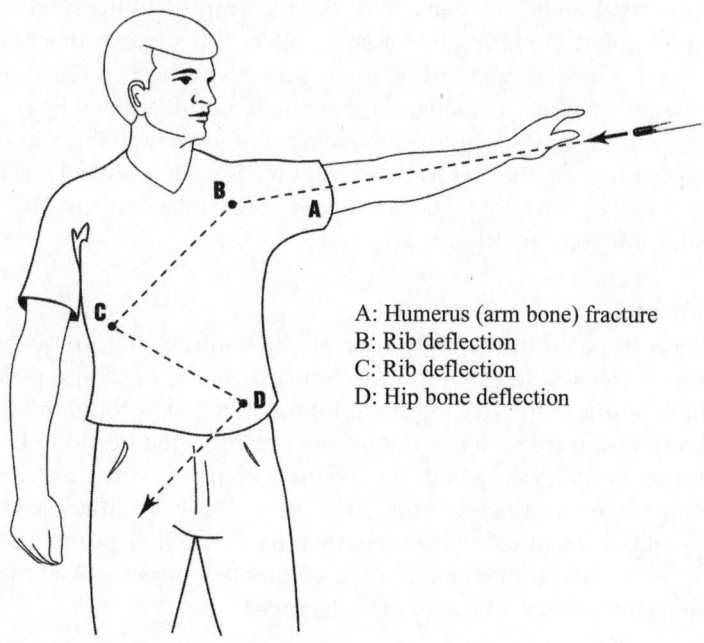

A: Humerus (arm bone) fracture
B: Rib deflection
C: Rib deflection
D: Hip bone deflection

Chest and Abdomen Trauma

Care of abdominal wounds in the field is easy: Cover any wound, even if there are exposed intestines, with a wet, sterile gauze (if possible), bandage, and transport. Chest wounds must also be covered in a similar fashion, and if there is a hole in the thoracic wall, a so-called "sucking chest wound," cover it with something to seal it off. Choices include cellophane or plastic with a rim of any ointment you may be carrying on your person. Wrap the chest and transport. Oxygen should be provided to any seriously injured trauma victim, especially one with chest trauma, when respiration is compromised.

Arm and Leg Trauma

Bleeding is easily controlled with direct pressure, and wounds may be cleaned gently and bandaged with sterile gauze. Dislocations of the hip need little intervention before transport to the hospital, while a knee dislocation should be aligned if possible by gentle traction to remove any compression of the artery to the lower leg. Fractures should be splintered, and the pulses below the fracture or dislocation site evaluated and documented, if possible. At least determine if the foot is warm or cool.

Bites

Cover and seek medical care. But before you do, obtain as much information about the biting agent as possible. If it's a dog attack, is it a known dog? Have it quarantined for possible rabies. Rabies is also possible with raccoon, fox, bat and other small mammal bites. Snakebites must be treated according to the degree of envenomation and the poisonous status of the disgruntled reptile. Speed is vital in seeking medical care as swelling, tissue death and infection at the fang penetration site may swiftly ensure.

Impalement

If the object impaled in the body is small, it should be left untouched as the victim is transported to a trauma center. If fixed, as with a picket or wrought iron fence, the fencing material must be cut within a foot or so of the body and transported without movement to the hospital. If some part of the body is impaled on a small sharp fixture, e.g., a bolt protruding from a concrete slab, the body must be lifted from the impaling object. In all of these scenarios, two potential problems exist: Will the removal or movement of the impaled object cause massive hemorrhage or further internal organ damage?

Traumatic Amputation

The stress of dealing with a traumatic amputation is similar to discovering someone impaled, in pain and in danger. The first responder has several specific duties:

- Stop bleeding from amputation stump. Apply wet, sterile (if possible) gauze. Wrap.
- Find the amputated part.
- Clean amputated part gently if dirty. Wrap in wet gauze or cloth, and place in a bag of ice — but *not* in contact with the ice.
- Transport victim and part to trauma center immediately. Minimal passage of time before an attempt at replantation is crucial.

Burns and Frostbite

Local care is adequate for small areas of skin involvement. This includes topical over-the-counter antibiotic ointment and frequent dressing changes. Larger burns or severe frostbite require hospital care. For affected areas covering more than ten percent of the body, frostbite or burns that involve the hands, feet, face or genitalia or local deep injury with obvious full thickness tissue death, care must be provided by the appropriate surgical specialist. Other issues such as body fluid loss, infection, and surgical cleaning of ongoing tissue loss justify hospitalization.

Diving Accidents and Altitude Sickness

Anticipation and prevention are the hallmarks of the style of serious climbers and divers. Where is the closest decompression chamber? Are there helicopter facilities to get an injured or sick climber off the mountain? Do you have oxygen? What special medications do you need to take at high altitudes? Do you have rope and extra tanks to execute a decompression dive? Do you have waterproof U.S. Navy Decompression Tables with you? Do you know the waters you're diving in? Do you need a guide for your proposed climb? Is everyone in the party in good physical condition?

Certain questions must be answered before any short or prolonged expedition is attempted. It's a matter of planning a fallback position if something goes wrong.

Assaulted Elders, Battered Women and Injured Kids

Underestimated over the years, domestic violence may be subtle or flagrant, occasional or agonizingly repetitive. No age group is spared. The resultant injuries may be trivial or quite serious. At times, doctors misdiagnose battered elders and children, especially if their caregivers or parents purposely scheme to keep the trauma concealed.

Clues to hidden injuries as well as to constant abuse from domestic violence abound, and the wise writer sprinkles them about her story like a delicate spice. One very productive source of conflict for writers in the arena of battered people is the dilemma of distinguishing accidental injury from malicious violence. Also, a history of battering—for the abuser and for the recipient—serves as a powerful ingredient of your character's back-story.

Sexual Assault

The victim of sexual assault usually brings herself to the hospital, although not all sexual assaults are reported. Many women feel embarrassed, frightened and, at times, responsible for the assault. If a victim is found injured, helpless, and possibly in shock, the first responder's task is to provide first aid, comfort and transportation to a hospital. But it is also the helper's duty to contact local law enforcement personnel. The first responder is in a crime scene, and certain procedures must be followed in order to preserve sensitive information for subsequent prosecution of the criminal.

Mass Casualty Management

Multiple injuries occurring in large numbers of citizens creates a nightmare all hospitals fear. Larger medical centers and Level One trauma centers (usually the same) are required to have in place a mass casualty disaster plan.

Disasters may be natural or man-made. Post 9/11, everyone fears further terrorist attacks. The definition of a mass casualty event is one in which the number of injured and dying victims far exceeds the capacity of the (closest) hospital to provide proper care. The process of mass injury management involves triage at the scene by paramedical personnel, further triage to floors, ICU, and the operating rooms at the receiving hospital, as well as the possibility of triaging the overflow to nearby hospitals. Other hospitals are usually needed because of the sheer number of patients as well as the complexity and number of multi-system injured patients.

How does one learn how to handle this level of emotional distress? The approach addressed in this book, namely the Advanced Trauma Life Support (ATLS) concept works well in the mass casualty setting. Trained personnel follow the guidelines established by ATLS in triaging victims according to degree of injury and expectation of a survival outcome. An expert will identify airway needs and shock states. The coordinator will provide or direct others in the use of simple methods of quickly establishing an airway and stopping bleeding. This directed triage and resuscitation will stabilize the largest number of victims.

Later issues of splinting fractures and dislocations, when salvageable patients have been sent to the hospital, are appropriately addressed. Terribly injured victims of the disaster may have to be left to die while care was being provided to more potentially treatable cases. This is where triage gets difficult. Someone left to die (considered too badly injured to make it) may still be alive at the end of the scramble to transport victims to definitive care. Your "expert" character - it may be a doctor, a paramedic, a nurse - will decide who lives and who dies. Post-traumatic stress disorders may arise from such problematic decisions, especially if the expected death doesn't happen immediately and raises the question: *Would this victim have survived if I had designated her to be transported immediately?*

Code Blue refers to victims who are dead or are expected to die because of the severity of their injuries. The dead are moved to an outpatient area and the dying are kept in the ER. Code Red covers victims with severe injuries thought to be treatable and survivable. They receive immediate treatment and are admitted to a ward or to the ICU. Code Yellow refers to victims who have sustained lacerations, non-critical head injuries or blunt injuries not associated with shock. A doctor treats these patients as one became available. Code Green patients have minor injuries and are assessed and treated by nurses in the outpatient area and discharged.

Physicians treating mass casualty survivors must address them with the same focus as any other patient - despite the chaos around them. As traumatic injuries are sutured, splinted and bandaged, the emotional scars must also be acknowledged. If the event is still evolving patients may not know if they have lost family members, close colleagues, or dear friends. This uncertainty must be spoken to and support for those who wait for word of the disaster's extent must be provided.

THREE

THE TRAUMA CENTER

More physicians than you might imagine dread the responsibility of caring for trauma patients. Even seasoned doctors hesitate before the broken body, held back by a twinge of doubt and a passing uncertainty about how they will behave in the presence of the torn-up body.

Like you, doctors dislike injury-associated gore. And that, in itself, may serve as a source of story conflict. The hospital course of a trauma victim is uncertain and the length of follow-up isn't well defined— nothing as predictable as elective surgery. The day after laparoscopic gallbladder surgery, you pack up your toothbrush and go home. A single follow-up office visit completes your care. Sadly, for the victim of uncontrolled injury, rehabilitation may go on for months, possibly years.

A heavy artillery of interventional diagnostics and treatment booms loudly in the modern high-tech hospital. A lot happens quickly. Within most specialties, controversy rages about which tests are most reliable, so you need to grasp a few key points in order to negotiate the trauma center when you write your hospital scene. This includes an appreciation of the interactions of the different players on the trauma team.

The Dynamics of Trauma Care

Despite the media's splashy, intermittent interest in acute hospital care, this part of the physician's world has not been delved into much by writers. It's an expansive vista of opportunity. And every day, it changes.

Lots of conflict can arise when you mix stressed doctors with sick patients. Mounting survival stakes flush adrenaline through your physician character's circulation and sweat drenches his clothes as he stands in the trauma room with a fresh broken body. What to do first? What's really wrong with this one? Are there others? Should he be operating on this patient?

In addition to learning how a trauma center functions, you'll become aware of a load of medical dirty laundry. Not an attempt to smear the profession, this information provides you with more ideas about how to create conflict when you write your hospital scene. Ugly turf battles, fear, and indifference all insinuate their unwashed hands into trauma care at all levels.

Why? Because doctors are human.

And while fifty million people are injured in the U.S. each year and are managed by trauma specialists as well as other doctors, there exists in this complex care system an underlying current of greed, ego and recrimination. Why does a young vascular surgeon in a small community hospital treat a child's severely compromised arm herself rather than refer the case to the nearby Level I trauma center? For the fee? For glory?

Why not?

You can take advantage of your own discomfort as you think about these issues, as well as the bothersome subjects of traumatic amputation, impalement and mutilation, and create a realistic tone in your injury scenes.

Of course, not all injury victims go to a Level I trauma center. Most are transported from the field to the local community hospital where they are treated effectively by a variety of physicians. The national trauma care system certainly isn't a seamless whole and many parts of the country still aren't set up to provide adequate care to everyone. It's constantly improving, and overall, the system works well. Still, there are flaws in the organization and provision of care to the injured. These areas of concern that have arisen over the years include:

- Appropriate levels of physician training
- Which victims to transport to Level I trauma centers
- How to prepare victims for transfer
- Who is responsible for the transfer

Which story elements from these issues might you write about? Where is the conflict? Here are a few suggestions:

- The surgeon on call is not immediately available when called by the hospital with a trauma patient. Does the ER doctor transfer the patient himself? Does he call the administrator on call? Does he report the delinquent surgeon for disciplinary measures?
- A specialist, say a neurosurgeon, isn't available to care for a head injury. Does the local doctor attempt to place burr holes in the victim's skull to evacuate the life-threatening blood clot? Or does she send the patient to the closest trauma center knowing he may not survive the trip?
- The local surgeon feels he can handle the injury himself despite the presence of injuries to three or more major organ systems. Is there anyone around to fight his ego-driven, ill-advised care plan?

- The local surgeon doesn't want to be bothered by what she expects to be time-consuming patient with no insurance. Does she dump the victim on the other hospital in town? Or is the ER doctor who works for the hospital trying to dump this "self-payer" — a euphemism you might hear in the ER back room for what are called street bums, slime balls, dirtballs — on the nearest trauma center? Who blows the whistle on the hospital?
- The local HMO says not to transfer the patient — it doesn't have a contract with the trauma center and wants its own surgeon to handle the case. Does the HMO administrator pressure the doctor into agreeing the injuries aren't really severe enough to warrant transfer? Do life-threatening injuries go undetected by the under-trained HMO physician?
- The local aging surgeon dislikes the young stud trauma surgeon at the local trauma center. Does he refuse to transfer the patient or do it in a sloppy manner with inadequate information sent with the patient?

There's no end to clinical chaos.

When a trauma victim reaches the local hospital, a lot of decisions must be made in a hurry. The ER doctor, unlike his pre-1980 predecessor, is trained to provide immediate trauma care. But not complete trauma care. That's where the trauma team comes in. This is one of the hottest areas of debate in trauma care. When a big crunch comes into the emergency room, ER residents and surgical residents man it. Who takes care of the patient? Well, the ER resident, physically in the ER when the patient comes in, can perform an initial assessment. Should he put in the various tubes? The surgical resident is better at it and can open the chest if necessary. The surgical resident has the good hands. So what happens?

Conflict.

All the way from the trauma room's bloody floor to the executive offices of the chairpersons of the departments of surgery and ER medicine, there is conflict about who should do what and to whom. Somehow it gets worked out, at least for the moment.

Thus, the trauma team or the emergency room doctor involved in the initial assessment of the trauma victim must:

- Rapidly assess the victim's condition, including vital signs — blood pressure, pulse rate, respiratory rate and temperature
- Stabilize and resuscitate the victim and treat life-threatening injuries immediately
- Decide if local (hospital) management is appropriate
- Arrange for transfer and transportation to higher level trauma center if local care is not adequate

- Be responsible for the transfer

The Level I Trauma Center

In Chapter One, we discussed the requirements for each level of care designated in the national trauma care system. Each level depends upon the local availability of doctors and technology. Linked by the needs of the trauma victim, these hospitals refer to each other when patients are triaged according to the severity of their injuries. In the field, the paramedic or EMT assesses the victim, calls the hospital, and describes the injuries. As well as giving the hospital lead-time to prepare for the victim's arrival, this communication also launches the triage process itself if several injured people are involved.

Lesser injuries may be sent to the local hospital, where such things as chest tubes may be placed, fractures set, and uncomplicated abdominal and head injuries observed. Victims of multiple organ trauma are usually taken directly to the nearest Level I facility unless resuscitation in a smaller hospital is warranted first.

The different levels of trauma care described in Chapter One are being integrated nationally into a regionalized plan of trauma care. The American College of Surgeons, over many years, has worked diligently to improve the plight of the trauma victim in America. Hardly complete, the aim of all states is to create a network of hospitals that function as parts of a universal care plan. In some geographical areas, trauma care is fine-tuned. In others, it is all but absent.

Next we will look at what is available at a top-notch Level I trauma center.

The Trauma Room

Readily accessible in all Level I trauma centers is a specially equipped room kept open for major injury cases. It isn't used to suture lacerations or to bandage abrasions or to reduce and cast fractures. This huge room (Figure 5) has two or three operating room tables and is filled with resuscitation equipment, including an oxygen source, ventilators, suction apparatus, emergency surgical instruments, and emergency cardiac medication and other equipment stored in wheeled carts. The walls are lined with drawers laden with suture material, sponges and surgical instruments as well as equipment used in the diagnosis and treatment of rapidly evolving, life-ending problems. Oral airways and endotracheal tubes are on standby ventilators and suction equipment is available for swift resuscitation. IV poles prepared with bags of lactated Ringer's and tubing are ready to be connected to large-bore catheters the surgeons will immediately place in the victim's arm veins on arrival in the trauma room. IV fluid resuscitation represents an essential part of the surgeon's first line of treatment.

Nurses specially trained in the immediate care of the trauma victim wheel the patient into the room from the ambulance or helicopter with the help of the paramedics who transported the patient from the field. There is no record taking, no search for identification, no asking for a history—the traditional steps in diagnosis. These critically ill patients are rushed into the trauma room, and, after assuring the cervical spine (neck) is protected with a rigid collar (it was probably applied in the field), an airway is established, ventilation started with an Ambu bag by hand or with the ventilator, and IV lines placed and fluid infused into the victim. As members of the team accomplish these initial tasks, the trauma surgeon, surgical resident, or ER doctor goes through the first of four phases of assessment to avoid missing a life-threatening condition, the four procedures are always followed in the same sequence, regardless of the patient's condition.

In Part II, you will become familiar with twelve nasty chest injuries that can kill the victim immediately or within hours of injury. It is the doctor's responsibility to make certain that the trauma patient doesn't have any of the "dirty dozen"—or, if present, that they are treated swiftly to reverse their lethal potential.

When these victims arrive in the emergency room, they represent the second wave of traumatic disasters. The first wave of killer injuries occurred in the field right after impact, terrible wounds that snuffed out life before anyone could respond. When death occurs within minutes or seconds of impact, the traumatic wounds sustained are usually:

- Severe laceration of the brainstem resulting in immediate cessation of breathing
- Severe laceration or contusion of the brain associated with massive increased intracranial pressure (on the brain) and compression of vital centers
- Transection or smashing of the spinal cord high in the neck with damage to the nerves to the diaphragm—death results from complete inability to breathe
- Laceration of the heart or aorta (off of the heart) or any other major blood vessel, causing immediate loss of blood volume, shock and death by exsanguination.

Figure 5 – The Trauma Room

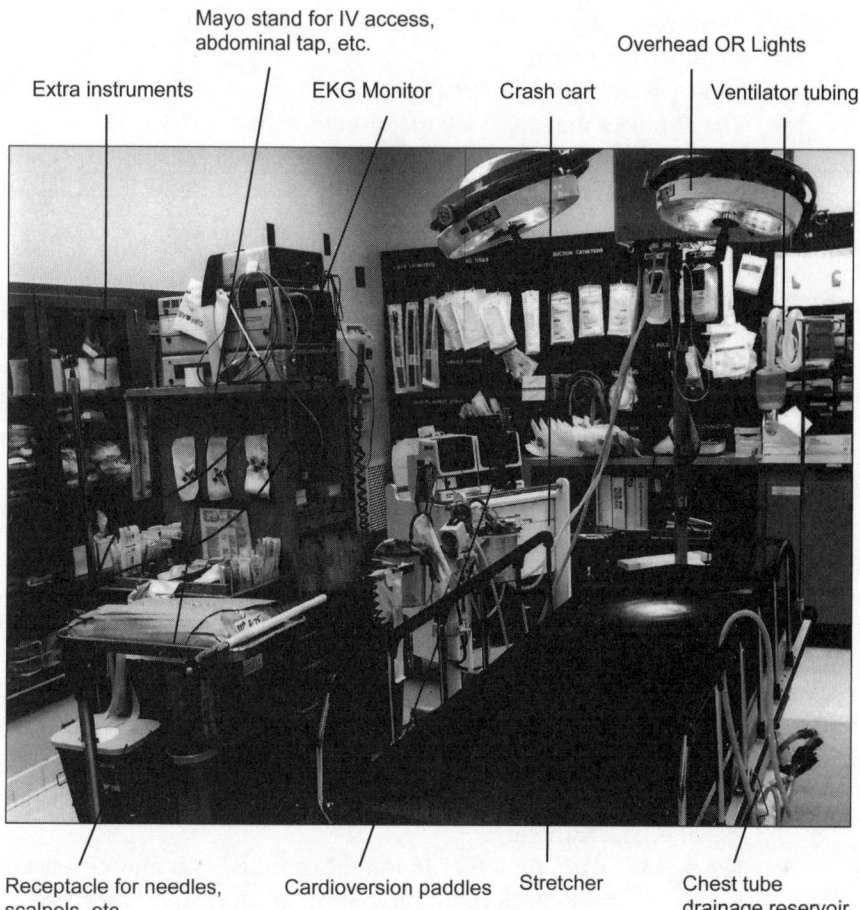

Mayo stand for IV access, abdominal tap, etc.

Extra instruments · EKG Monitor · Crash cart · Overhead OR Lights · Ventilator tubing

Receptacle for needles, scalpels, etc. · Cardioversion paddles · Stretcher · Chest tube drainage reservoir

The Four First Steps in Trauma Care

Out in the field, your hero should use these same steps in assessing the victim of a traumatic injury. Whatever the setting, the sequence of steps is always the same—unless you want an injury to be missed.

Step One: The Primary Survey

In the ER, the doctor who first evaluates the victim follows these steps. The trauma surgeon, for example, arrives at the side of the stretcher and begins this quick drill. As the doctor makes his initial assessment, nurses start IV lines and remove clothing to permit careful examination. It all happens at once.

The trauma surgeon's initial brief examination is performed to identify life-threatening injuries. The elements of the examination are to:

- Establish an airway
- Make certain victim is breathing
- Check pulses and stop any major hemorrhage
- Look for head and spinal cord damage, surface wounds, chest injuries, abdominal tenderness or any other findings that suggest hidden injuries

Step Two: Resuscitation

- Place two large-bore (caliber) IVs in the arms — usually forearm veins — or legs if needed. If neither is available, use neck veins (this is called a *central line*). Last choice is a "cutdown" on an ankle vein.
- Administer lactated Ringer's IV solution as fast as possible, anywhere from two to ten liters in the first hour. Place IV bag inside pressure cuff for faster infusion of fluid in cases of severe shock.
- Draw *labs* (blood tests) to cross and type for blood transfusion and to determine specific organ function, body chemistries and blood count.
- Place a nasogastric tube to decompress stomach, a Foley catheter in the bladder to measure urine output (and thus judge how much fluid and blood to administer) and, in the ICU, special lines to measure blood pressure (arterial line) and heart function (Swan-Ganz catheter).
- Emergency surgery, either in the ER or in the OR, may be part of the act of resuscitation; nothing short of operative intervention will save the victim's life. In the ER, the surgeon may open the chest (cut between the ribs on the left) and suture a bullet or stab wound to the heart (twenty-five percent of these warriors will live to fight another day). In the OR, any surgery designed to halt massive hemorrhage may be needed to catch up on blood volume.

Step Three: The Secondary Survey

With lines in place and life-threatening injuries treated for the moment, the trauma surgeon now goes back and starts to examine the victim all over again. A meticulous head-to-toe evaluation is carried out to check for broken bones, dislocations and deep soft tissue injuries. Appropriate x-rays will now be performed, with extra films taken of areas of concern based on this second exam. Also, if no injury mandates a rushed trip to the operating room, CT scans and other special x-rays may now be done.

Regardless of the types or pattern of the injuries, in all multiple-injury victims the following x-rays are performed routinely:

1. Chest x-ray—Any evidence of the "dirty dozen"?
2. Cervical spine x-rays—Fractures or dislocation of neck vertebrae?
3. Pelvis x-rays—Fractures? How many?

If the original abdominal examination reveals significant tenderness, or if the tenderness seems to be increasing on subsequent examinations, the trauma surgeon will perform a test called a *peritoneal lavage*. This involves placing a plastic tube into the abdominal cavity through a tiny incision near the belly button and infusing saline solution. The peritoneal lavage test is positive and leads to emergency abdominal surgery if:

- Frank blood comes out of the tube when first placed in the belly—something is bleeding massively.
- Feces come out of the tube mixed in the saline—it means the colon (large intestine) is ruptured.
- Food—ruptured stomach.
- Urine—ruptured bladder.
- Bile comes out in the fluid—gallbladder, liver, bile ducts or duodenum (first part of small intestine) are ruptured (perforated).
- Many red or white blood cells are present in a sample of the saline when examined under the microscope.

Note: If the abdomen is swelling up before the surgeon's eyes in the ER, no test is required as the assumption is that massive bleeding is occurring in the belly. An urgent operation is mandatory, so a peritoneal lavage isn't needed. The FAST test (Focused Assessment Sonography in Trauma) is an ultrasound examination of the abdomen. The ultrasound-scanning test looks for blood.

Step Four: Management of All Major Injuries

After a detailed secondary survey of the victim, the trauma surgeon knows what's wrong or has a high index of suspicion for certain injuries. Specific operative or non-operative treatment may be started or further tests may be ordered to chase additional diagnostic possibilities. Injury severity and the need for specific organ support determine what happens next. Basically, the patient goes to the OR or the ICU. With lesser injuries, some trauma patients may go directly to a surgical floor for careful monitoring. Which floor depends on the injury: "neuro" floor for a head injury, orthopedic floor for a fractured femur, or a general surgical floor for lesser degrees of both. For patients who do not require a surgical intervention, observation becomes the name of the game.

It is, at this point, when conflict may arise among members of the surgical team. Does the trauma surgeon repair the torn bladder or should an urologist be called in? Should the trauma surgeon fix the fractured femur or ask for assistance from an orthopedic colleague? Is the chest injury severe enough to warrant the services of a thoracic surgeon or can the trauma surgeon handle it herself? Who repairs the child's torn bladder—a pediatric urologist or an adult trauma surgeon? Or an adult urologist or a general pediatric surgeon?

Turf battles rage all over the country. Somehow it gets worked out and excellent care is provided in a timely fashion. Despite the conflicts, trauma care in the U.S. is becoming consistent and more universally available.

CARE OF THE TRAUMA IN THE OPERATING ROOM

Trauma surgery is almost never elective, not unless the patient is well down the road to recovery from the original night of horror. Follow-up operations are usually undertaken to fix broken bones, remove screws and pins, debride (clean away) dead tissue from open wounds or place skin grafts on beds of burned flesh. This sort of follow-up surgery may be performed more leisurely than the chaotic emergency procedures. Nonetheless, the mood in the operating room during surgery for the first big crunch and subsequent surgery is never casual.

Before writing an authentic operating room scene, you need to know who works in this hallowed and horrid corner of the hospital. Who are they? What do they say? What is the mood in surgery? Does it change when things get tense? Who's in charge? Also, you need to have a handle on the equipment.

First, who is the trauma surgeon?

All surgeons, other than those whose specialties you recognize— orthopedics, neurosurgery, plastics, urology, vascular—are *general surgeons*, not general practitioners, not primary care docs. A general surgeon is the board-certified surgeon most people refer to when they say "surgeon." A general surgeon does everything except the more complex and specific procedures done by specialists. In some circumstances, and in many small communities, the general surgeon performs all of the basic duties of the specialist, referring the complex cases to a larger medical center.

A *trauma surgeon* is a general surgeon with five years of residency and extra training or a fellowship in trauma surgery. Able to perform a variety of lifesaving operations as well as the usual general surgical procedures, the trauma surgeon sees all major injuries admitted to the hospital through the emergency room. Of these creatively smashed-up souls, only about fifteen percent require a major operation.

Other than the lifesaving kinds of things done in the trauma room that you've already learned about, the remainder of the trauma victim's surgical care is rendered in the OR, the surgical ICU and on the surgical floors. Unlike elective cases where a specific procedure is prepared for and a defined area of the body shaved and prepped with specific instruments picked and sterilized, in trauma cases the victim's status is unknown. The surgeon expects and often finds bizarre injuries.

The trauma surgeon expects to operate in all body cavities. All tissues are potential areas of injury. Nothing's a given.

The Operating Room

The operating room (Figure 6) is a familiar place to most readers. Movies and television productions portray realistic, well-researched hospital scenes. Your readers know intuitively that there's a lot going on in that clean, well-lighted place. When you write about the operating room, it's the drama that counts, not a detailed description of the hardware. Sprinkle a few details onto your reader's visual screen. She'll fill in the rest.

You may choose a splash of authenticity from any of the following items on this OR list.

Anesthesia machine: Bulky and on wheels with a screen that displays the patient's blood pressure, pulse, temperature, oxygen saturation; dials that control the "inhalation" gases to keep the patient asleep; plastic tubes going to the patient; other hoses connected to a wall oxygen source; large corrugated hose from machine to patient; suction apparatus.

Anesthesia cart: On wheels, with drawers containing everything from vials of drugs, syringes, plastic tubing, instruments and gauze pads to anesthesia journals, the most recent stock market report and a copy of *your* last novel.

OR table: Narrow with thin plastic mattress, restraining belt, foot pedals to adjust height and tilt, small pillow.

Back table (or two): Stainless steel tables draped with sterile sheets, laden with all of the instruments to be used during surgery; manned by the *scrub tech*, the person who hands the surgeon instruments and whatever else is needed.

Suction apparatus: Usually one for the surgeon and one for anesthesia; consists of tubes coming out of the ceiling or walls, going to huge disposable plastic containers that seal for the disposal of body fluid.

Cautery machine: The electrocautery has several settings for cutting or cauterizing tissue; the current varies and different levels of intensity may be used from a setting of twenty to what the residents call "stun" at fifty or more.

Laser machine: Used much less often than the cautery, the laser is an excellent source of energy for delicate surgery such as fixing a detached retina; not much use in trauma.

Small prep table: Covered with a sterile towel, holds two or three stainless steel cups or bowls to hold antiseptic solution; scrub tech puts a sponge stick (a clamp to hold sponges when the surgeon cleans the skin) on the prep table from his bundle of instruments.

TV cameras and associated technology: For laparoscopic surgery: one or two screens and multiple cables and hoses.

Figure 6 – The Operating Room

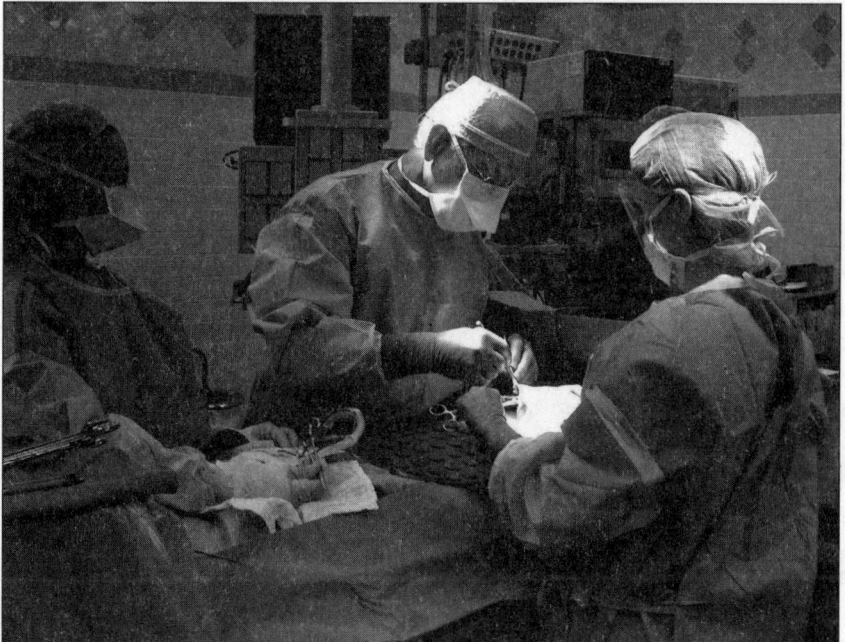

The OR Personnel

What's the maximum number of people who might be involved in a trauma case? For a Level I trauma center, the number of personnel is considerable, and within the ranks seen in the OR are many young doctors and medical students. In smaller community hospitals, the team to be described may shrink considerably.

Most or all of the following medical personnel will participate in the care of the trauma victim in the OR:

Trauma surgeon: The leader, a general surgeon whose life is devoted to the care of the injured.

Surgical residents: One or more; often do the procedure under the supervision of the trauma surgeon; may be at any level of training. The big secret: these unsung heroes do all the grunt work, are in the ER when the trauma victim comes in and save the lives that are nearly shattered at the scene; they have never been given credit by the public who so desperately and unwittingly rely on them.

Third and fourth year medical students: One or more observe, scrubbed and crowded about the OR table or in the way somewhere else. They see life from the "other side" often for the first time on the trauma service.

Anesthesiologists: One or more monitor vital signs, give anesthesia, support volume with blood and IV fluid; may leave the room periodically to let the anesthesia resident sweat the case.

Anesthesia residents: They are actually doing a lot of things under the supervision of the anesthesiologist; they try to give an alternate explanation to the surgeon for the patient's blood pressure dropping when the surgeon knows it's because of the hole in the bloody spleen in his hand.

Circulating nurse: One or two RNs. Gets supplies; coordinates the room internally and with the front desk regarding the progress of the case, anticipated ending time, when the next case starts, etc.; gets "stuff" for the annoyed surgeon; keeps the equipment in the room functioning properly; gets more "stuff" for the anesthesiologist; answers the resident's beeper, calls central supply for the one instrument the surgeon doesn't have but needs *now*.

Scrub tech: Stands within elbow distance of the surgeon and, unlike in American football, is not permitted to wear protective equipment. Hands instruments to the surgeon, including sutures, in a swift cadence.

OR assistants: Sometimes called orderlies. They help move patients onto the OR table before the case starts and off of the table at the conclusion of surgery; clean rooms (mop floors, stuff laundry, move the table, etc.) between cases and keep supplies available; go to preadmission for elective patients and return the gurneys to the surgical floors; know a lot about sophisticated OR equipment and how to keep it running.

Front desk personnel: Nurses or secretaries. They coordinate elective and emergency cases as well as all of the calls coming into the OR, some of which must be passed on to specific rooms. When the place heats up, there is no more stressful place in the world—for air traffic controllers, a plane *might* get into difficulty if something isn't done immediately; in the OR, trauma patients are wheeled down from the ER who are *already in the act of dying*; while this is going on, five other surgeons can't understand why they've been delayed; oh, and a patient in radiology having his coronaries reamed out just "crashed" —which means the chest boys will soon dance on the front desk person's head and will drown out the rest of the noise.

How Cases Are Listed:
The "Bumping" Scenario

Most of the multiple trauma cases come in a night. Booze, drugs and barrel-bottom human behavior kick in when the sun sets. It is then that the world turns more slowly and groans on its axis.

It is at night when the blood flows.

Last night, as I prepared my notes to write this section, I discovered yet another human had died in our trauma room of savagely inflicted stab wounds to the chest. Lest you believe this to be purely theoretical, I remind you there is a head injury sustained somewhere in the U.S. every seven seconds, a stab wound inflicted every fifteen minutes, a woman raped every six minutes. Operating room time is needed for the "knife and gun club," as doctors call them, as they unpredictably slash and maim each other. Within hours, a schedule of elective surgery booked for the next day must be completed. Someone has to make time. Also, other non-traumatic emergencies, such as perforated ulcers, burst appendixes, fractured hips, dog bites, etc., must be squeezed into the schedule, night and day.

Where do the trauma crunches go?

At least one operating room is kept open for dire emergencies. When the trauma surgeon calls from the ER and says, "We're coming down with a gunshot to the chest, in shock . . . oh, we may need bypass," he doesn't ask for the next available room. That's a different kettle of physical insult. The next available room is for a lesser type of distress, the perforated intestine cases that can stand a little "buffing up," a few hours of IV fluids and antibiotics.

Big trauma goes to the operating room immediately.

Stat.

Sometimes, the victim isn't *in extremis*. There's nothing to wait for because in this circumstance, surgery is part of the process of resuscitation. If the hole in the heart isn't patched, it doesn't matter how much IV fluid you administer to the patient. On the other hand, a stab wound to the belly, like the busted intestine, may need stabilization and fluid resuscitation, then an operation.

And sometimes a room just isn't available.

That's when *bumping* comes into play.

Often the surgeon, who books an emergency, doesn't know exactly what the problem is with his patient. Alas, the diagnostic rub! Although the surgeon knows something bad is going on in, say, the patient's belly, he *never* knows for certain the nature of the problem. Honesty is imperative to make bumping work.

Bumping refers to the selecting of one case over another to go directly to surgery because of the perceived acuteness of the emergency. The second case, although also urgent, is considered to be less so. That patient is taken to the next available operating room and everyone gets the care that's needed.

It's another wonderful source of conflict for a story.

Doctors milk the system for their own advantage. Often, bumping becomes an issue because everyone wants to get home. If the patient is stable, the wait for OR time is usually no more than an hour or two—a little time for a stable patient, an eternity for an impatient surgeon.

The following is a representative system of rating cases in order to determine what order emergency cases will be performed:

Designation of case: 1-4

1. A case designated a "one" must be done within two hours - highest priority, e.g. a patient with a perforated intestine and peritonitis
2. A case designated a "two" must be done within three to six hours - e.g. a patient with acute (uncomplicated) appendicitis
3. A case designated a "three" must be done within six to twelve hours - e.g. re-look after damage control surgery, a skin graft, or cleaning up a traumatic wound
4. A case designated a "four" must be done within twelve to twenty-four hours - e.g. a patient admitted with an infected gallbladder on antibiotics who needs a cholecystectomy before discharge

There's a final chapter in the bumping story.

The OR personnel—the anesthesiologists and nurses—talk to the surgeons involved about their patients and set up the order in which the cases will be done. If the surgeon who must wait disagrees, she must discuss it with the surgeon listed to go first. Listen to the conversation: The pediatric surgeon asks the neurosurgeon if it were *his* (the neurosurgeon's) child with the perforated appendix, would he want the pediatric surgeon to be bumped? The neurosurgeon counters with a demand that the pediatric surgeon tell him what he would want the neurosurgeon to do if this were *his* (the pediatric surgeon's) mother with the clot in her brain.

You take if from there.

Easy Cases

Most trauma victims never go to the operating room. Only fifteen percent need surgical treatment. For example, the drunken kid who bumps his head in a car crash and has a negative CT scan will be observed in the ICU and eventually discharged when stable. He may need a chest tube to treat a pneumothorax (collapsed lung, more on this in Part II), or his fractured fibula may require a cast before he goes to the ICU or special neurology unit for observation. But no major operation is needed.

Single organ trauma is the buzzword for uncomplicated cases. A broken thighbone represents a major injury with lots of rehabilitation in the wings. For the orthopedic surgeon, it's a matter of placing a rod into the bone (marrow cavity) to stabilize the fracture and encourage early ambulation.

A smashed spleen may be preserved by follow-up serial abdominal CT scans to make certain there is no further bleeding. Or the trauma surgeon may find blood in the abdomen when he performs an abdominal "tap" in the ER, which leads to exploratory surgery. There the issue becomes saving the ruptured spleen (less complicated than saving the whales) for its immune function. If terribly lacerated, the trauma surgeon may be obligated to remove the spleen.

But single organ trauma can also be horrible.

Take the case of a lacerated liver. Although most liver lacerations are small and the bleeding stops spontaneously, some livers are shattered and massive blood loss may spell eventual death, even though only one organ is damaged. So it depends which one. Woe to the poor soul with a major isolated head injury who slips into the persistent vegetative state.

Complicated Cases

Multiple organ system failure is the end point in trauma care gone wrong. The vital organs that ultimately fail—heart, lungs and kidneys, as well as the immune system, brain and intestines—may not be the organs injured. Thus, *multi-system trauma* refers to badly hurt people with some combination of broken bones, chest injury, brain trauma, ruptured abdominal organs, and shock on admission to the ER trauma room. Not all systems on this list must be injured for the victim to be in serious difficulty.

Let's see what happens with a complicated case in the operating room. Two or three teams of surgeons swell the OR ranks and everyone is screaming "priority". Who actually operates first? If you've got an OR scene in your story, you need to know who gets to fix his or her system first.

Here's a guide:

- Any serious bleeding must be handled first. If the surgeon is in a small hospital, she will do most of this work alone (with an assistant). In a level I center, the specialist, in whose anatomic territory the bleeding occurs, will stop the hemorrhage, unless the trauma surgeon decides to handle it (remember the turf battle issue?).

- Any acute head injury with brain compression from a blood clot or a depressed skull fracture must be handled next.

- Any chest injury that wasn't handled in the trauma room must now be fixed, and the thoracic or trauma surgeon will work simultaneously with the neurosurgeon on the multiple injury victim.

- The abdominal part, if not approached earlier for exsanguinating hemorrhage, is next.

- Lastly, the orthopedic surgeon does what's needed for extremity damage except when there's a vascular injury and the orthopedic surgeon operates first to fix broken bones (stabilize with rods, pins or screws) or reduce and stabilize dislocated limbs before the vascular surgeon attempts to suture delicate disrupted blood vessels.

- Somewhere in the course of the trauma victim's multiple, simultaneous operations, the plastic surgeon may become involved, as might an ENT surgeon, for maxillofacial smashes. The urologist works with the abdominal surgeon if the kidneys, bladder or other parts of the victim's plumbing are disrupted.

Multiple trauma is a team endeavor.

Major trauma occurs most often because someone took a calculated risk and lost. Enter the trauma team, the dedicated group of specialized doctors, nurses and other technicians—the "expensive care" team. A hospital with high-tech facilities and a dedicated staff of surgeons, nurses, OR personnel, ICU staff and regular floor nurses greet and care for the trauma victim.

When Things Go Wrong in the OR

Not all surgery ends happily.

Not all victims of trauma, treated at a dedicated facility, get better. Some don't make it out of the hospital alive. Not all injuries are treated successfully. Disabilities often linger long after all efforts have been exhausted to return the victim to a state of sound health.

Sometimes excreta strikes the flabellum.

Your stalwart surgeon hero may feel the nibbling pangs of fear when up from the depths of the opened abdomen, blood appears in huge clots and dribbles over the drapes. "Oh my God!" he cries, before catching himself. "Quick! Suction . . ." The controlled atmosphere of the OR abruptly disappears, replaced by panic and uncertainty.

Experienced surgeons get rattled?

It happens.

A sudden, unexplained fall in blood pressure, a cardiac arrest, a heart rhythm change, an unexplained rise in airway pressures suggesting a blocked windpipe, massive bleeding from the depths of a body cavity—all of these cause rapid acceleration of emotions among members of the operating team. Not all surgeons react with emotion. Most move through their planned emergency drill, step by calculated step. But the atmosphere is never the same again in that OR on that day.

At time, frustration creeps up on the surgeon. It's more of an insidious unraveling of the doctor's expectations. He can't locate the bullet in the belly. He can't actually find the blood vessel in the torn lung that's hemorrhaging. He can't get adequate exposure behind the liver where fresh blood keeps puddling.

OR Atmosphere

You've just had a taste of a panic scene—something that doesn't occur very often in the OR. At times, things heat up for other reasons. Surgeon and anesthesiologist may disagree about what constitutes adequate abdominal or chest wall muscle relaxation (permitting easy access to organs), how much fluid to give, which antibiotics to administer, where the patient should go after surgery (ICU versus the floor), and on and on.

Maybe the front desk calls into the room to see how much longer the surgeon thinks he'll be before closing. "Why are you asking?" fumes the surgeon. Is he late for the trauma clinic? Did his boss refuse to consider a raise? Is his wife out shopping as they speak? Did his favorite stock drop twenty-six points? Or was it because the resident doing the case is a klutz and the surgeon gets chest pain watching? It's anyone's guess why the surgeon loses his temper.

Often in the easier cases, music plays and everyone in the room begins to talk once the tough part of the operation is over. The scrub tech asks the circulating nurse for a recipe for chicken François or the name of her boyfriend's brother who fixes mufflers. The surgeon hits on the intern who asked if she could try to close the skin. Use your imagination. Most of the time it's just solid professionals doing their jobs.

Worked into these various levels of communication is the ever-present question asking ("pimping", as the residents call it). Anything in the surgical field or facts related to the case is fair game if a medical student is scrubbed. These obtuse questions are asked in the name of education.

Many exchanges, both with instruments and verbally, occur during a case. In the OR there's a doe's-eyelash distance between harassment in all forms and accepted behavior. Sometimes it's just harassment. In this case of on-the-job education, excreta obeys the laws of gravity. It flows from the trauma surgeon downhill to the intern. It's a wonder they're not all on antibiotics.

PACU: The Recovery Area

The severity of the injury determines where the trauma patient goes after surgery. Most post-op injured go to the *post-anesthesia care unit* (PACU) to recover from the affects of anesthetic drugs, the shock state caused by the trauma and the impact of major surgery. Monitors are used to watch heart and lung function (EKG, blood pressure, pulse, respiratory rate) as well as record urine production and keep track of bandages and drain output. When extubated (breathing tube removed from the windpipe), awake and stable, the patient is taken to the surgical floor.

Sometimes the trauma victim will go directly to the ICU from the operating room. In the more severely injured, there is no need to stop in PACU as the ICU serves the same purpose and the patient cannot be extubated anyway. Intense monitoring and care is begun in the surgical ICU beginning in the immediate postoperative period.

The Intensive Care Unit

Special medical services and personnel are available to ICU patients. Also available on the surgical floors, these services and treatments are given priority in the intensive care unit.

Special medical services available in the ICU include:
- The intensivist—a doctor specially trained in critical care medicine
- Specially trained ICU nurses
- Multiple high-tech machines to support ventilation, blood pressure, kidney function, nutrition, etc.
- Residents (in teaching hospitals) who work around the clock at the bedside, making minute-to-minute adjustments in sophisticated treatments
- Doctors and nurses with special training
- There are also special critical care units in the hospital that function like the main ICU in providing specialized care. These include cardiac surgery ICU, coronary care unit, pediatric ICU and dialysis unit

The Surgical Floor

Depending on the body system most injured, the trauma victim may be transferred from the PACU or ICU to a regular surgical floor. Some go to a specialty floor. For example, the hospital may have a neurological care floor to manage all head trauma, stroke victims and postneurosurgical patients. The orthopedic floor handles all of the bone and joint cases. If one of these is the predominantly traumatized system, the patient then goes to that floor.

Other trauma patients recover from their injuries on a floor designated as a specific unit for certain surgeons. Most are cared for on a general surgical floor, which manages a variety of cases. This includes elective operations.

Trauma patients go through a series of steps in their recovery. As each phase of recovery is completed, a number of possible complications are treated or the likelihood of getting a particular complication passes. Eventually, the patient "turns the corner". What does this mean?

Here is a list of *general phases of recovery* that every trauma victim passes through on her path to renewed health.

The acute injury phase: Stress hormones make the body retain fluid to fight shock and to use energy efficiently; much IV support is needed. The patient is ill in this phase for days.

The turning point: When the body decides the threat to survival is over, the patient feels better and begins to get rid of excess body fluid via increased urine production, temperature returns to normal, appetite improves, walks become longer, stairs seem less treacherous.

The anabolic phase: A natural buildup or anabolic replacement of lost body protein associated with major gains in strength, resumption of activities of daily living, and a return of interest in hobbies and work; even sex drive returns now (assuming it didn't reestablish itself moments after leaving the operating room).

The fat gain phase: Convalescence melds imperceptibly into normalcy, the metabolic piper has been paid, structural damage is repaired, extra calories become fat and life goes on.

Rehabilitation and Going Home

Some trauma victims don't go home.

Fifty percent of all head-injured patients die, and almost half of the survivors have a neurological deficit. Often, these poor souls must be cared for in long-term or chronic care facilities. Unable to perform activities of daily living, the brain-injured patient must rely on constant nursing care. There are institutions around the country that specialize in caring for head-injured and spinal cord-damaged patients.

If your story includes a victim of trauma to the nervous system, here are a number of chronic problems you may wish to visit upon your character:

Quadriplegia: Results in inability to use one's arms or legs due to paralysis. Patient may have limited upper arm movement; some are on ventilators, no control over bowels and bladder.

Paraplegia: Paralysis of the lower extremities; control problems of bowels and bladder; patient can get around in a wheelchair.

Pelvic or genital trauma: May result in permanent colostomy if bowel-controlling anal sphincter muscle is seriously damaged.

Disfigurement: Affecting face, hands or other parts. May include exaggerated scarring, amputations, tissue loss with skin grafting, burns, fused joints and a useless arm or leg.

Loss of voice: Neck trauma with permanent tracheotomy or paralysis of vocal cords.

Other rehabilitation issues include management of chronic bladder catheterization, treatment for urinary tract infections, cleaning and bandaging chronic open wounds, managing feeding tubes (through the abdominal wall into the stomach), bathing of patients with muscle weakness, physical therapy, occupational therapy and psychiatric evaluation and support. Most of these begin in the hospital and must be continued at home. Home care has replaced longer hospital stays in order to complete the rehabilitation process.

At home, the trauma patient begins to see the course of his illness. Lost time, perhaps lost job security and difficulties he has pressed on the family with such a complicated clinical course may cause depression. Anger at the random nature of the accident and at the doctors and nurses who performed so many unpleasant tests and treatments may push the recovering patient to despair. Of course, many find solace and a genuine sense of gratitude that they are survivors.

Lastly, the trauma victim is evaluated in the surgical clinic several times following discharge from the hospital. In addition, the patient may need to see an orthopedic or neurosurgeon for more specific follow-up. At times, the patient must be readmitted for additional surgery. These procedures include skin grafts; removal of pins, screws and other orthopedic hardware; or plastic surgery to revise scars and repair poorly healing wounds.

The areas of the trauma center of most concern to the victim of major body injury are the operating room, the intensive care unit, the rehabilitation unit and the hospital's surgical clinic. Each of these settings provides you with an opportunity to weave another thread of uncertainty about recovery into the fabric of your story.

PART II

SPECIFIC TRAUMATIC INJURIES BY ORGAN SYSTEM

FIVE

HEAD TRAUMA: FROM CONCUSSION TO THE PERSISTENT VEGETATIVE STATE

> This is where those writers are mistaken who write books called *Generals Die in Bed*, because this general died in a trench dug in snow, high in the mountains, wearing an Alpine hat with an eagle feather in it and a hole in the front you couldn't put your little finger in and a hole in back you could put your fist in, if it were a small fist and you wanted to put it there, and much blood in the snow.
>
> — Ernest Hemingway, *A Natural History of the Dead*

Man and his animal companions developed solid bone shields over eons to protect their brains. The skull bones, a double layer of armament, protected the victim from all sorts of trauma, including, no doubt, getting clobbered with a bison femur by a cave neighbor. But no one in charge of designing skulls back then anticipated the gasoline engine, gunpowder or American football. Man-made weapons infused new meaning into words like *deceleration* and *impact*.

In the United States, someone suffers from a head injury every fifteen seconds and someone dies of a head impact every twelve minutes. Although the skull affords adequate protection to the brain for the kinds of forces experienced over the years of our evolution, it cannot deal with the types of impacts encountered in the twenty-first century. More than sixty percent of all auto accident fatalities are from head injury. In this chapter, we will learn about lesser as well as major head trauma, a theme reflected in each chapter in this section via the Master Injury Lists. To make it easier to grasp the spectrum of head injuries, we'll divide them up in the list according to what structures get smashed. Because there are so many elements of anatomy in the head and neck, only common injuries are presented.

Each of these head injuries will be dealt with in some detail as no other group of injuries are as critical to full recovery. And they are no strangers to literature.

It was in this cave that a man whose head was broken as a flowerpot may be broken, although it was all held together by membranes and a skillfully applied bandage now soaked and hardened, with the structure of his brain disturbed by a piece of broken steel in it, lay a day, a night, and a day.

Few writers will express surprise at the words Hemingway chose (again, in *A Natural History of the Dead*) to depict man's traumatic plight, and few could match his ability to take essential medical principles involving the consequences of impact and translate them into a true, timeless description of the savagery of war. The quote above includes a reference to the meninges, the membranes enveloping the brain; a shattered, open compound fracture of the skull, and its essentially futile field treatment.

A flowerpot, a bandage. A shattered brain, a wasted life. Accurate, timeless, it is visual. Disturbing, it is literature.

Skull fractures are *open* if they are found with a scalp laceration or *closed* if the scalp is intact. The underlying brain may be compressed, lacerated or both. Buried beneath the flowery cerebral cortex lies the reptilian brainstem, which also suffers from the increased pressure in the cranium as the brain swells above it. Designed to regulate unconscious body functions, the brainstem may be the only survivor of a major brain insult, thus becoming a central neurological headquarters of sorts for the *persistent vegetative state* (PVS).

A few immediate steps must be taken when either a fracture or lacerated scalp is identified:

- Clean scalp wound and suture if no other injuries exist.
- If a compound (open) skull fracture is present, suture the dura (brain membrane) closed and elevate any depressed skull bone. Remove loose bone fragments. Place the patient on antibiotics.
- The most important task for the trauma surgeon treating a head injury is to decide if there is a *focal* or *mass lesion*. If a blood clot is forming inside the skull, it must be identified immediately and evacuated by a neurosurgeon. To find a clot hiding inside the skull, the surgeon looks for the following *lateralizing symptoms* (i.e., only found on one side of the body) in addition to drowsiness or frank coma:
- Enlarged pupil (usually on the same side as the clot)
- Paralysis on the opposite side (arm and leg)

Also, blood pressure may rise as heart rate (pulse) drops. If these signs are present, or if a head trauma victim becomes drowsy after having been awake, the surgeon must perform a head CT scan and search for a subdural, epidural, or intracerebral blood clot (Figure 7). The massive clot exerts pressure inside the skull, literally squeezing the victim's brain and, eventually, life away.

Severe impact affects all layers of the head, setting off destructive waves of energy that are transmitted to the deepest, oldest ganglia of the

Master Injury List For the Head I

Injuries involving the brain and skull (victims may be awake, lethargic or unconscious with any of these skull fractures)

Skull Fractures

- Simple "straight line" non-depressed: treat underlying brain injury
- Depressed: some need neurosurgical elevation of fragment to avoid seizures in the future
- Open: need immediate surgery to close meninges (membranes) to protect brain from infection (brain exposed)
- Base of the skull: often not seen on x-ray; treat conservatively

Diffuse Brain Injuries

- Concussion
- —Mild: temporary confusion, amnesia
- —Severe: nausea, headache, dizziness, amnesia
- Diffuse brain injury: also called a closed head injury or a brainstem injury; prolonged coma for days or weeks

Focal Brain Injuries

- Brain contusion: small or large, single bruise or multiple; prolonged coma, confusion and if large, may cause brain compression and serious neurological deterioration
- Bleeding into the brain
- —Surface: tear in epidural artery with major clot formation and brain compression or bleeding under the membranes (meninges); called a subdural hematoma (clot)
- —Deep: bleeding into brain substance; impalement or bullet wounds

brain where the brain becomes the spinal cord at collar level. We'll work our way through these injuries in a little more detail.

Almost seventy percent of trauma victims with multiorgan system impacts will have a head injury, anything from a torn scalp to lacerations and clots inside the mysterious mind cave, the cranial vault. You may combine single injuries to create horrible results or merely mix and match lesser insults to create a state of confusion about story outcome— adding a ticking clock to your plot.

If your character strikes the windshield of his car, he might sustain a *simple linear skull fracture*. On x-ray it appears as a dark line engraved in the whiteness of the bone, undisplaced, reducing the likelihood of underling brain damage—unless the fracture crosses a part of the skull (temporal bone) where a large blood vessel (the middle meningeal artery) lies embedded in the cranium. Major hemorrhage inside the skull may occur when the artery is torn.

There is no specific treatment for a simple linear skull fracture not associated with an epidural clot, unless road dirt became caught in the fracture found with a scalp laceration. At the instant the skull is smashed, the bone opens several millimeters. When it shuts, debris may get caught in the fracture line, and the neurosurgeon must clean it up.

If the impact dents your character's cranium, she has a *depressed skull fracture*. The neurosurgeon must decide whether or not he needs bone fragments elevated (lifted free of the brain surface) or pieces of the broken skull removed. The underlying dura membrane must be closed as well. With all skull fractures, management is subservient to the underlying brain injury.

Figure 7 – Brain Hemorrhage (Hematoma)

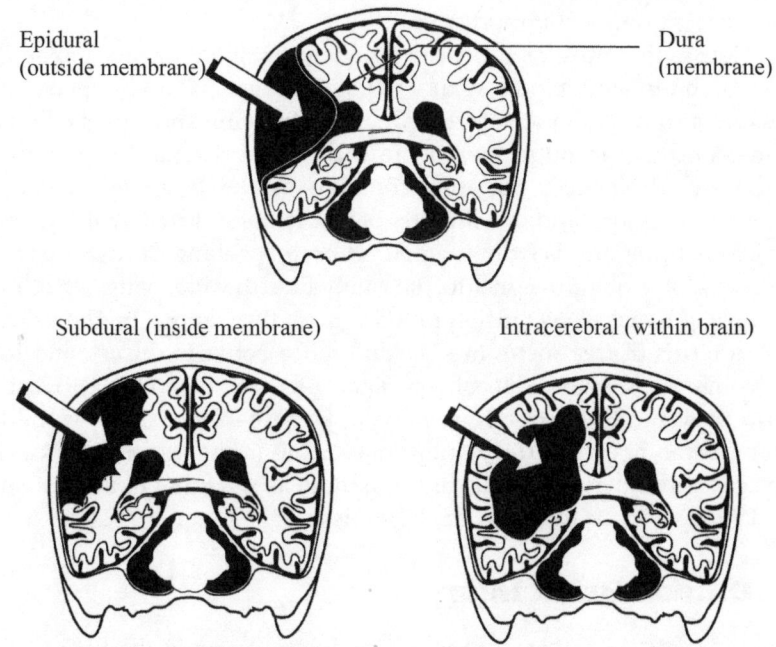

Epidural (outside membrane)

Dura (membrane)

Subdural (inside membrane)

Intracerebral (within brain)

In particular, *open skull fractures*—where the lining of the brain (dura mater) is torn leaving the brain exposed—must be repaired as an emergency. Torn meninges (dura mater, Hemingway's "membranes") allow leakage of cerebrospinal fluid (CSF). This unique clear liquid is the waterbed of the brain and infection will almost certainly ensue if the membranes aren't surgically closed. The patient will also be placed on antibiotics.

Your unfortunate character may have hit something or was struck in an attack and suffered a *basal skull fracture*. The mass of bone at the base of the skull is complex and fractures are sometimes difficult to diagnose in this location. Instead of a dent in his "squash"—that's what the intern calls your character's noble cranium—the poor fellow arrives in the ER dripping fluid the color of pink zinfandel from his ear. Not blood, mind you, but something suspicious, which the intern mops up with a gauze pad.

A faint pink halo forms about the blood spot from the victim's ear and represents cerebrospinal fluid leaking from a basilar skull fracture. Bruising behind the ear is called *Battle's Sign* and suggests the same diagnosis. *Raccoon eyes* refer to periorbital (around the eyes) bruising, which may be from direct facial trauma or from a basilar skull fracture.

Treatment of the other injuries your character suffers from won't matter much if the cerebral sepulcher isn't handled properly. The squash must be intact. For some head injuries, immediate neurosurgical treatment is of utmost importance.

Here's the physiologic deal: Unyielding skull meets expanding mass of brain and blood with no place to go. What happens? The pressure in the system shoots up, squeezes the brain and squirts the vital brainstem down through the hole in the base of the skull like so much toothpaste. Prolonged, the imprisonment of the brain gives way to dysfunction, injury and, eventually, death. It doesn't matter if increased intracranial pressure is from the injured brain swelling diffusely or from a blood clot expanding inside the skull like the big bang, creating a universe of treacherous tension pitted against the trapped brain tissue.

In terms of treatment, the big difference between diffuse and focal brain injury is that a focal problem (e.g., a blood clot) requires neurosurgical intervention to remove it. Diffuse injuries may be mild or severe. Some brain injuries require only a *bolt* (a monitoring device that is placed through a small hole in the skull to assess intracranial pressure) and IV medications to shrink the brain tissues.

Diffuse Brain Injury

Woof—something, someone, struck her square in the back. The blow knocked all the breath out of her . . . It happened again . . . Kate was in shocking pain . . . He swung hard and struck her in the forehead.

She heard a metallic *ring*, and felt herself falling, toppling. Felt herself *vaporizing*, actually. Then her body bounced off the wooden floorboards . . .

She stayed conscious for a long time. She fought with all her strength. She was stubborn, willful, and proud as hell. The light finally went out for her like a tube in an old-fashioned TV set. A blurry picture, then a small dot of light, then blackness. It was that simple, that prosaic.

James Patterson's point-of-view character in *Kiss the Girls* is attacked by two men and slips into a coma. The brutal assault bridges the end of one chapter and the beginning of another. Like the terse chapters, his short choppy sentences mimic the assault itself. Kate's "Off" button is punched, the wiring of her brain disrupted, and her visual light, like the TV cathode ray tube, fades.

Kate will be back. She's merely suffered from a concussion. She'll be a little confused, perhaps. She doesn't have a blood clot swelling inside her skull.

A *concussion* is a diffuse brain injury that produces coma and, often, amnesia, with rapid recovery. This insult, as well as the more severe form, is the result of rapid flexion-extension of the head and neck, impact of the brain against the inside of the skull with rotation of the brain. This motion disrupts several areas of neurologic tissue. A concussion may be associated with nausea, headache and/or dizziness, but the examining doctor usually doesn't discover the specific lateralizing (present on one side of the body only) neurologic signs mentioned above.

During the 1994 National Football League season, there were ninety documented concussions. Called "bell-ringers," these injuries may be followed by what is termed the *second impact syndrome*, another head hit which aggravates the initial injury and cause severe brain swelling. In some victims, the second impact results in death. At least one hockey player's career ended that year because of a severe concussion, and more than a few baseball players got "dinged" by an errantly tossed ball. Concussions probably happen more often than is documented in and out of sport.

Treatment?

If your character was knocked out cold for more than five to ten minutes, you'd better have a doctor admit him to a hospital for twenty-four hours of observation. Admit any kids who've been in a coma from a head injury regardless of length of time—unless, of course, your character can't or won't seek medical care and the brain injury becomes a source of story tension.

Diffuse (axonal) brain injury refers to prolonged coma and implies severe injury to different parts of the brain and brainstem. The coma may last for weeks. A third to a half of these poor souls will die of their injuries. Only a CT scan of the head will clearly distinguish this insult from the next group of brain injuries, many of which require emergency surgery.

Focal Brain Injury
Brain Contusion
A brain bruise, or contusion, may be of any size, number or location and may occur at the point of impact or at a distance (contrecoup injury), thus producing a spectrum of confusing clinical signs. You can get away with almost any story of foreshadowing with this one. Create any neurologic deficit (e.g., paralysis or blindness) by choosing the mechanism of injury and the impact point on the skull.

Intracranial Hemorrhage
Bleeding on the brain surface occurs inside the skull between the unyielding dura mater membrane and the soft brain surface and causes damage by creating increased intracranial pressure as we have seen. This clinical picture is characterized by coma followed by:

- A lucid period during which your character's window of consciousness may not be marked by full awareness
- A second period of unconsciousness
- Clinical findings of paralysis on the opposite side of the body and enlargement of the same side pupil, which doesn't react (become smaller when exposed to direct light)

For the writer, an *acute epidural bleed* is arterial (so bleeding is brisk) and raises the heat of the scene as the stakes soar. An epidural hematoma collects between the bony skull and the dura mater, the outer brain membrane. Without urgent neurosurgical intervention, the victim will die.

Similar to the acute epidural bleed is an acute *subdural hematoma*, which results from a tear of veins under the dura mater and above the cortex. Lethal in over sixty percent of patients, this injury may also occur with a skull fracture where bone fragments cut brain tissue and lacerate surface arteries or veins. Three types of subdural hematoma are seen according to when they require surgery:

1. Acute subdural hematoma—operated on within twenty-four hours
2. Subacute subdural hematoma—to OR within two days to two weeks
3. Chronic subdural hematoma—operated on after two weeks

How a Doctor Evaluates a Head Injury

Glasgow Coma Score less than 8
If . . .
Pupils unequal or other lateralizing signs present (paralysis; decreased reflexes; decerebrate or decorticate posturing*)

Could be . . .
- Large mass (blood clot)
- Diffuse axonal injury

The doctor will . . .
- Admit to ICU
- Give mannitol and steroids to shrink brain
- Put on ventilator
- Get CT scan, stat
- Operate for mass, stat
- Observe if CT scan negative

Glasgow Coma Score 8 or greater
If . . .
No pupil inequality or lateralizing signs present

Could be . . .
- Mass (blood clot)
- Basilar skull fracture
- Brain contusion
- Brain concussion
- Minor injury

If open skull fracture, the doctor will immediately . . .
- Admit patient to hospital (ICU)
- Get urgent CT
- Operate if there's a mass or CSF leak

If closed skull fracture, the doctor will . . .
- Observe if no bad neurological signs

Decerebrate posturing means continuous spasm of extensor muscles of both arms and legs because of injury at the brainstem level (very bad sign). *Decorticate posturing* with flexed arms and extended legs means injury at the cortex level (bag sign).

Bleeding Inside the Brain

Bleeding may occur in the substance of the brain tissue, deep in the tangle of pathways and ganglia, disrupting the essential cerebral wiring. A blunt strike on the skull, impalement of a sharp object or a gunshot wound may, through different mechanisms, all result in a central brain blood clot.

By the way, you *never* remove an impaling object from the skull. The neurosurgeon will do so in the operating room where all hell may break loose if more bleeding is unleashed.

Bullet wounds to the skull are frequently wrongly invented in contemporary fiction. Improbable entry and exit locations are often chosen, which, in reality, would cause disruption of nerve pathways followed by paralysis, prolonged coma or death. Yet, the character walks and talks.

So it's important to remember the following two bad prognostic signs with penetrating head injuries:

1. "Through and through" (entry and exit wounds visible) wounds are ominous.
2. The lower down on the skull (closer to the vital brainstem functions) the bullet hole, the worse the prognosis.

Also, most bullets leave small entry wounds and blow off the back of the skull (huge exit wound). Hemingway got it right. But regardless of which of these brain injuries is suspected, the doctor will assess each patient in the same fashion. The easiest, most productive method of neurologic evaluation tests the victim's ability to open her eyes, talk, and move.

The Glasgow Coma Scale (GCS) is also part of the revised trauma score and describes the method doctors use to assess the trauma patient's present level of brain function. You now understand how important it is for the paramedic to document this information in the field. If the victim's level of consciousness changes, the trauma surgeon may not be aware of it unless proper documentation in the field was carried out. The basic principle is for the examiner to determine what the best response is at that time:

Function	Stimulus/Response	Score
Best eye opening	spontaneous	4
	to voice	3
	to pain	2
	none	1
Best verbal response	oriented	5
	confused	4
	inappropriate words	3
	nonsense words	2
	none	1
Best motor response	obeys commands	6
	localizes pain	5
	withdraws to painful stimulus	4
	flexes with painful stimulus	3

extension with painful stimulus   2
none   1

The best GCS score is 15 while a 3 signifies an overwhelming brain injury. Other grave findings in a head injury victim are seizures, restlessness and severely elevated body temperature.

The sidebar on page 71 gives you a sketch of what steps the surgeon takes to triage a head-injured victim.

Scalp Injury

Scalp lacerations vary from trivial but bloody cuts all the way to what doctors refer to as degloving injuries—a literal ripping of the scalp from its bony cranial attachments like stripping off a glove. In the Old West, it was called scalping.

The scalp is the thickest skin in the body; more cushion for the squash. Because scalp arteries run in dense connective tissue and are "held open" by this fibrous net, scalp lacerations bleed like swamps, especially in children. You may recall someone in your childhood, blood dripping into her eyebrows, hair matted, wailing in fear. Scalps can bleed a lot. Use this fact to create drama, uncertainty about prognosis, or a major life-threatening hemorrhage.

How the doctor treats a scalp laceration
- Washes (irrigates) wound with lots of normal saline
- Clamps massively bleeding blood vessels and ties them off
- Examines the wound with gloved finger looking for a skull fracture; orders skull x-rays as needed (maybe a CT scan with prolonged coma)
- If uncomplicated by a fracture, sutures scalp closed
- If complicated, calls neurosurgeon

You can remember the layers of the scalp from the outside in by using the mnemonic SCALP. See Figure 8.

Facial Injuries

The three types of fractures of the face and cheeks are fractures of the lower jaw, upper jaw and the zygoma or cheekbone. Any fracture of the bones forming the orbit (the bony circle about the eye) must be referred to a plastic surgeon for immediate repair. This is also true for cheekbone breaks. The zygomatic bones, which give the cheek its loft, are

Master Injury List For The Head II
Injuries not involving the brain and skull
Scalp Wounds
- Minor: Bleeding may be impressive; lacerations small, require only sutures
- Major: Most of scalp ripped from skull; needs careful assessment of skull before closure

Facial Fractures
- Orbital (eye) fractures
- Nasal fractures
- Cheekbone fractures

Jaw Fractures
- Lower jaw (mandible): Various patterns
- Upper jaw (maxilla): LeFort I, II and III

immediately beneath the skin and get smashed with some regularity. These injuries also require the skill of a plastic surgeon to elevate the fragments and wire them back into proper alignment. Fixing a broken nose is optional. Fractured nasal bones may need to be pried back into position; undisplaced breaks are left to heal by themselves.

The upper jaw fractures may also involve other facial bones and reflect extensive facial trauma. Called LeFort fractures, they occur with major facial smashes (Figure 9) and are Types I, II and III.

Lower Jaw Injuries
Bruising of the chin as well as sore jaw joints result from being struck in the jaw. More serious is a fracture of the jaw, as shown in Figure 9. Jaw fractures are treated by stabilizing the jaw, using the teeth to hold the fracture together with bars, wires, and rubber bands. Your "wired" character will spend several weeks eating through a straw.

The best way to diagnose a broken jaw is to find the tender point and move it. A crunching noise called *crepitus* tips off your doctor character, who should don gloves for this exam. It's performed with both hands, one inside the mouth, one outside. Will his patient bite him?

We'll finish with a few head odds and ends that can be useful in characterization.

Figure 8 – Layers of the Scalp

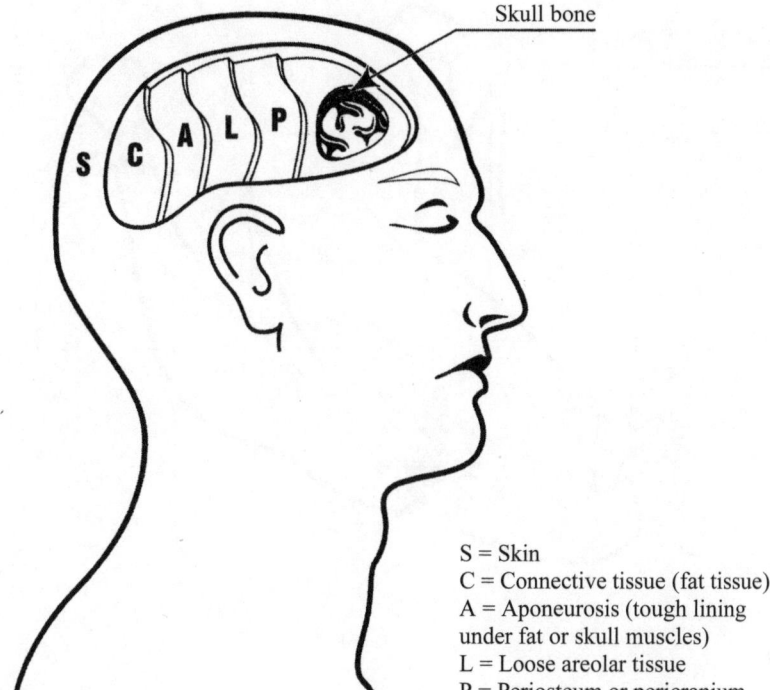

Skull bone

S = Skin
C = Connective tissue (fat tissue)
A = Aponeurosis (tough lining
under fat or skull muscles)
L = Loose areolar tissue
P = Periosteum or pericranium
(tough lining of the skull bones)

Patterns of Baldness

Baldness coupled with evidence of a hair transplant may help develop character or reflect how one deals with aging. Does the CEO walk into the boardroom with plugs of one-inch hair creating a new hairline above his bushy eyebrows? Are the surgeon's indelible ink marks still evident at the base of each tuft? Does anyone in the room dare ask?

Figure 9 – Lower and Upper Jaw Fractures

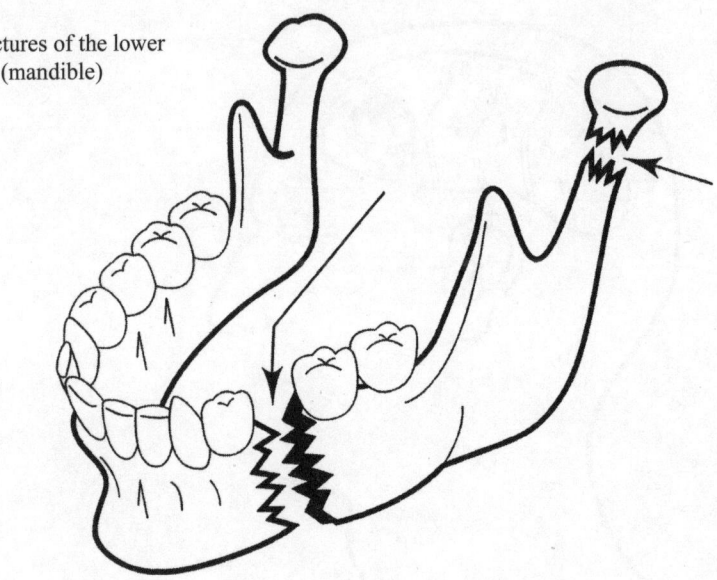

Fractures of the lower
jaw (mandible)

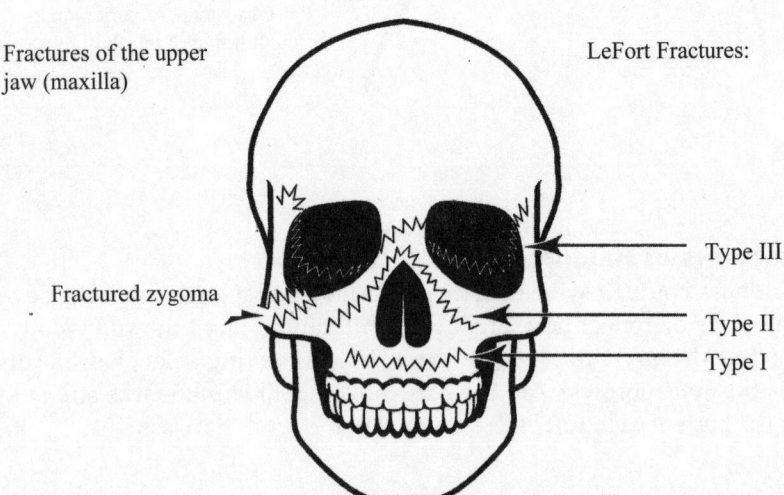

Fractures of the upper
jaw (maxilla)

LeFort Fractures:

Fractured zygoma

Type III

Type II

Type I

Eye Signs From Local Trauma

Subconjunctival hemorrhage: Bleeding under the red inside part of the eyelid. Usually heals without treatment but looks terrible for a while.

Scleral hemorrhage: Bleeding beneath the white part of the eye that abates slowly. May suggest other more serious eye injuries.

Orbital cellulitis: Infection of the soft tissue about the eye with swelling, redness and pain in the eye; often must be treated in the hospital with IV antibiotics. This is a good problem to get a character out of the way for a few days. A managed care plan may not allow hospitalization.

Ruptured orbit: Fluid drains from eyeball, which collapses. Usually from impalement of eye with sharp object, results in blindness if not repaired and may cause blindness regardless of treatment.

Cut Facial Nerves and Facial Paralysis

Upper facial laceration: A cut lateral to eye on cheek may produce a permanently open eye with drainage—a one-sided vacant stare.

Lower facial laceration: If anywhere near jaw margin, this can produce a depression ("droopy") deformity at the corner of the mouth.

Bizarre Things

Stephen King hits the high-water mark for the medically grotesque in the prologue of *The Dark Half* when he describes a neurosurgeon opening the skull of a patient whose twin was all but absorbed during embryological development. Left on the surface of the brain, the fascinated surgeon discovers, is an eyeball that "looked as if it were trying to wink at them", three fingernails and two teeth.

This, from the master of aberration.

Do what you will with the noble head. Create new injuries, bizarre scars. Make your readers remember your friends any way you can.

NECK AND SPINAL CORD INJURIES: SNAPPED, STABBED AND STRANGLED

Witness expert trauma care at an accident scene and you will notice how obsessive paramedics are about protecting the neck in cases of *potential* cervical spine injury. Not only is head trauma often associated with neck injury, but also the neck injury is potentially *unstable*.

Potentially. That means conflict.

Angular with soft muscular cords framed by brunette locks or massive from the fullback's hairline to his shoulders, the neck conceals a vital tangle of tubes, nerves and blood vessels. These essential structures travel from the head to the chest or arise from the heart and shoot upward in a sprig of branches to the head, neck and arms. Size does little to afford the neck protection from injury.

The neck is also a common target for assault. Weapons such as a knife, screwdriver, ice pick, piece of glass, and length of wire or gun may be used to slash, stab, and garrote or shoot the neck. A maddened, mindless attacker may not use a penetrating weapon. Grabbing anything in sight to bludgeon his victim, or employing his fists, the villain may smash repeatedly at the neck. Blunt trauma, in the form of strikes or compressive force by hands, arm, wire or rope, produces different injuries from those seen with penetrating trauma. A stranglehold may be used to frighten human prey as well as to kill.

While the spinal cord isn't always at risk, major blood vessels in the neck frequently come under attack. A lot of anatomical structures stand in the path of a neck assault, and most of them don't take kindly to being cut open. Before we get to specific injuries (e.g., those produced by blunt vs. penetrating impact), consider what's at risk regardless of the traumatic agent:

- Larynx (voice box)
- Trachea (windpipe)
- Jugular vein
- Carotid artery
- Esophagus (gullet)
- Spinal cord
- Vertebrae

The neck encompasses an impressive number of vital organs, and the injury of any of these structures, could result in death. Both blunt and penetrating neck trauma cause major injuries, and some are associated with prolonged disability.

As always, it's a matter of degree.

Direct Trauma to the Neck

Penetrating Neck Trauma

The treatment of any neck injury begins with two questions: (1) Is there an actual or potential spinal cord injury? (2) Does the victim have an adequate airway?

Assume, for the moment, that we're dealing with penetrating neck trauma from a knife assault. Most neck injuries result from a stabbing attack. Sharp, penetrating attacks to the neck often come from in front and are aimed at the anterior neck or chest, and frequently, structures in both anatomic areas become injured with a single assault. Attacks from behind are still directed for the most part at the throat. With a "reach-around" knife assault, the intent is to slash open the major neck blood vessels.

Thus, as a general statement, muscles, ligaments and vertebrae (including the spinal cord) are seriously injured by indirect neck trauma, while superficial anterior structures are at risk from sharp weapon assaults. On the other hand, gunshot wounds may rip through any part of the neck.

Master Injury List for Neck Trauma
Minor Neck Injuries
- Neck sprain
- Minor fracture of vertebral process
- Stable ligament tear
- Contusion of neck
- Minor lacerations
- Temporary spinal cord injury

Major Neck Injuries
- Laceration of the jugular vein
- Laceration of the carotid artery
- Perforation of the larynx
- Perforation of the trachea
- Perforation of the esophagus
- Unstable neck fractures
- Permanent spinal cord injury

A discussion of penetrating injuries centers on whom the trauma surgeon should take to surgery in order to explore the neck structures for serious injury. But with neck fractures, the issue is what method of stabilization is most advantageous.

In a study on penetrating neck wounds, those victims explored immediately had a six percent mortality rate. Victims of a neck stab injury either not operated on at all or for whom surgery was delayed during initial observation had a thirty-five percent death rate—almost a six-fold increase.

Quite a difference. And while we don't know how many of the operated patients developed complications after surgery, the number of patients who had a neck operation with no findings of a major injury ranged from forty to sixty-three percent. Still, this large negative exploration rate wasn't enough to discourage most trauma surgeons from an aggressive approach to these injuries. And these injuries are not a new problem. A French surgeon tied off the first lacerated carotid artery in the 1500's!

To resolve the issue of whom to operate on and whom to observe, a system is used that divides the neck into three zones, as shown in Figure 10. The zone involved does not determine treatment decisions.

Zone I: Root of the neck, from the collarbone to the lower edge of the larynx (Adam's apple). This is the most dangerous neck zone as serious injuries to the great vessels arising from the heart occur with downward-directed knife assaults. An innocent-looking stab wound above the collarbone may lacerate the aorta in the chest. Beneath the skin in the middle of the neck lies the trachea (windpipe) and just behind it the esophagus (gullet). A knife attack may cut open the esophagus, spilling terrible bacteria into the chest. Immediate or delayed infections can occur if these injuries aren't recognized.

The surgeon may ask for an *arteriogram*, a special dye study (an x-ray) of the arteries in the region of the wound. This will indicate if there's a blood vessel leak. Other studies include an *upper GI series*, to examine the gullet for a perforation, and *bronchoscopy*, a look inside the windpipe with a fiber optic instrument.

If a major injury is diagnosed, the surgeon will have to "crack" (surgically open) the chest. Midline sternum-splitting incisions as well as horizontal incisions beneath the collarbone are used.

Zone II: From the lower edge of larynx to angle of the jaw. Many of the stab wounds in this area are evaluated in the trauma room where a decision about further surgery depends on a few reliable physical findings. Because most of the vital structures are not deep in this zone, special x-rays are used less often.

Figure 10– Zones of the Neck

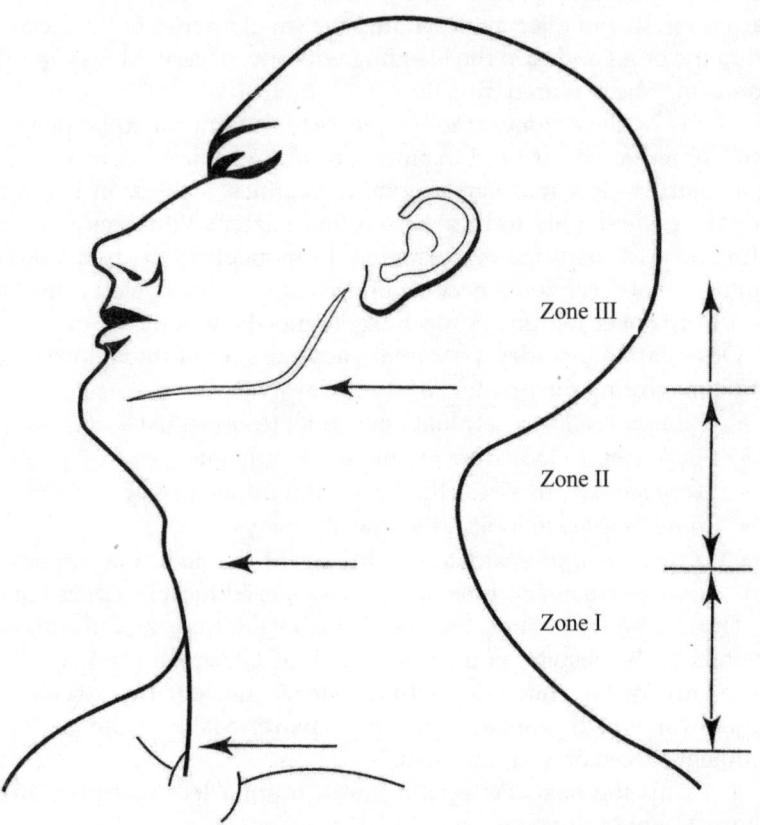

Acute physical findings that require emergency surgery include:

- A hematoma (blood clot) that's expanding or growing as it is observed, the implication being that a major blood vessel continues to bleed and the airway may become squeezed.
- Major bleeding from the wound not adequately controlled in the trauma room
- Air in the neck tissue (subcutaneous emphysema), which means the larynx or trachea has been perforated
- A major wound that must be debrided (cleaned up) surgically and inspected carefully (bleeding and poor lighting in the ER means that not all wounds are properly assessed there).

Zone III: The area above the jaw up to the base of the skull. It's not easy for a surgeon to dig around in the tight spaces of the upper neck and face without inadvertently causing more damage than already exists. If major hemorrhage is the problem, the radiologist will perform an arteriogram and inject material into the small arteries of the facial area to plug the holes and stop the bleeding without surgery. More superficial wounds may be explored directly.

In any of these zones, the wound may not appear to be deep, and careful observation—if local exploration in the trauma room reveals no major injuries—is a reasonable option. At times, a decision is made to observe a patient, only to be reversed hours later. With neck wounds, a healthy dose of suspicion is warranted. Proponents of the two schools of thought—to observe some neck wound victims or operate on everyone— cross swords over whose approach represents the best medicine.

Observation includes performing any number of the following tests at any time during the first few hospital days:

- *Barium swallow* to evaluate the gullet (esophagus)
- *Endoscopy* to look directly into the esophagus
- *Laryngoscopy* to assess the throat and upper airway
- *Bronchoscopy* to look at the lower airways
- *Arteriogram* to evaluate the arteries of the neck and upper chest (x-rays are never done on the veins), used most in Zones I and III

During your victim's trauma room evaluation, and through the uncertain early hospital course, the clock just keeps on ticking. If you need a subplot for your injury-strewn story, consider two doctors who disagree on which stabbed neck to explore. Make it the neck of a prominent citizen or a supermodel.

Turn up the heat. Penetrating neck trauma lets you play around with treatment options.

Blunt Neck Injuries

These are usually less severe, although it's possible to clot off a carotid artery with blunt neck trauma, sometimes resulting in a stroke. Near hanging, garroting as a threat, or an interrupted choking attempt all leave soft tissue swelling and the possibility of airway blockage.

It may not happen immediately; your heroine may turn purple at midnight.

Tick tock.

Indirect Trauma to the Neck
Neck Fractures and Dislocations

A broken neck can kill your character quicker than a jab in the throat. But the trauma patient who suffers from quadriplegia—loss of function of the arms and legs—may be the most unfortunate victim of chance. For the writer, a neck injury with the *potential* for neck damage opens unlimited possibilities.

For example: paralysis—if that's the end point you are seeking—may occur:

- At the time of the accident
- When emergency personnel or a well-meaning friend first attempts to move the victim
- During transportation to the hospital
- When the ER doctors move the patient into the trauma room
- When the victim is being moved to x-ray for view of his cervical spine
- During a surgical mishap

The neck bones may splinter in numerous ways, but we're interested in two patterns only: (1) stable neck fractures and (2) unstable neck fractures.

Stable neck fractures are present when the majority of the vertebral bone is intact, the ligaments are still holding and there is no x-ray suggestion of dislocation. On the other hand, an *unstable fracture* is characterized by smaller bone fragments, torn ligaments, and the overriding of one vertebra on the next. This sliding of one bone on the one above or below creates a shearing effect and pinches the spinal cord. The result is a damaged cord and interruption of information traveling to the brain and back down to muscles and other organs. It can lead to paralysis.

In any area of the vertebral column from the neck to the sacrum, any two vertebral bodies can slide on each other or *dislocate* without actually being broken. Held in place by massive ligaments running up and down the spine in front and behind the vertebral bodies, the bones are also anchored by shorter ligaments between bony projections on the vertebrae and by accessory joints. The smaller stabilizer joints are the ones that pop and crack like firewood when a chiropractor manipulates a patient's neck.

Severe flexion-extension motion of the neck causes most of the unstable as well as stable cervical spine injuries. "Whiplash" is a legal term. It's descriptive. A vivid image of forward bending of the neck with sudden force applied from behind followed by backward motion, or hyperextension, of the neck becomes indelible in your mind. Only the deep ligaments of the neck and the strap muscles can arrest this action.

The automobile headrest is designed to modify this sort of movement of the head and neck should impact occur. Pain is often in proportion to the other person's insurance policy.

A blow to the top of the head may cause fracture of the first cervical vertebra, the *atlas*. If there's no nerve damage, the treatment is conservative with immobilization and rehabilitation. The situation becomes a little more complicated at this point with fractures and dislocations as well as combined fracture-dislocations. Any of these neck injuries may be unstable and therefore critical.

You may have heard of a youngster who became paralyzed after diving into a quarry, empty pool, or shallow pond. Cervical spine injuries carry the potential to kill, or to maim for life. These injuries may cause one of two basic types of spinal cord injury: (1) contusion (bruise) of the spinal cord or (2) compression of the spinal cord.

Most severe cord injuries don't resolve. They may occur anywhere down the vertebral column, and as the distance from the neck increases, the degree of paralysis decreases. So the victim of a broken low back (lumbar fractures) would suffer from *paraplegia* if the cord damage was permanent. This involves loss of leg, bowel, bladder, and sexual function.

Of course, many people have suffered from neck spasm at one time or another. Although quite painful, there is no neurological deficiency. A diagnosis of *neck sprain* can only be made after a careful physical examination and negative neck x-rays. Damage to soft tissues, muscles, ligaments and joints causes decreased range of motion and pain. Treatment involves immobilization with a cervical collar, rest and physical therapy.

Uncertainty *always* surrounds the exact nature of a cervical spine injury, and x-rays are needed to make the diagnosis of a fracture, dislocation, or both. The victim may experience any number of symptoms, including numbness, incontinence, paralysis and pain. Neck pain is the most consistent complaint.

The Treatment of Neck Fractures

A broken neck may require a collar to restrict motion and relieve pain. A larger "halo" collar with rigid fixation, which permits limited neck motion, is used for less stable fractures. For very unstable fractures, inline traction in bed with skull tongs and weights is needed. It depends on what bones are broken and which ligaments are disrupted. The more severe the injury, the more rigorous the traction or immobilization.

Other treatments range from IV steroid medication to a more aggressive open surgical approach. The latter involves surgical fixation (wires, pins and rods) of unstable spine fractures to avoid spinal cord compression and paralysis.

Three time frames for death after an accident also apply to neck injuries, and therefore these traumatic insults carry a ton of anguish and conflict for your story. Death may occur:

- Immediately because of sudden loss of respiratory function
- After an hour or so from spinal cord compression (which may or may not be recognized)
- Following months of rehabilitation because of complications such as urinary tract infections or pneumonia

Death by hanging occurs as an act of homicide, suicide or autoerotic asphyxiation. We are interested in the botched hanging that doesn't cause death. A clean jerk at the end of the rope represents the preferred hanging method to fracture or dislocate the cervical vertebrae, compress the spinal cord and/or cause sudden death by asphyxiation.

In his novel *Acceptable Risk*, Robin Cook describes the hanging of the witches of Salem, one of whom was Elizabeth Stewart, the wife of Ronald, a friend of Reverend Cotton Mather. Unable to prevent Elizabeth's hanging because of the horrible evidence against her, the good Reverend, we are led to believe, does the next best thing. Elizabeth is on the ladder leaning against an oak tree:

> For a brief second Ronald saw Elizabeth's eyes rise to meet his. Her mouth began to move as if she was about to speak, but before she could, the hangman gave her a decisive shove. In contrast to his technique with the others, the hangman had left slack in the rope around Elizabeth's neck. As she left the ladder, her body fell for several feet before being jerked to a sudden, deathly stop. Unlike the others, she did not struggle nor did her face turn black.

Robin Cook dramatically and accurately depicts the different effects of a slow, painful hanging and a sudden, compassionate death. Because our discussion centers on *near death from hanging*, it's crucial to understand that suicide often fails because the rope, belt, electrical wire, or whatever only partially strangulates the victim. If not sufficiently far above ground or the floor, the would-be suicide gags, passes out and then recovers. Near-death hanging creates swelling and tiny hemorrhages in the eyes, a circular bruise on the neck and an open-ended question: What to do next? Did the person really want to die or merely send a message?

Hangman's Fracture (Or is it Hanged-Man's Fracture?)

While the first title above is the usual one, the actual incidence of fractures to the second and, at times, third cervical vertebra and associated spinal cord crush or transection, is less frequent than often stated in medical reports. To the writer the two terms of course reflect point of view. The first is an occupational goal, the second (as we will see) a desired terminal event. There are congenital malformations of the neck bones that may mimic a hangman's fracture.

It's all about knots and drop distances. And because this book is about non-lethal injuries the inclusion of this section would be incomplete without mention of botched hangings. In a 1992 report in *Forensic Science International*, RYK James and Rachael Nasmyth-Jones describe fascinating aspects of the dubious art of judicial hanging. The authors report the exhumation of thirty-four bodies between 1882 and 1954 in Britain and the examination of the necks for injury patterns. Surprisingly, only eleven criminals were deemed to have died from cervical fractures (hangman's fractures). Almost a half died of strangulation or asphyxia and ten percent died entirely of asphyxia. Thus, the hangman's noose does its damage in more than one way.

James and Nasmyth-Jones reveal that many judicial hangings produced "dancing" on the end of the rope. Drop distances from a beam between two trees or formal scaffolding varied between two to as much as seventeen feet. An occasional decapitation resulted. Half hanging did occur, ropes broke, relatives dragged on the victim's legs to speed death, and others attempted to procure the bodies for dissection. Placing the knot beneath the chin caused severe hyperextension of the neck and more fractures and spinal cord damage with a quick death. This injury pattern was inadvertently reproduced with seatbelts and cars lacking a head support. When the knot was placed beneath the ear, the criminal was often strangled to death.

Other medical explanations for the swift loss of consciousness with most judicial hangings include: compressions of the carotid arteries cutting off oxygen to the brain, stimulation of special receptors in the carotids (carotid sinus/bodies) causing cardiac arrest, blockage of the jugular veins and obstruction of the trachea. The "rope dancing" seen was probably decerebrate positioning or unconscious muscular activity as the spinal cord became progressively damaged.

There are many cases of the hanged person being resuscitated. Some were cut down and recovered. Thus, it is fitting to include this section here.

Autoerotic Asphyxiation

A risky way to increase one's sexual pleasure is to *almost* hang oneself. Presumably, the confusion that results from one or more of the mechanisms mentioned at the end of the last section cause altered consciousness and a heightening of sensations. A trusted partner is advised. This rather spectacular way to have an orgasm is also presumably tied to the despicable act of "snuff" sex.

Neck injuries reflect many of the unsavory aspects of violence. Victims of clinical depression who feel the compulsion to attempt self-destruction often attempt hanging. Neck trauma may also be a by-product of uncontrolled rage, attempted homicide, domestic violence or accidental strangulation during autoerotic asphyxiation. Regardless of the cause, nothing challenges a character's character like the loss of all ability to move, breathe and control one's destiny.

The possibility of paralysis, suffocation, and major neck hemorrhage raises the stakes in your plot. It is indeed gruesome when someone takes it in the neck.

SEVEN

CHEST TRAUMA: THE DIRTY DOZEN MAIMING INJURIES

Whether you end up writing about a potentially lethal injury or about the cause of death—followed by crime scene investigations, how to deal with the body, disposal, etc. —depends on how you handle the window of opportunity for treatment. This moment is brief, variable. But your characters glimpse at it with the desperate intent of being saved.

For the fiction writer, this dread-drenched interval between life and death defines the ultimate ticking clock. Chest injuries, more than any others, possess their own self-limited course. The threat is death or a life-altering mishap. Only correct emergency medical decisions are acceptable to Madame Fate.

Because we're interested in injuries in this book, we'll now examine the kinds of things that can go wrong inside your character's heaving rib cage. With unexpected death, you fire off a cascade of emotional events that create or aggravate conflict and change the direction of your plot. But by *not* killing your character, you step back in the story's time line to the traumatic event itself and create even more conflict because of the uncertainty of the outcome of the injury.

> His instinct and every fighting fiber of his body favored the mad, clawing rush to the surface. His intellect and the craft thereof, favored the slow and cautious meeting with the thing that menaced and which he could not see. And while he debated a loud crashing noise burst on his ear. At the same instant he received a stunning blow on the left side of the back, and from the point of impact felt a rush of flame through his flesh.

Moments later in *All Gold Canyon*, Jack London's tense short story about a miner shot in the depths of a seven-foot-deep hole, the wounded man escapes after killing the intruder. The author's brief description of the miner's relief when he realizes the wound was not fatal rings of authenticity for the era as well as for its medical verisimilitude. Relieved to be alive, the miner opens his shirt and examines himself. "Went clean through and no harm done!" he cried jubilantly. "I'll bet he aimed alright, alright; but he drew the gun over when he pulled the trigger."

Sometimes not knowing the outcome of an injury is more unnerving, more difficult to deal with than the certainty of a loved one's demise. *What will happen next?* The big story question is always open-ended with a serious injury and (almost) always shut tight in death—except for *who*dunit, and we're interested in *how*dunit.

Chest trauma is unique because so many insults may occur to the cavity that conceals your character's vital structures. Outcome becomes a literal crapshoot. How marvelous for you, the writer.

One-quarter of the victims of chest injuries die, often after reaching the hospital. Fewer than fifteen percent of these unfortunate souls need an operation, and their lives may be saved by your hero's actions before the ambulance arrives.

The basic organization of this chapter centers on the "dirty dozen" bad chest injuries and a few other common problems about which you are almost certainly already aware. Before we get to the bad stuff, remember that a bump on the chest may only cause rib bruises, which can be extremely painful, or broken ribs with no underlying injuries. These impacts get your character out of action for days as opposed to weeks or months.

Then there are the twelve terrors. This material is a little heavy, but hang in there. Once you get the basics, you can imply the rest.

The Dirty Dozen

Described below are twelve chest injuries that may threaten your character's life immediately or cause delayed death. The ultimate medical ticking clock is a serious but reversible injury that, when survived, may alter the course of your plot or a character's view of life. The only real difference between the first six chest insults and the rest is time.

All of these injuries can be survived. It's the threat of death that makes them so terrible and so remarkable when the patient walks out of the hospital alive.

Basic Treatment Plan

No matter the specific injury, your hero should follow certain steps as he evaluates the chest trauma victim. Familiar by now, they are repeated with each new trauma problem. Remember, if you want to create more conflict, let someone forget to do something.

Steps in evaluating and treating the chest trauma victim:
1. Conduct primary survey—a quick search for major injuries.
2. Have a high index of suspicion for certain injuries based on history and visible marks.
3. Do simple lifesaving things.

4. Do a secondary survey—go back and look again for other injuries.
5. Get the victim to a medical facility.

Injuries That May Kill Within Minutes
Airway Obstruction

Imagine you are a molecule of oxygen attempting to travel from room air through the mouth, down the windpipe into the terminal air sac in someone's lung. (If you can envision this peripatetic oxygen outing, you can write anything.) Airway obstruction is anything that impedes the molecule's progress down the road to the bloodstream; it usually involves what doctors call upper airway blockage. Anything from a smashed face, swollen lips-mouth-throat from an allergic reaction, the tongue "falling back" to block the inlet to the larynx (voice box) or a chunk of foreign material, such as a piece of meat, will clog the airway.

Master Injury List For The Chest: The Dirty Dozen

Chest injuries that may kill within minutes:

- Airway obstruction—blockage of the windpipe
- Tension pneumothorax—lung collapse with increased pressure inside the chest from broken rib (blunt trauma), knife, bullet
- Open pneumothorax—the so-called "sucking chest wound", which means a chunk of the wall is missing
- Massive hemothorax—a large amount of bleeding (a quart or more) inside the chest cavity
- Flail chest—a floppy section of chest wall caused by ribs becoming broken in two places and leaving a "floating section" in between
- Cardiac tamponade—the heart sac floods with blood and squeezes the heart, leading to shock

Chest injuries that may kill within hours

- Lung bruise—from a direct hit (blunt trauma)
- Heart bruise—from direct blunt trauma
- Torn aorta—large artery coming off heart gets lacerated
- Torn diaphragm—the thin muscle layer separating the chest and abdomen is lacerated
- Torn windpipe (or its branches) -- air leak; lung may collapse
- Torn gullet—esophagus is lacerated, leaks and causes infection from swallowed bacteria; if the tear isn't treated, death may take days or weeks

Be creative. Imagine the special world of your story. What's in the environment that could be accidentally "inhaled"? At a banquet, someone plummets to the ground. Heart attack? No, she's suffered from what is called a *café coronary*. It's sudden upper airway obstruction from a chunk of food and mimics a true heart attack.

As you know, the treatment is the Heimlich maneuver. Swift pressure is exerted on the upper abdomen (by someone behind the victim who encircles her with his arms, pressing the "pit" of her abdomen) to increase the pressure inside the chest to force air in reverse up the windpipe and blast out the food gob.

The most common form of sudden upper airway obstruction occurs when the tongue falls back and blocks the free flow of air into the windpipe. Treatment involves lifting the chin or elevating the angle of the jaw.

Always, your rescuing hero should check inside the mouth for foreign material.

Tension Pneumothorax

It's pronounced *new-mo-thor-ax*. A pneumothorax is simply a collapsed lung. Young people get them from ruptured blebs, or weak "ballooned" regions on the surface of their lungs that burst after exertion. It presents as shortness of breath with gasping, and is often accompanied by severe chest pain on the side of the collapse. The victim is treated with a chest tube. That's a *simple pneumothorax*. As the interns say, you "buy" a chest tube for a few days, and then go home.

With a *tension pneumo* (that's doctor talk), a one-way valve effect develops, usually from a stab wound, bullet or the jagged end of a broken rib tearing the lung. Now we have a problem. One-way means *out*. Air flows down the windpipe, out through the hole in the torn lung tissue and out into the closed chest cavity, the pleural space (Figure 11).

What happens rather quickly is that the lung collapses and the heart and great blood vessels in the chest are pushed to the opposite side. Everything gets kinked. The heart now doesn't pump enough blood, oxygen delivery to vital tissues stops and your character's got a big problem.

Treatment involves putting a plastic hose, a chest tube, between the ribs of the victim's chest wall. To make the diagnosis, the smart paramedic or doctor inserts a big needle between the ribs just below the collarbone as soon as she considers the possibility of a tension pneumothorax. If air under pressure doesn't hiss out immediately, the small puncture doesn't cause any harm.

Open Pneumothorax

This is referred to as the sucking chest wound, and is also shown in Figure 11. Instead of a buildup of pressure inside the chest, as in the tension pneumothorax, the open chest wound is characterized by a hole in the chest wall through which air flows with every inspiratory effort. It's truly a case of lack of inspiration. The victim exchanges air through the chest wall hole instead of being able to create enough negative pressure to draw air into his airways for a deep breath.

Treatment in the field is a bandage to cover the hole. We'll have more on this later. In the hospital, the trauma doctor will place a chest tube and repair the defect in the chest wall.

Massive Hemothorax

Heme, as in hemoglobin, refers to blood—in this case, blood loss into the chest cavity. Does it require blood replacement? Well, a hemothorax is a condition in which blood from torn blood vessels fills the chest cavity. The chest can hold a lot of blood, and transfusions are often part of resuscitation for these injuries.

The blood can come from several sources in the lung or chest wall and occurs with both blunt and penetrating trauma. The source is not important. But the chest is a pretty good bucket, and it can overflow with a lot of your victim's precious heme. The victim has difficulty breathing and shock from blood loss.

Have you figured out the treatment?

Two things, right? Place a chest tube (or two) and resuscitate, eventually administrating blood to reverse the shock state. And if the bleeding doesn't stop and the red stuff continues to pour out of the plastic hose, you might hear the intern cry, "Damn it, Luke, we gonna crack this chest or what?" (Ten years of higher education.) Cracking a chest means a chest operation: an emergency *thoracotomy*—cut between the ribs, pry open the bony struts, and peek inside. The trauma surgeon sees what's bleeding and stops it.

Flail Chest

A flail chest means the same rib is broken in two places with a floating piece of chest wall in between. Usually more than one rib gets the double whammy during blunt chest trauma.

Figure 11– Chest Trauma

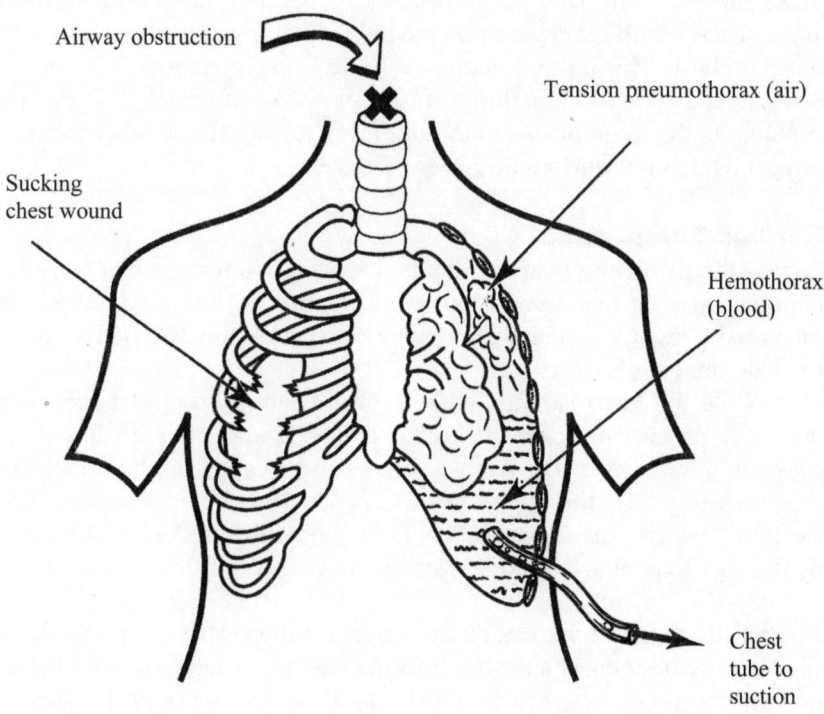

Airway obstruction

Tension pneumothorax (air)

Sucking
chest wound

Hemothorax
(blood)

Chest
tube to
suction

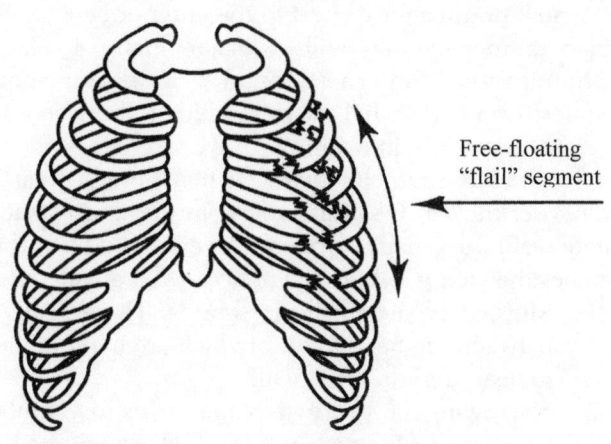

Free-floating
"flail" segment

Figure 11 shows the chest wall with a floating segment with several broken ribs all next to each other. The pressure changes inside the chest make this segment *move paradoxically* (i.e., balloon out with inspiration and collapse with expiration). It moves in the opposite direction of the normal chest. The injured segment "flails." Oxygenation is hampered because the victim's breathing efforts aren't economical. But the real problem is the huge bruise to the underlying lung tissue from the blunt impact, which interferes with oxygen delivery.

Cardiac Tamponade

Picture the throbbing heart inside its fibrous sac, a tomato inside a small balloon. Imagine the balloon filling with water as the tomato resists the increased pressure, water that compresses the tomato and then expands the balloon. Here's the rub.

While the heart sac fills with serum or blood, the heart constantly works at its task; it contracts and expands, filling up with blood and propelling it forward. The heart squeezes and swells from before birth to death. Ceaselessly, the fabled heart expands with blood, contracts with ejection. Diastole, then systole. Ebb, flow. Driven by emotions, pummeled by disease. Expands, demands. Ejection, rejection.

Cycles.

Suddenly your character's car rattles off the road and crashes into a doublewide. Her chest smashes into the steering wheel. Directly behind her sternum lies her heart, which, in this steering wheel injury, is bruised. For the moment, we're interested in only one of the consequences of blunt chest trauma: flooding of the pericardial sac with blood.

It's referred to as cardiac tamponade.

A stab or gunshot wound to the anterior chest will often result in a cardiac tamponade, as will a major injury to the heart. In both penetrating and blunt chest trauma, the doctor should consider the possibility of a pericardial sac full of blood. It doesn't take a lot of blood to squeeze the pump into failing.

Do you have a doctor character that's pretty smart? (They're not all clever, you know.) OK, this is how he picks up (that's doctor talk for "diagnoses") a cardiac tamponade everyone else in the ER missed. He examines the victim's chest and notices what is called *Beck's Triad*:

1. Muffled or distant heart sounds. There's now a wall of blood between the heart valves (which are making the noises he wants to hear) and the chest wall.
2. Narrowing of the two blood pressure numbers. Because the heart can't fill and empty as well, the maximum and minimum

pressures are closer together; instead of 120/80, blood pressure might be 90/70.

3. Enlargement or distention of the neck veins. Blood is "backed up" in the big veins because the heart is less efficient while trapped inside the pericardial sac.

The doctor inserts a huge needle between the ribs near the breastbone directly into the pericardial sac and removes (aspirates) the blood squeezing the heart.

Injuries That May Kill Within Hours

Lung Bruise

Most commonly associated with blunt chest trauma, a lung bruise is an area where blood and fluid collect within air sacs and interfere with oxygenation. If the bruise is small, it will heal spontaneously. If it's massive, your victim may require intensive care on a ventilator. It may take weeks to heal. The injury may even progress to the point where the lung tissue becomes solid—like liver.

Any degree of disability your story requires may be created by a whack in the ribs. A bunch of ribs may be busted. These fractures may be the usual one-crack-per-rib variety or they may become broken in two places producing a flail chest. Still, the ribs aren't the problem. They heal with rest. It's the ugly underlying lung bruise that can sneak up on your heroine and strangle her oxygen supply. Treat it with a ventilator, diuretics (IV water-pill-type drugs to dry out the lungs), and antibiotics if needed.

Heart Bruise

All you need to remember about this injury is that it's exactly like a heart attack. That's correct. A heart attack means a patch of cardiac muscle died beyond a blockage in one of the coronary arteries. In the care of a bruise, the muscle is injured by impact, but it dies nonetheless. As with a lung bruise, the heart is not very creative and, regardless of the cause of the injury, the tissue response is always the same.

If the patch is huge, *cardiogenic shock* occurs: The pump fails to propel enough blood to the body's vital tissues. Your character's now in big trouble and special cardiac drugs are needed to support heart function. For lesser injuries, the patient is treated like a heart attack victim—with rest, medications and a graduated exercise program.

Torn Aorta

Not much imagination is needed to create this potential disaster. This huge blood vessel comes off the heart and is attached by a ligament to the chest wall as it arches over and down toward the back of the chest cavity. Now imagine, after a decelerating impact your character's aorta continuing in a straight line according to Newton's first law of motion — until it's acted upon by that little ligament, which tears the pulsating blood vessel.

You'll recall that this is one of the causes of immediate death at the scene of the accident. But that's only if the full thickness of aorta tissue rips open, pouring the victim's entire blood volume into his chest cavity. Often these trauma victims arrive in the ER in shock from bleeding from this injury or from hemorrhage from other impacts. Because the smaller tear is only partial thickness, the remaining tube holds and the victim lives until your hero either makes or misses the diagnosis.

The middle compartment of the chest is the *mediastinum* and contains the heart and great blood vessels. So the red flag with blunt chest trauma — particularly a steering wheel injury — is a widened mediastinum on chest x-ray. To prove the aorta is torn, your character orders an arteriogram, an x-ray of the heart and aorta performed with special dye. If dye leaks out of the blood vessel, there's a tear in there somewhere.

Torn Diaphragm

You'll remember the diaphragm is the muscular sheet that separates the chest from the abdominal contents. It looks like a parachute with the strings anchored to the walls inside the belly. It helps you breathe and is traversed by the aorta heading south with fresh blood and the *vena cava*, the huge abdominal vein, returning old blood from the lower body to the heart. Also, your esophagus (gullet) passes through the diaphragm.

Injury to the diaphragm can be subtle. As with an aortic tear, a ruptured diaphragm is suggested by a chest x-ray that shows fluid or intestine in the left chest. Blunt trauma causes the diaphragm to "burst" with a large radial tear, whereas penetrating wounds, e.g., from a knife stab, cause small holes.

Often the diagnosis isn't made until weeks or months later when the chest x-ray doesn't improve or a trapped loop of intestine causes bowel obstruction (blockage). You can use this injury to get someone out of the picture *again* after his convalescence from the original accident is over.

Torn Windpipe

Do you have a karate expert in your story? Suppose she defends herself by striking her attacker in the throat. He becomes hoarse and develops crackles in the tissues of his neck. A grating sound is produced when someone pokes his neck, which is now swelling.

He's got a broken voice box, a fractured larynx.

Chest trauma may burst the windpipe lower down or even rupture one of the branches (bronchi) of the windpipe. This may cause labored breathing, depressed level of consciousness or a tension pneumothorax. The doctor makes the diagnosis by looking into the windpipe and its branches (bronchoscopy).

Immediate surgical repair is mandatory.

Figure 12– Effects of Gunshot Wound to Chest

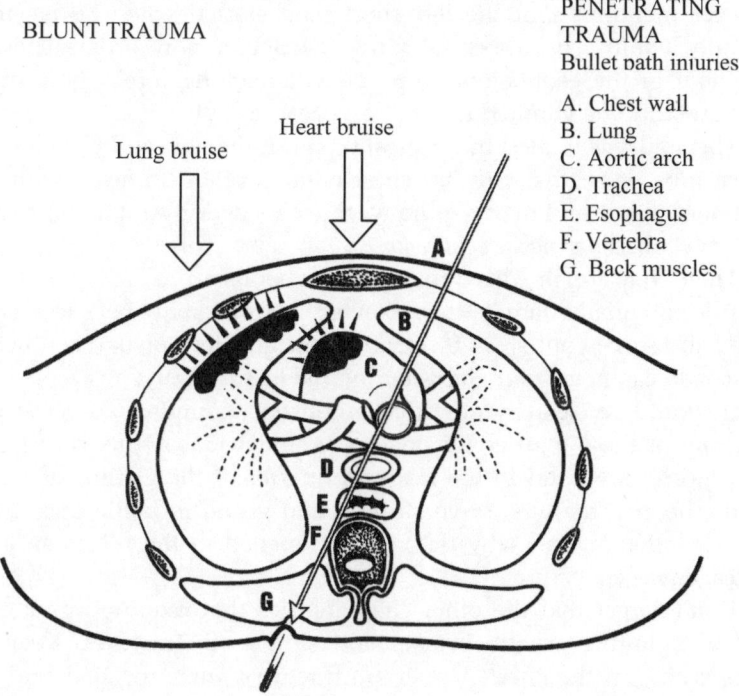

BLUNT TRAUMA

PENETRATING TRAUMA
Bullet path injuries

Lung bruise

Heart bruise

A. Chest wall
B. Lung
C. Aortic arch
D. Trachea
E. Esophagus
F. Vertebra
G. Back muscles

Torn Gullet

This one's both dull and fascinating.

By now you need little imagination to picture a long kitchen knife slicing between the victim's ribs, penetrating the back of the chest cavity, narrowly missing the aorta but nicking the esophagus. Saliva, bacteria, booze, and food drip into the sterile chest cavity, and if the injury is missed, the patient can insidiously slip into *sepsis*, an infected state with fever, pus formation and an urgent need for surgery.

It's subtle. It's a useful "missed diagnosis" ticking clock.

Now here's the really fascinating possibility. (Hopefully, you've blunted any tendency toward squeamishness by this point.) Suppose you've got a character that has just been admitted to the hospital with pneumonia. Two days later, he slips into shock from infection and his chest x-ray looks horrid. Finally, the doctor asks him how this all started (doctors are supposed to take the history first, but being as smart as they are, they often make the diagnosis first, and when it's wrong, they go back and do it right the second time around—don't tell anyone). Your character mentions that the left chest pain started when he began to forcefully vomit. The upper GI x-ray the doctor now orders shows a huge hole in the esophagus. Yep. Violent retching tore a hole in his esophagus, and he vomited into his left chest cavity!

This injury is treated by surgical repair of the hole and placement of a chest tube. It begins with left chest pain, is often confused with left-sided pneumonia and may require weeks of recovery. And if you have to know, it's called *Boerhaave syndrome*.

There they are: the dirty dozen. And a bonus.

All potentially lethal, these severe injuries may be successfully treated and serve your story by creating intrigue, tension and conflict. Of course, you can have your character injured less severely.

It should be clear by now that a gunshot wound of the chest may cause any of these injuries (or ones very similar), as depicted in Figure 12, including a wound in the heart. A quarter of the victims of a blast into the heart actually survive surgery and go on to battle once more. This is another reason why the chest is opened in the ER as an acute surgical emergency.

Don't forget that the other chest injuries that require only a chest wrap or splinting are rib bruises and simple rib fractures. Keep the fractures low in the chest. Upper rib fractures are associated with the dirty dozen.

Also, remember to use this material sparsely. Imply what you don't describe.

Next, we'll discover that some so-called chest injuries are actually a problem in the belly.

EIGHT

ABDOMINAL TRAUMA: BEWARE OF HIDDEN DAMAGE

Unlike the chest wall, propped up like a mountaineering tent by rib struts, the abdominal wall is soft, pliable, and vulnerable. Gentle curves and powerful muscles mask injuries, conceal bleeding, and confuse the doctor who attempts to diagnose a belly injury. In fact, it is so difficult to identify abdominal cavity problems (called intra-abdominal injuries) that most medical texts beg the physician who initially sees the patient to *cultivate a high index of suspicion*.

A trauma surgeon is ready for any kind of belly injury. For example, if a victim of a street fight comes to the ER in shock, one of the first places on the belly wall the surgeon examines is the right upper quadrant. Why? Because when a knife is employed in a premeditated attack, a right-handed assailant typically grasps the weapon with the blade pointing up. Then, he rips up and in, smack into the right upper quadrant—and the liver. (By contrast, someone attacking out of sudden, blind rage is more likely to jab downward, holding the knife's point down.)

Here's good news for the writer. Unlike the specific and rather complicated injuries you learned about in the previous chapter, belly trauma is easier to understand because most abdominal organs become injured in the same way. Instead of listing a dozen quite distinct injuries, we'll be looking first at a method of understanding all intra-abdominal traumas, no matter which organ is involved.

Pattern of Intra-Abdominal Injury

Two types of intra-abdominal organs make up the belly contents—*hollow* and *solid*—and so only two basic patterns of injury can occur. Most of these organs have something to do with digestion, although the kidneys, spleen and reproductive organs are also implicated in trauma. Before examining specific organ trauma, which you know as an *internal injury*— a nebulous collection of terrible things only the doctor is allowed to see—we'll first look at how hollow and solid organs become smashed up.

Figure 13– Hollow Organ Trauma

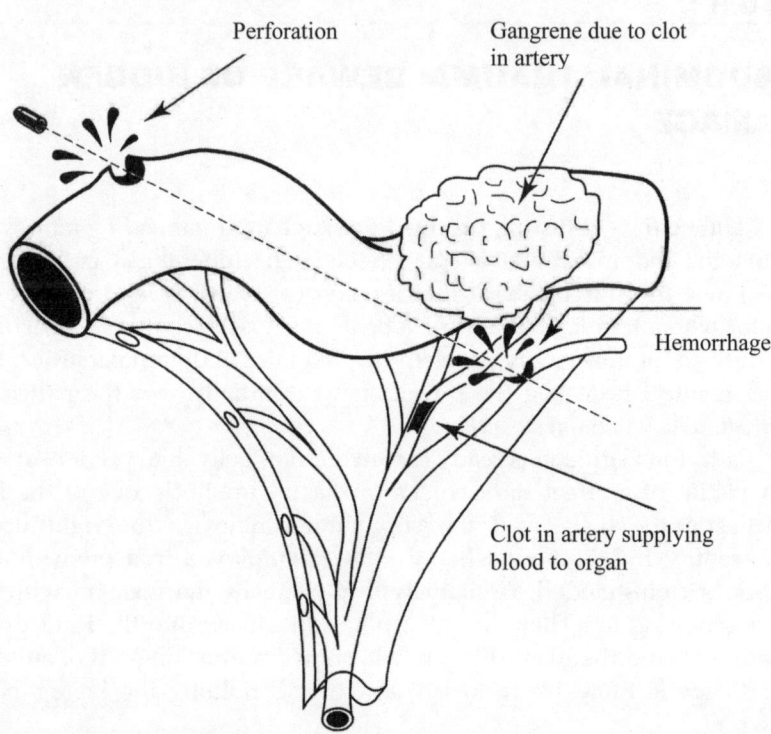

Perforation

Gangrene due to clot in artery

Hemorrhage

Clot in artery supplying blood to organ

Hollow Organ Damage

A long time ago, "living tubes" became necessary to permit the concept of a multi-organ human, a complex living creature distinguished from single-cell globs by complex internal support systems. Living tubes carry a variety of fluids (and some notable solids) about the body. If injured, these tubes leak, bleed or become gangrenous.

As Figure 13 explains, the basic living tube unit consists of an artery carrying blood to the tube, veins transporting old blood away, and the tube. With both blunt and penetrating trauma, the artery and vein (being close to each other) are often injured as one. Thus, the three basic patterns of injury are:

1. Cut or torn blood vessels that hemorrhage.
2. Cut or torn blood vessels that leave the tube without a blood supply, resulting in dead tissue, or gangrene.
3. A cut or tear to the tube (a traumatic hole called a perforation) resulting in body fluid leak.

Figure 14– Solid Organ Trauma

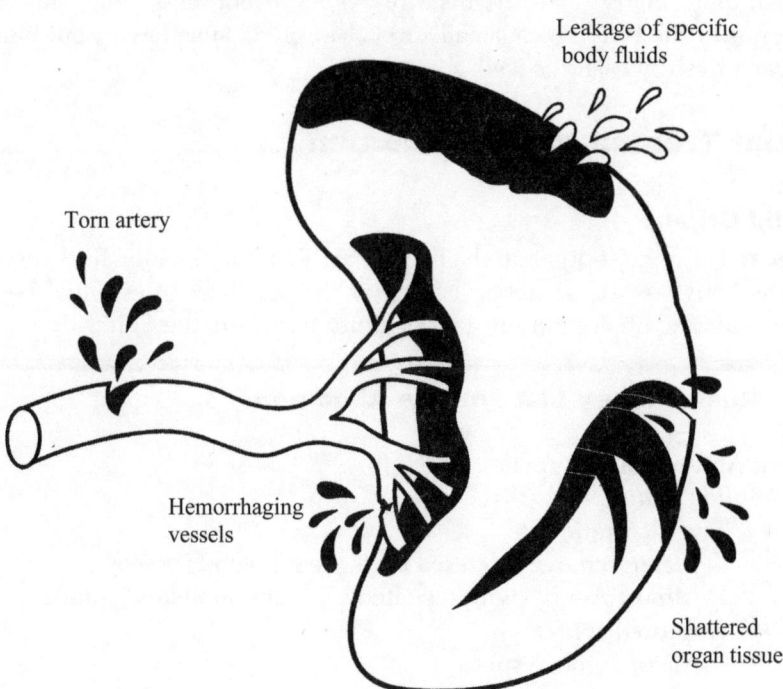

Leakage of specific
body fluids

Torn artery

Hemorrhaging
vessels

Shattered
organ tissue

Solid Organ Damage

The human body specialized by developing sold organs that assist in the
various survival functions of excretion, digestion, and procreation—all
tied together by the heart, lungs and a massive tree of branching blood
vessels. Many solid organs have more than one role. When injured, these
solid organs and their special functions become compromised. Thus, loss
of organ function is a possibility.

Figure 14 depicts a working model for a solid organ and its injuries.
Again, the artery carries blood to the organ while veins permit old blood
to exit. Most solid organs have the consistency of liver, and the basic
injuries to these organs are:

1. Cut or torn blood vessels that hemorrhage
2. Cut or torn blood vessels that leave the organ without a blood
   supply, resulting in partial or complete organ necrosis (means
   dead tissue, as in necrotic liver, and is pretty much the same as
   gangrene)

3. Cut or shattered organ tissue, resulting in hemorrhage
4. Leakage of specific body fluids

At first you might think blunt trauma is less destructive than a penetrating injury. Not necessarily so. Gunshot and other missile wounds to the belly do cause all sorts of unpredictable havoc, but blunt impacts destroy tissue as well.

Blunt Trauma to the Abdomen

Solid Organs

Liver: The biggest organ in the body other than the skin, the liver serves as the body's waste scrubber as well as the producer of essential body chemicals and other vital substances. Blunt trauma to the right side

Master Injury List For The Abdomen

Blunt Abdominal Trauma
Solid Organs
- Liver laceration
  - Major: remove shattered parts, tie off blood vessels
  - Minor: observe with repeated CT scans and blood counts
- Ruptured spleen
  - Major: remove spleen
  - Minor: repair spleen
- Pancreas
  - Bruised: observe or drain
  - Lacerated: remove injured segment and drain

Hollow Organs
- Bladder: repair; drain with suprapubic catheter
- Small intestine:
  - Major: remove segment and sew back together
  - Minor: observe
- Colon/rectum
  - Major: remove segment, perform a colostomy (temporary)
  - Minor: observe
- Kidney
  - Major: remove all or part
  - Minor: observe

Penetrating Abdominal Trauma
Solid Organs

- Liver, spleen, pancreas, kidney
  - Knife trauma: clean (debride), drain and conserve tissue
  - Gunshot: clean extensively and remove dead tissue (bullet damages tissue beyond immediate track), drain extensively

Hollow Organs

- Small intestine: remove any damaged part and sew together (called an anastomosis of the bowel)
- Colon/rectum: extensive removal of any torn tissue, may close small holes but remove segment; always a protective colostomy

---

of the lower ribs or abdomen results in various types of liver lacerations. Some are innocent and require no treatment; others cause a "burst" liver where the tissue literally explodes and hemorrhages so badly that survival is barely possible. In-between degrees of liver damage are often seen and require suturing to control bleeding.

Spleen: Unlike the liver, the spleen may be salvaged even it if is split in two after major trauma. Surgeons always make an attempt to preserve this portion of the body's immune system. At times, a chunk is removed surgically and the remaining portion saved with its blood supply.

A *ruptured spleen* occurs with trauma to the left side of the body, either to the lower ribs or flank. Hiding under the protective shield of the tenth, eleventh and twelfth ribs, the spleen may be split open by a hockey check, from a fall on slippery sidewalk ice, or after what seemed to be an innocent tumble at home, particularly if the spleen is abnormally enlarged. The victim will suffer from light-headedness, will become pale, and may slip into shock from blood loss.

Splenic injuries from blunt trauma are classified into *five categories* according to severity. Liver injuries are similarly classified. To keep things uncomplicated, let's describe the groups in general.

Class One: Injury to the spleen means a torn, non-bleeding capsular tear with a small blood clot.

Class Two: Injury is a bigger clot, a more extensive tear, and active bleeding.

Classes Four and Five: Injuries involve major blood vessels actively bleeding, a large blood clot and in the case of a Class Five, a shattered spleen. Classes One and Two require observation, not surgery; Classes Four and Five often require removal of the spleen (splenectomy).

Class Three: Is on the fence.

It's a judgment call by your surgeon character.

What happens next?

Anything you want. Her coagulation system can kick in and eventually stop the bleeding, or you may choose to let her ooze and ooze until hospitalization and multiple transfusions are needed. Even if she does stop hemorrhaging initially, she may start bleeding uncontrollably later.

A ruptured spleen serves as a flexible plot tool in your devious hands.

Pancreas: A soup bowl full of enzymes is produced each day by the pancreas, the firm organ tucked behind the stomach. Attached to the duodenum (of ulcer fame) by a duct (tube), the gland's secretions are designed to digest protein, carbohydrates, and fats. Also, the pancreas has scattered little islands of cells that produce insulin.

The pancreas poorly tolerates even trivial injuries. If you need someone hurt by an innocent assault, for example, a playful punch in the gut, give the poor dolt a bruised pancreas and three months of lingering near death in the ICU from progressive multiple organ failure.

Leaking pancreatic enzymes can *autodigest* your favorite character by eating her alive from the inside out. It's the perfect setting for a lingering disability and a slow, painful recovery.

Hollow Organs

Large and small intestines: Both are hollow organs, or transport tubes, for your Chateaubriand for two. The differences between the colon (large intestine) and the small intestine are their size, location and contents. Foul feces are stored in the colon, the last station along a tortuous digestive system. If accidentally ripped open, the colon will leak feces into the sterile abdominal cavity and produce *peritonitis*.

In the trauma room, the doctor makes the diagnosis with peritoneal lavage: He places a plastic catheter in the belly, runs in saline, and out comes saline and usually something ominous. If the fluid retrieved suggests feces, the victim goes immediately to the operating room for bowel repair and a colostomy.

The small intestine contains partially digested food products as well as bile and digestive juices from the pancreas upstream. A small intestine tear, much more subtle, can easily be missed. If not treated, a leaking gut causes peritonitis and big-league infection. Also, both colon and small bowel have supporting tissue called the mesentery that carries the blood supply. Major or minor hemorrhage may result when the *mesentery* and its blood vessels are severely torn.

Inappropriately worn seat belts can cause intestinal rupture by trapping a loop of intestine internally, causing the pressure in the loop to rise abruptly and burst the wall. Blunt abdominal trauma is anything but benign.

Seemingly innocent bumps on the belly can damage major intra-abdominal structures, and the appearance of pain, bloating, or other symptoms may be delayed. You can use this subtle type of traumatic injury to create a ticking clock, leaving a trail of small clues.

Kidney: The kidney is partly solid (the urine-forming, water- and salt-saving part) and partly hollow (the collecting system to transport urine to the bladder). Injuries include bleeding from a solid part laceration or urine leakage from a tear in the collecting tubes.

Penetrating Trauma to the Abdomen

The result of penetrating abdominal injury is similar to that produced by a blunt impact. For the uninitiated, a thrust with a butcher knife into the gut seems more ghastly than the by-product of slipping and falling on the ice. Sometimes it's the penetrating wound that's trivial.

Instead of listing each organ system again, we'll outline wounds, which will permit you to create an injury time line to suit your plot. Much of it has already been described above. Penetrating trauma may lacerate solid organs, causing bleeding and loss of function, or put a hole in a hollow tube, which then leaks its contents. Remember, with a penetrating wound, you need only trace the normal anatomy in your

---

Symptoms and Signs of Peritonitis
Subtle physical findings on exam with minimum complaints
- Elevated pulse rate
- Low-grade fever (99 or more)
- Mild swelling of the belly

Obvious symptoms
- Complaints of severe abdominal pain made worse by moving, coughing, jumping up and down, hitting a bump in car (on the way to the hospital)
- Nausea, vomiting, bloating

Obvious signs
- Severe pain during doctor's examination when abdomen is pushed, then quickly released; location suggests the organ injured
- Mass or lump in the belly
- Bowel sound (via stethoscope) absent
- Major abdominal swelling
- External markings suggesting injury, such as tire marks, cuts, bruises, abrasions; evidence of a knife wound or gunshot entry or exit wound

mind, decide what will be injured, then write about the ghastly visible results of that injury.

A stiletto stab wound in the right upper abdomen may hit the liver, causing trivial bleeding, which your villain survives in his room on the fifth floor of an abandoned building in the barrio. Or it might slice through the hepatic artery and throw the fellow into hemorrhagic shock. Sure, he can survive. Aren't you at the controls of the novel?

This is where cross-sectional anatomy comes in handy. A knife's path is direct, short and predictable. Some stab wound victims don't require surgery, just careful observation. A bullet wound, on the other hand, may ricochet anywhere in the belly, bounce off ribs, vertebrae or pelvic bones, and shatter everything in its path. Refer to Figure 15 and imagine a bullet nicking the liver, ripping through the stomach, smashing a rib and becoming redirected into the spleen or intestines.

Figure 15– Abdominal Cross-Section With Bullet Course

L = Liver
S = Spleen
St = Stomach
K = Kidney
A = Aorta
P = Pancreas

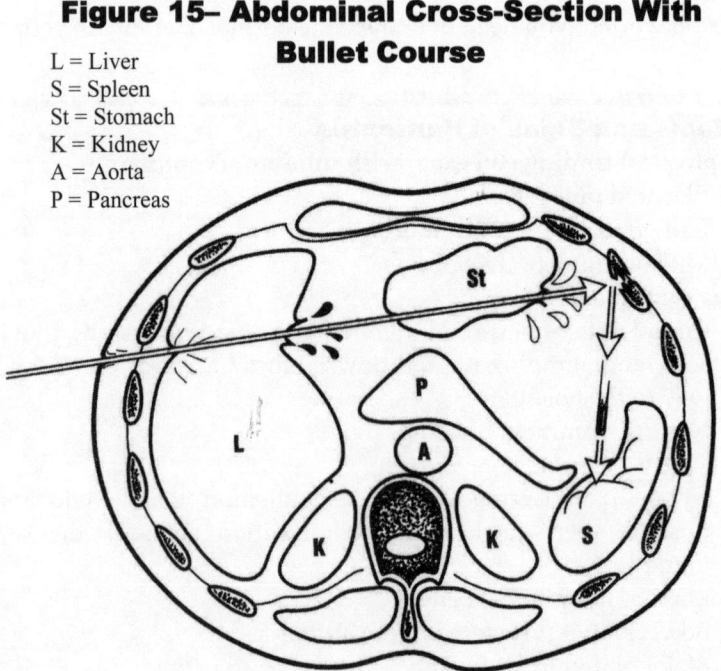

Suppose your character, carelessly playing with a gun, accidentally drills his kid brother in the buttocks. Buttocks? Probably a trivial wound, right? The ER doctor cleans out the wound and sends the patient home on antibiotics and a rubber donut.

Or did the .38 hollow point tear into the kid's gluteus maximus, smash his hip joint, nick his rectum and then lodge in his flank muscles? This time line of this more involved injury includes transport to a hospital, emergency surgery complicated by the need for a colostomy, and extensive tissue loss from an infected hip wound. Eventually, he'll need either extensive home care with visiting nurses or management in a chronic care facility. At the writer's discretion, this tale may be followed by months of further care, including a total hip replacement, which may become infected requiring removal of the hardware and . . .

Anything can happen with a gunshot wound.

You decide.

The trauma surgeon handles small and large intestine injuries differently. Injured small intestine may be removed, a segment cut out, and the ends sewn or stapled together. However, in cases other than minor nicks or tears, the victim with a major perforation of the colon or rectum needs a temporary *colostomy*. This procedure (Figure 16) involves bringing the working end of the colon out through an opening in the belly wall, to which is it sewn. A colostomy bag or appliance is worn for months, until the intestine can be safely and electively prepared (cleaned of stool) and put back together.

A colostomy may create dread, depression and disillusionment. Many patients think the stool collection bag is forever, and sometimes, the colostomy cannot be reversed. For transient distress and a test of deep character, a colostomy appliance full of feces in your heroine's lap could be distressing indeed.

A summary of what happens with penetrating abdominal trauma is listed below:

- Solid organs bleed.
- Hollow organs perforate and leak irritating body fluids.
- Virtually all gunshot wounds to the abdomen must be explored: The victim must go to surgery and have the trauma surgeon search for any and all possible injuries in the bullet's path.
- Some stab wound victims may be observed in the ICU if the wound is superficial and there are no signs of peritonitis.
- Deep stab wounds of the belly are usually explored (exploratory surgery).

- A stab or gunshot wound of the lower chest may cause damage in the belly.

Figure 16– Colostomy

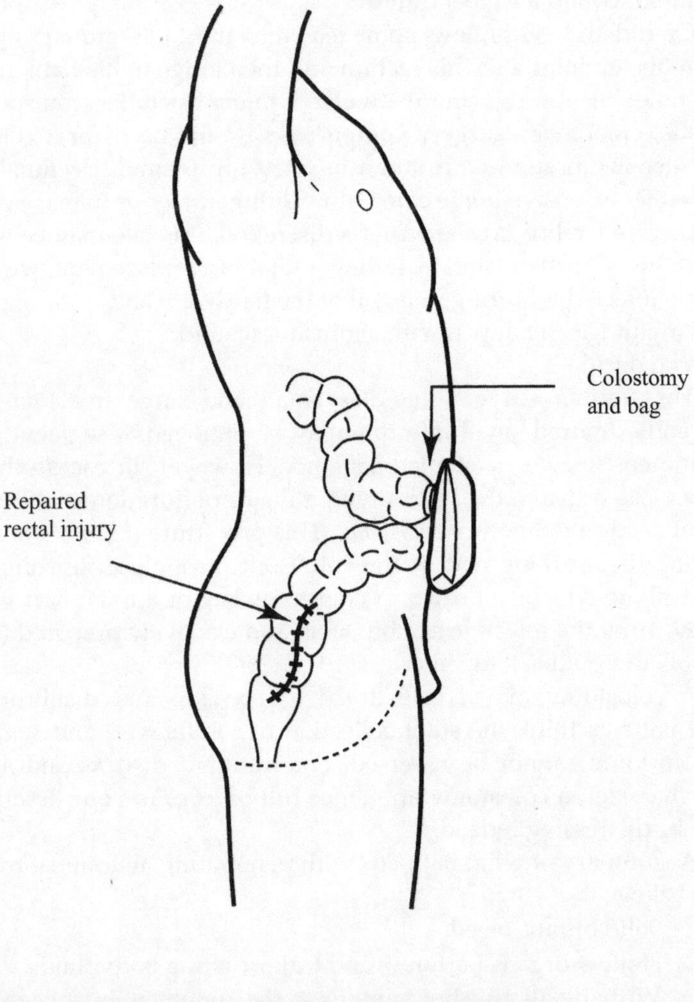

Colostomy
and bag

Repaired
rectal injury

Diagnosing a Major Abdominal Injury

The injured belly (one of the causes of what is called an acute abdomen) can be a diagnostic snake pit for the trauma surgeon. Notice how many of the problems listed above have similar symptoms and pain location? Twenty percent of major abdominal injuries are *not* associated with significant symptoms or physical findings. A lot of blood may hide in the belly without detection. The trauma surgeon's job is to always suspect a missed injury, particularly if surgery isn't performed immediately.

The victim's history may be helpful in blunt trauma. Information about the injuring object, weapon, speed of the car on impact, or details from the scene of the accident all help to determine the likelihood of certain injuries. Skin abrasions, bruises, or cuts may suggest deeper injury. In penetrating trauma, the availability of the weapon is useful in gauging depth of penetration. Any obvious external findings, such as a knife wound or gunpowder burns, will help direct further special tests.

When the surgeon examines the victim, she looks for tenderness, particularly increased soreness when she presses in on the belly wall, then releases suddenly. The sudden movement of the underlying peritoneal lining will hurt terribly if there is peritonitis. Severe pain produced by this maneuver ("rebound" tenderness) leads to emergency surgery. A belly that is swelling before the surgeon's eyes means massive bleeding and immediate surgery.

Clinical Picture of Abdominal Injuries

Minor abdominal injuries

- Bruised kidney: blood in urine, flank pain
- Small liver laceration: skin abrasion over upper right abdominal skin with deeply located pain
- Small spleen laceration: left lower rib pain or upper left abdominal pain
- Mildly bruised pancreas: central abdominal pain that may radiate into the back
- Minor tear of bowel: abdominal pain

Major Abdominal Injuries

Usually associated with shock; any of these injuries may be heralded by diffuse or generalized abdominal pain.

- Massively bleeding liver lacerations: upper right or diffuse abdominal pain
- Shattered spleen with extensive bleeding: left rib or abdominal pain or diffuse abdominal pain associated with shock
- Leaking small intestine (perforation): diffuse abdominal pain
- Leaking colon or rectum (perforation): diffuse lower abdominal pain
- Shattered kidney with bleeding or urine leakage
- Ruptured urinary bladder (perforation): lower abdominal pain
- Torn, bleeding aorta or vena cava: massive abdominal swelling, hemorrhage in belly, shock

Three special tests may lead the trauma surgeon to recommend an emergency operation:

1. Peritoneal lavage, a "washing out" of the abdominal cavity with saline solution, looking for blood, stool, bile, or urine
2. CT scan of the abdomen to look for leaking fluid, gas outside the gut, a mass or a lacerated solid organ.
3. The FAST test or "quickie" abdominal ultrasound is performed to determine if there is fluid in the belly; if there is, it is presumed to be blood, and the amount (and the patient's general condition, e.g. stable or unstable vital signs) will determine if an operation is needed.

Armed with information derived from the clinical examination, multiple tests and x-rays, the surgeon decides whether to explore the patient's abdomen or observe the patient for further clarification of the clinical picture. Also, the surgeon searches for the appearance of new findings.

The Outcome of Abdominal Injury

Abdominal injuries, with or without exploratory surgery, usually heal without major complications, permitting a complete recovery and return to one's usual diet and activities. If a colostomy was needed, it will be closed at a later date. Drains may be left in for a prolonged period of time and removed in the surgeon's office or in the clinic. Wound infections occur sometimes.

Unlike the residual limps, lapses and language deficits seen after neurological damage, recovery from abdominal surgery is quite uncomplicated. Nonetheless, the major focus of the abdominal surgeon remains fixed on deciding whether to explore the trauma victim's abdomen at all. The surgeon cultivates a high degree of suspicion even if there is no obvious belly injury.

Some diagnoses are difficult to make, particularly when other injuries, such as coma, complicate the picture. The trauma surgeon will return to the bedside over and over to reevaluate the patient until he is certain no injury exists.

Some belly injuries are subtle. Some diagnoses are delayed.

After major torso trauma, there may be heard inside the victim's belly, without the assistance of a stethoscope, a loudly ticking clock.

Damage Control Exploratory Surgery

The standard of care has always been to rush trauma patients dying of massive hemorrhage to the operating room. Once there, it was routine to stop the bleeding and repair any and all injuries to solid organs such as the liver, spleen and kidney, as well as injuries to the intestinal tract. Immediate control of bleeding and suturing of torn bowel was the standard of care. Until recently, it's what surgeons traditionally did with a multiple trauma patient.

Things have changed dramatically. It turns out that you can kill patients by doing too much.

Victims of multiple chest and abdomen stabbings, high-energy blunt trauma to the torso (auto, motorcycle accidents, falls, etc.), *develop a deadly trio of body function disruptions:*

1. They become profoundly cold (hypothermic).
2. They develop acidic body fluids from poor oxygen delivery to tissues (metabolic acidosis)
3. The patient's coagulation ability - the capacity to create blood clots to stop hemorrhage - deteriorates. Any attempt to perform complicated, time-consuming resections and repairs in these patients will usually kill them.

Thus, a *three-step approach* to the severely injured patient is now used. The trauma surgeon (or the general surgeon preparing a trauma victim for transport to a Level One facility) must make a difficult judgment. Does he complete the needed repairs at the first operation, or perform "damage control" and transfer the patient to the ICU to stabilize and warm up? It depends on how sick the patient is when brought to the operating room. If definitive surgery isn't in the cards, here's what the trauma surgeon does:

Damage Control Step One:

- Control bleeding - suture any tears or huge holes in the aorta, other large arteries, or major veins
- Control contamination - close holes in the intestines with sutures, staples or a huge tie with umbilical tape; suture holes in bladder; remove or drain gallbladder; drain (use special plastic hoses that exit the abdominal cavity) pancreas and other disrupted organs
- Pack (using large sterile OR pads) the entire abdominal cavity
- Close the skin only or apply or suture into the incision a sheet of sterile plastic for temporary closure

Damage Control Step Two:

- Warm the patient using special blankets, over-the-bed heaters, warm IV fluid, flush Foley bladder catheter with warm saline, or use a heating unit with dialysis or extracorporeal (bypass) devices
- Give IV fluids, blood and/or blood components and cardiac drugs to optimize heart function and blood circulation

- Correct coagulation problems - warm patient, give fresh frozen plasma and other coagulation blood factors as needed
- Provide total ventilatory support
- Look for additional (missed) injuries
- Return to the operating room and carefully remove the packs and suture all bleeding points
- Resect (remove) any dead or dusky bowel; remove any other dead, torn, or smashed tissue
- Close the abdomen, usually with mesh (all tissues are swollen and there's not enough room for the abdominal contents)

The Abdominal Compartment Syndrome

This entity refers to enormously elevated pressure in the belly cavity. It occurs most often after major intra-abdominal injury or after prolonged, complex, and extensive abdominal operations. When the intra-abdominal pressure (IAP) skyrockets, vital organs don't get enough blood (because the increased intra-abdominal pressure causes compression of the veins and congestion), and kidney failure occurs, soon followed by lung and heart complications. The intestinal tract and brain may even be affected. If, for example, the IAP rises after a damage control exploratory operation, it is assumed that there is persistent hemorrhage somewhere in the belly that must be addressed, or that the abdominal wall (incision) closure was too tight.

Intra-abdominal pressure is measured with a transducer attached to the Foley catheter in the bladder. When the pressure exceeds 20 mmHg, the patient's belly must be decompressed. This problem can be avoided by not closing the abdominal wall incision tightly over swollen intestine.

NINE

EXTREMITY TRAUMA: CRUNCHED ARMS AND LEGS

Most writers have suffered a painful impact at some juncture in their lives. Perhaps an awkward stumble resulted in a twisted knee, or a slam in the thigh produced a painful muscle knot. The injuries discussed in this chapter — lumps, bumps, abrasions, twisted ankles, broken bones and dislocations — are undoubtedly familiar maladies.

In some ways, arm and leg injuries are more useful than catastrophic injuries of the trunk as subjects for characterization. All sorts of potential characters come to mind. Think of Uncle Wheezer with his gimpy leg. Or Cousin Billy's annoying trigger finger, the one he snaps incessantly. What about Grandma's hammer toe? Or Martha's unresolved sciatica?

In *Madame Bovary*, Charles is about to splint a man's broken leg; the scene occurs in a small farmhouse. Gustave Flaubert describes Charles observing Mademoiselle Emma's hands as she prepares strips of sheets for the splint:

> Charles was surprised at the whiteness of her nails. They were shiny, delicate at the tips, more polished than the ivory at Dieppe, and almond-shaped. Yet her hand was not beautiful, perhaps not white enough, and a little hard at the knuckles, besides, it was too long, with no soft inflections in the outlines.

Perfect nails, imperfect fingers. A reflection of the young woman's work on the farm? Flaubert carved intrigue into her knuckles to be read by the perplexed Charles, subtle indications of deep character, polished by repetitive minor trauma.

We are known by our hands and feet.

Engineers often build a prototype when working on something new, a model of the real thing. The prototype is really a physical scheme with essential elements crafted and enjoined. Thus, a prototype arm or leg could be represented as a cylinder of concentric layers of tissue through which course a variety of tubes and cables, all supported by a central rod with joints. Figure 17 demonstrates all of the elements of a human limb. With this model in mind, you'll easily understand the effects of common injuries. For a particular scene, you may choose an isolated injury or a combination of afflictions. These elements represent the trauma prescription for an injured arm or leg. Or both.

For both extremities, we'll discuss acute impact injuries first. At the end of the chapter, you'll discover ways to employ chronic injuries from repetitive motion, often occupational, to create back-story and establish character verisimilitude. For example, envision the cracked, grease-filled fingernails of a mechanic or the stained fingers of the ever-suffering woman working in a dingy print shop. Sometimes old injuries—for example, loss of a fingertip from frostbite—reflect a forgotten passion for adventure. Arm and leg injuries may be major or minor, and the time line of each injury determines how each plays out in the plot.

Figure 17– Prototype Limb and Basic Injury Types

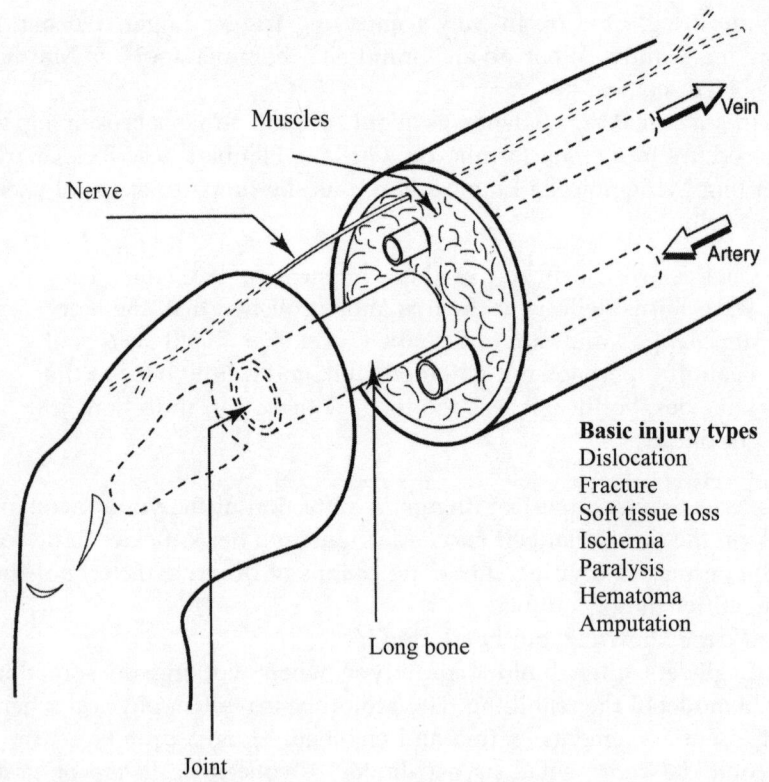

Muscles

Nerve

Vein

Artery

Basic injury types
Dislocation
Fracture
Soft tissue loss
Ischemia
Paralysis
Hematoma
Amputation

Long bone

Joint

The Upper Extremity

Shoulder

Several direct and indirect impacts create problems in the shoulder. Lesser shoulder injuries include contusion (bruise); tendonitis (e.g., inflammation or damage to the rotator cuff); or bursitis (inflammation of the tiny bags of fluid around any joint, which act as cushions for tendons). Repetitive motion as in swimming, in throwing a baseball or in various occupations produces diseases of wear and tear — the arthritis-bursitis-worn-out-old-tendon syndromes.

The most common acute shoulder injuries are fractures and dislocations. Fractures occur in the neck of the upper arm bone (humerus) or in different parts of the shoulder blade (scapula), part of which forms the shoulder socket. A bone-shattering impact may result from a fall directly on the shoulder, from force transmitted to the shoulder from a fall on the outstretched arm or from direct trauma (e.g., a club strike).

It's possible to *dislocate* the shoulder with a fall on the arm, or by yanking or striking the shoulder while it's relatively unprotected. The worst position (most susceptible to dislocation) is when the arm is held away from the body and rotated backward. Most shoulder dislocations are anterior, or in front of the joint, and may be *reduced* in the field or in the ER with sedation. Basically, the dislocated head of the humerus (contrary to the sound of that name, there's nothing funny about a shoulder dislocation) must be replaced into the socket before the shoulder muscles go into spasm.

Mechanisms of Extremity Injury

Acute injuries occur by:
- Direct trauma to the injured area
- Indirect force transmitted up or down the arm or leg to the injured area

Chronic injuries occur by:
- Direct, repetitive low-level intensity impact
- Indirect irritation associated with repetitive motion
- Deterioration of the limb from an acute injury

A dislocated shoulder is diagnosed when:
- There is a flat angular shoulder profile (loss of gentle shoulder curve)
- Shoulder pain is severe (except in the case of a chronic dislocation, which may not be painful)

- The elbow is bent slightly away from the body with the forearm turned in (palm down)

There are two ways to reduce a dislocated shoulder:

1. Place the stocking foot into the armpit and apply steady traction on the arm until the head of the humerus "clunks" back into the socket.

2. Apply the Kocher maneuver's four moves; first, pull down on the bent elbow; second, rotate the arm out (externally); third, slide the elbow in toward the middle of the chest with the victim's hand still out; fourth, cross the hand over the body, or rotate the arm medially.

The owner of a chronically dislocating shoulder may be able to reduce the slack joint without assistance. Some acute dislocations cannot be reduced with the two conservative methods mentioned above. Part of the joint capsule or a chunk of the rotator cuff (muscle or tendon) may become stuck between the joint surfaces. Open surgery is then needed.

Fractures of the shoulder blade, which result from a major direct smack on the shoulder or back, are not common. It takes an impressive direct hit to break the flat part of the scapula, and other major injuries, such as damage to the arm nerves, may also occur.

Connecting the scapula (shoulder blade) to the sternum (breastbone) is the bony strut called the clavicle (collarbone). It's a good one to break if your hero attacks a villain using a karate chop to the root of the neck. Severe pain and deformity result from a *fractured clavicle*. It gets the bum out of the picture for a few weeks.

A *shoulder separation* (AC, or acromioclavicular, separation) may be slight or may result in disruption of all of the complex ligaments that tie the lateral end of the collarbone to the shoulder. These injuries are seen frequently in contact sports.

The *sternoclavicular joint* is where the collarbone attaches to the breastbone and rarely is the site of a dislocation. If the dislocation is anterior (in front of the sternum), it's not dangerous, but if the end of the collarbone dislocates posteriorly, it may damage blood vessels in the lower neck causing major hemorrhage.

Any of these orthopedic problems may be associated with a significant tissue tear and disruption of the joint anatomy. Thus, some injuries become chronic. If so, open surgery may be the only solution to persistent pain or disability. Surgery is the only solution to a major fracture or dislocation.

Arm

Not to be confused with the forearm (below the elbow), the arm extends from the shoulder to the elbow crease and is known best for its cultivated biceps and massive triceps. Common *acute* injuries to the arm include fracture of the shaft of the humerus, tears of the biceps or strains of the triceps. An interesting acute injury occurs when the long head of the biceps tears away from the shoulder area where it inserts, leaving the belly of this impressive muscle to curl up like a burrowing rodent beneath the arm skin.

Five nerves arise from a tangle of interconnections in the neck and go south to the arm, forearm, and hand. Each has the task of supplying sensation to specific areas of skin as well as innervating specific arm and forearm muscles. For example, spiraling behind the middle of the arm (hugging the humerus bone) lies the *radial nerve*, which controls the extensor (bending backward) muscles of the wrist and fingers. These muscles form the mass below the elbow and can be knocked out of commission in two interesting circumstances:

1. The radial nerve may be damaged acutely by a broken shard of bone following a fracture of the midhumerus.
2. The radial nerve may be damaged by direct pressure or a smack on the back of the arm by a club. For example: A drunk falls asleep on a park bench (be warned, this is an often-told tale in the halls of academic medicine, so alter the telling) and compresses his radial nerve against the back of the bench as he flops his arm over the bench. It's called Saturday night palsy and it may become chronic.

In both situations, the injury produces radial nerve damage and what is called "wrist drop." The victim can't extend the wrist or hand, and varying degrees of paralysis are possible. The acute injury may disappear quickly; the more chronic problem may become permanent.

Master Injury List For The Arm

Minor Injuries

- Shoulder: bursitis, first-degree AC (acromioclavicular) shoulder separation, muscle strain, arthritis, shoulder bruise
- Arm: biceps or triceps strain, muscle contusion (bruise)
- Forearm: "tennis elbow", bursitis of the elbow
- Wrist: sprain, cyst, tendonitis
- Hand: minor abrasions, laceration, nail injuries, arthritis, trigger finger

Major Injuries

- Shoulder: fracture of neck of humerus, dislocation, third-degree AC shoulder separation, sternoclavicular separation, rotator cuff tear, injury to nerves to the arm and shoulder
- Arm: fracture of shaft of humerus, fractures at elbow with artery damage, injury to radial nerve at midarm, tear of biceps tendon
- Forearm: fracture of one or both bones, fracture of one with dislocation of the other at the elbow, severe "tennis elbow"
- Wrist: Colles' fracture of wrist, dislocated navicular bone, fracture of scaphoid bone, dislocation of carpal (wrist) bone, fracture of carpal bone(s)
- Hand: severe infections, lacerations, "degloving" (stripping off of skin) injuries, crush injuries, amputation of fingers, broken fingers

Elbow

It seems there's nothing in-between about the elbow. Either you break it and risk catastrophic damage to the nerves and blood vessels to the forearm and hand, or you just cause all sorts of pain and annoyance for yourself. Not much else happens at this dingy hinge joint.

Take the minor problem of "tennis elbow," which is not so minor if you've ever had it and is certainly not restricted to racquet enthusiasts. Inflammation of the origin (from the bone) of the extensor muscles of the forearm, tennis elbow occurs because of repetitive pronation and supination of the hand and wrist. Place your palm facedown: That's pronation. Now rotate your hand until it's facing up, as if you're holding a bowl of soup in your palm: That's supination. Tennis elbow often becomes chronic and may require steroid injections or the application of an external compression band.

Bursitis of the elbow can occur in the pocket of fluid located posterior over the bone. It's diagnosed as an acute inflammation or infection when the bursa becomes red, hot, and tender. It may need to be drained by an incision or by needle aspiration, and antibiotics are often required. At times, it must be removed if the inflammation becomes chronic.

Kids can easily dislocate the *radial head* (the end of the forearm bone at the elbow) because the flare part of the bone doesn't develop until later in life. An adult could cause this injury by yanking a child by the arm.

As with the knee, the most terrible injury to the elbow is a *dislocation* or *fracture-dislocation*. The artery and nerves are at risk because they hug the bones, and major hand complications can follow these injuries. At times, the neurovascular bundle (as the blood vessels and nerves are called when considered together) is severely injured despite the orthopedic surgeon's best efforts.

Forearm

Two bones form the framework of the forearm where a galaxy of muscles weaves its way to the wrist and fingers. Complicated beyond reason, forearm anatomy may be summed up by thinking of it as two groups of muscles: flexors on the inside and extensors on the outside. Well, there are a few more muscles that rotate the forearm (that pronation and supination thing), and a couple of outcropping muscles that control the thumb.

Imagine the forces exerted against the muscles and bones of the forearm when a blow is deflected by the raised forearm. Any injury can occur from a muscle contusion, to a bone bruise, to a fractured ulna (the ulna is the bone directly beneath the forearm skin; check it out on your self). Also, the radius may break alone or with the ulna. A stab wound to the forearm may cut nerves, muscles, and large blood vessels.

Forearm injuries occur in folks who tumble and try to break the fall as well as in those attempting to defend themselves. Chronic forearm muscle strain may occur in people performing repetitive occupational tasks. More commonly, the forearm is spared and the wrist (carpal tunnel syndrome) and elbow (tennis elbow) take the brunt of the insult.

Wrist

Fractures and sprains occur commonly at the wrist. The classic wrist fracture, perhaps the best-known bone break in the body, is the *Colles' fracture*. These injuries meld with those of the carpal bones, those eight stone-size bone lumps between your forearm struts (radius and ulna bones) and the delicate finger bones that elongate to form your hand. The proper diagnosis can only be made with an x-ray.

A couple of other traumatic injuries characterize the wrist area and provide you with methods of sidelining a character with a pesky problem for weeks or months.

The scaphoid bone in the wrist is subject to fracture from direct violence, such as a fall on the outstretched hand, or by direct impact. Because of the unique blood supply to this funny little ossicle, one of the broken fragments may die, and thus begins an oft-protracted tale of orthopedic surgical care. Whether pinned, screwed, or casted, the broken bone stone may eventually need to be removed and replaced with a plastic implant.

The other more or less common wrist bone injury involves the scaphoid's next-door neighbor, the navicular bone. For reasons of ligament design, this baby doesn't break easily; it dislocates. Squirted out of alignment, the bone creates acute and chronic pain and may ruin the plans of the professional athlete and concert pianist alike.

Carpal tunnel syndrome is a well-known chronic wrist problem. Many people, particularly folks such as writers who use their hands in repetitive tasks, develop numbness, tingling and aching of the hands. Trapped in a tight tunnel at the wrist, the median nerve becomes compressed and often surgery is needed to release the carpal ligament. This may be done with a special scope (closed surgery) or with open surgery.

Hand

Some orthopedic and plastic surgeons do nothing but hand surgery. And though palm reading is intriguing, what Flaubert accomplished in the passage quoted at the start of this chapter represents more clearly what we are seeking to emulate creatively. On the parchment of a character's fingers and palms, you may write a life history. What can the hand tell you about your character?

Lots.

Scars, knobby arthritis, missing digits, crooked fingers that won't straighten, flushed palms and splintered fingernails all imprint the individual with a unique back-story. Arthritis and scar tissue contractures may distort the tissues until the hand becomes a gnarled knot, a contorted, impotent fist.

A number of hand infections may put your character out of action for days or weeks. Treatment may include antibiotics, elevation, rest, and, in some conditions, surgery. Often in a story, the writer wishes to take someone out of the action for a short while, usually someone who needs his or her hands, such as a musician, artist or surgeon. These hand infections can do the trick.

If someone gets stuck in the hand or finger with a sharp object—look at the story's environment and pick something appropriate, such as a garden tool, rose bush, hunting knife, or an exposed nail in a barn—an infection called *cellulitis* may result. It means a red, tender swollen body part with a diffuse infection with bacteria. A simple cellulitis may turn into a *deep hand space abscess*. The hand cellulitis may be accompanied by streaks of red traveling up the arm and is often mislabeled as blood poisoning. Actually, the red marks represent *lymphangitis*, which is an infection running up the lymphatics of the arm, and they mean things are definitely out of control. Treatment at this stage includes intravenous antibiotics, rest, and elevation in the hospital. If a specific swelling occurs, say, in the palm, then surgical drainage of the abscess becomes an emergency.

From the humdrum cellulitis your pianist picked up trimming her Presidential roses a day before the big concert, there evolves a nasty swollen index finger full of pus. The *tendon sheath* abscess becomes a ticking clock.

Other hand injuries include:

- Ruptured tendons: require surgical repair; may be from wear and tear or sharp trauma
- Ruptured ligaments: tearing of ligaments that hold the finger bones together; may need surgery
- Dislocated fingers: painful; short term (two to four weeks) disability; may require surgical reduction if closed reduction takes too much force.

Degloving injury of the hand refers to the traumatic stripping off of full-thickness skin from the top (dorsum) of the hand, where it is less well fixed than in the palm. Ripped from its attachments, the curled skin flap remains attached at one end. It must be replaced surgically, although if the blood supply is severely damaged, the flap may not survive. Then a skin graft is needed.

Finally, there are congenital deformities of the hand that are quite striking. A *claw hand*, for example, occurs when a huge cleft develops between the third and fourth fingers, leaving a truly clawlike (lobster) appearance. Two or more fingers may fuse together before birth, or six fingers may develop.

These types of injuries will be echoed in the discussion of lower limb injuries.

The Lower Extremity

Hip

In a young person, the hip is a sensual signal of firmness, physical health and allure. In the elderly, the hip strains to carry the load of accumulated poundage that overloads an already crooked back. The youthful woman's hips rock as she walks and suggest a generous pelvic cavity friendly to new life and birth. The old woman's hip shatters when she tumbles to the floor, her foot caught on a rug, her eyesight dim. There is an insidious degeneration that the hip joint endures as age creeps into our bones.

It does not respect gender. Hips do not age well.

Falls and fractured hips in the elderly and hip "pointers" or contusions, with skin abrasion in younger people, make up the lion's share of acute hip pain. *Bursitis* and *degenerative arthritis* play a role in chronic suffering in middle and old age. A lifetime of bearing the body's weight wears down the hip joint and thins out the cartilage designed to keep the joint running smoothly. Thin bones break at or near the angle between the vertical thigh bone (femur) and the short neck of the bone that supports the head (ball of the ball-and-socket joint). Limping may result from any of these lower extremity injuries.

With a *hip dislocation* the thigh bone (femur), positioned horizontally in a seated driver, is driven posteriorly with direct impact of the knee

Master Injury List For The Lower Extremity

Minor Injuries

- Hip: acute pain from bursitis; a "hip pointer" or skin abrasion from scraping injury; chronic degenerative osteoarthritis resulting from "wear and tear"
- Thigh: acute and chronic groin pull or adductor muscle tear (minor or major), quadriceps (anterior thigh muscles) contusion, abrasions, hamstring pull (posterior muscles)
- Knee: acute minor sprains or strains involving the four major ligaments with localized pain: medial collateral, lateral collateral, anterior cruciate, posterior cruciate; minor meniscus cartilage tear; fluid in knee (joint effusion); chronic osteoarthritis
- Leg: minor acute "shin splints" and minor anterior compartment syndrome, bone contusion ("bone bruise"), simple fracture of the fibula, abrasions and lacerations, chronic tendon or muscle strains
- Ankle: minor acute sprained ankle, acute partial tear or tendonitis of the Achilles tendon (may become chronic), chronic degenerative arthritis, tendonitis of long tendons to toes
- Foot: fallen arches (flat feet), bunions, fracture of metatarsal bone (so-called "stress" or "march" fracture), Morton's neuroma (painful swelling of a nerve to the toes), gouty arthritis of great toe, hammer toe, plantar warts—all chronic

Major Injuries

These injuries are acute but may have chronic, painful complications.

- Hip: fractured hip, posterior dislocation of hip, pelvic fracture through hip joint.
- Thigh: fractured femur with major blood loss, major torn quadriceps muscle, major hamstring tear, major soft tissue injury or crush injury (direct trauma), traumatic amputation of leg through thigh.
- Knee: fractured patella (kneecap), complete tear of one of the

four ligaments, complete tear of two ligaments, dislocation of the knee with damage to artery supplying the lower leg, fracture of femur or tibia through knee joint.

- Leg: compound (open) or comminuted (many broken bone fragments) fracture of tibia with or without a fibular fracture, major soft tissue trauma with vascular or nerve damage, crush injury to leg.
- Ankle: trimalleolar fracture (all three bones making up the ankle are broken), complete rupture of the Achilles tendon, open (compound) fracture of the ankle, major laceration of tendons, nerves or arteries to foot, traumatic amputation of the foot.
- Foot: traumatic amputation of part of the foot, severe lacerations with tissue loss "degloving" injury), major crush injury.

---

against the dashboard (or by any major force against the flexed hip). The weak posterior hip joint capsule ruptures and the head to the femur dislocates backward. Surgical correction is required.

Hip fractures occur almost exclusively in the elderly and require hospitalization and surgical fixation with special orthopedic prosthetics, plates and screws or "superglue." Often the patient must wait a few days after the accident for operating room time to become available. The big postoperative risk is *phlebitis* (blood clots forming in the legs) because of the patient's immobility. After surgery, prolonged rehabilitation is needed to help the patient regain muscle strength, balance, and maneuverability.

Thigh

Fractures lead the list of severe thigh injuries, and although a hip fracture technically occurs in the neck of the femur bone, it is a *shaft* fracture that we refer to in the thigh. Two common patterns may be seen, each with a different impact on the patient. Besides the disability experienced because a major bone has been broken, a bone that ordinarily supports much of the body's weight, these two fractures carry additional ominous complications:

1. A midshaft fracture of the femur may be associated with major blood loss—up to one or two units of blood lost into each thigh. Bilateral (on both sides) thighbone fractures can cause shock from blood loss.
2. A fracture of the femur above the knee (called a supracondylar fracture) may cause disruption of the artery to the leg, producing a cold foot. This is a vascular emergency, and the fracture often requires surgical fixation (with pins, plates, or screws).

The basic principles of emergency treatement for fractures of the femur include:

- Clean and bandage any open wound and cover with a dry sterile dressing
- Place a traction splint, manipulating the fracture only enough to straighten severely angulated bones
- Transport to a hospital with an orthopedic surgeon

Crush injuries to the lower extremity are especially devastating when the meaty thigh muscles are smashed, creating increased IV fluid volume requirements and releasing toxins. Major lacerations require extensive debridement (surgical cleaning up) and suturing of torn tissue. Major tissue loss must sometimes be filled in by rotation flaps from elsewhere (done later when the threat of infection is less). Other plastic surgery techniques may also be required, but that would be much later in the hospital course.

Lesser thigh injuries include contusions (bruises), groin pulls (a tear of the adductor muscles) and strains or major injury to the quadriceps tendon at the kneecap (patella). Chronic "quad" contusions seen in football, lacrosse, soccer, and hockey players occasionally will become calcified and mimic a chunk of bone with the muscle. And, of course, your character can get shot or knifed in the leg.

In John Sandford's novel *Mind Prey*, the cops find bad guy John Mail's house and attempt to corner him as he runs out of the cellar. Police Officer Sherrill jumps out from around the corner of the house and Mail shoots her in the thigh with a shotgun.

> Del was kneeling over her, had ripped open her pants leg. Sherrill had taken a solid hit on the inside of her left leg between her knee and her hip; bright red arterial blood was pulsing into the wound.
> "Bleeding bad," Del said, his voice was cool, distant.

Mail nailed Sherrill's superficial femoral artery, and the subsequent description of the cop applying pressure, then whisking her off on a helicopter, rings true. And there's no mention of the artery, but Sandford knew it was there.

Knee

Acute knee injuries, ligament strains or tears, or torn cartilages often occur during strenuous sports activity. Each supporting structure may be mildly or severely injured. The damage may occur during vigorous activity in the highly-trained person as well as in the untrained weekend athlete. Tissue tears are partial or complete. Any of these injuries may become chronic.

The following acute knee injuries may be the result of a direct or indirect impact on the knee:

- Medial collateral ligament strain/sprain/tear
- Lateral collateral ligament strain/sprain/tear
- Medial meniscus tear
- Lateral meniscus tear
- Anterior cruciate ligament tear
- Posterior cruciate ligament tear
- Patellar (kneecap) ligament strain

When a knee structure is repeatedly strained or torn, a chronic knee problem results. This is often seen in athletes who strain or tear the aforementioned ligaments or cartilage that then may wear out and snap or tear. Like old rope, the ligaments may become frayed and weak and often must be replaced by prosthetic material or other ligamentous tissue from the patient's body. With time, the cartilage lining the knee joint becomes worn because joint mechanics are thrown off by ligament imbalance. *Traumatic arthritis* results.

An additional potentially devastating knee injury is a *dislocation of the knee* (with or without fracture). While this injury is quite rare, it must be treated immediately because of the potential for damage to the nerves and artery to the lower leg. Remember the neurovascular bundle? These structures pass behind the knee in close proximity to the joint and are stretched or torn when the femur-tibia joint relationship is disrupted. As with any injured joint, it is impossible to determine if a fracture has occurred in association with a dislocation without an x-ray.

Leg

There's not much tissue between the tibia (bone) and the skin, and if you run your finger along your own shin, you'll notice your anterior leg is all skin and bones, except lateral to the bone where there's a fleshy muscle mass.

Two serious leg injuries are related to these observations, and each may be uncomplicated or quite involved. As with all damage, it's a matter of how much traumatic force is applied to the region. There are two leg bones, the larger weight-bearing *tibia* and the recessive *fibula*, which is clothed in muscle. You can't feel the fibula unless you crack it.

The two injuries we'll consider are fractures of the tibia (with or without a fractured fibula—simple, complicated or compound) and anterior compartment syndrome.

Tibial fractures are common.

Boot-top ski breaks involve the tibia and/or fibula and often require casting, possibly complicated orthopedic surgery, and a lot of healing time. A fractured leg from sliding and crashing a motorcycle usually breaks both bones, and it's often a compound fracture (i.e., the broken ends often stick out of a nasty jagged laceration). Chances are your "hog"-riding character will wear a complicated stainless steel jungle gym fixator on the broken leg for months. With any luck, he'll walk again, perhaps with the slightest limp.

Blunt trauma to the leg may also cause a compartment problem. In a lesser form, "shin splints" are a result of repetitive trauma to the fleshy (as opposed to the more resilient tendinous) origin of the toe and ankle extensor muscles. As these muscles swell within the closed space in the front of the leg, the pressure in the compartment rises. Blood vessels are squeezed. If the problem isn't diagnosed, pulses may be lost and muscle death (necrosis) can occur. This so-called "anterior compartment syndrome" may occur following severe exercise, such as marathon running, or after blunt leg trauma. It may even occur in the postoperative period following reconstruction of the arteries to the leg when blood flow increases to the leg.

Treatment for the compartment syndrome involves filleting open the leg, a *fasciotomy*. The procedure is directed at cutting open and releasing the natural fascial envelope (tough anchoring tissue for the muscle) of the leg. Muscle then bulges out of the surgical incision until the swelling dissipates, at which time it recedes and the incision heals. But the scenario leaves an ugly scar on the side of the leg.

There is a posterior compartment (and a small lateral one, too), but it is less well developed and compression is not often seen in the back of the leg.

Ankle

Sprains, strains and tears of the ankle ligaments occur on the less severe side of the trauma equation. Fractures and fracture-dislocations with open wounds lead the major trauma list for this region. Treatment requires emergency reduction of the fracture/dislocation and plate or screw fixation of the break with suture repair of torn ligaments. Open traumatic wounds must be closed. Antibiotics are given for days. Late complications include nonunion (bones fail to knit together), bone infection, and traumatic (chronic) arthritis.

Foot

From stepped-on toes to traumatic amputation of the foot, injuries below the ankle may be trivial or devastating. A variety of lesser injuries cause pain and limping. These may be self-treated or may require surgery.

As with the hand—but to a much lesser degree—arthritis, infection and wear and tear on tendons cause a laundry list of foot complaints. Pain in the foot leads the list of laments. Abscess (from stepping on sharp object), cellulitis, tendon rupture, etc., all occur in the foot and produce pain.

A few unique problems add to the whimpering wrought by foot discomfort. Foot pain may be caused in the heel by Achilles tendon bursitis, under the foot by plantar fasciitis (inflammation of the tough tissue supporting the arch), a broken foot bone (metatarsal), a benign tumor of a small nerve to the toes (Morton's neuroma), ingrown toenail, bunion, or an occult foreign body (stepped-on glass or wood) in the foot. These may arise acutely or in the setting of chronic irritation.

Speaking of stepping on a rusty nail, ever wonder how that rust is suppose to cause gas gangrene in your foot but never bothers you when you're rubbing it off of your fender? Rusty nails often are found in old buildings where there's lots of dirt and *Clostridium bacteria*, the ones that are responsible for gas gangrene infections. They live in the soil, hate oxygen, and love misbehaving after they've been pushed into the sole of the foot. If diagnosed early, surgical cleaning (debridement) and antibiotics are all that's needed. If missed, removal of major muscles or amputation may be the only way to save your character's life. It's not the rust; it's the bugs in the dirt.

Finally, treatment for acute upper and lower limb impact injuries seen in sports and daily activities include the modalities reflected in the mnemonic *PRICE*:

- *Protection* from additional insult
- *Rest* (stop sports activity)
- *Ice* (cryotherapy) to reduce pain and swelling
- *Compression* to reduce swelling
- *Elevation* to reduce swelling

Chronic injuries also respond to rehabilitation such as muscle training, electric stimulation, massage therapy, ultrasonic and deep heat therapy, and icing down area before and after activity. Steroid injections into painful "trigger" points are sometimes required to get an athlete or active person back to full activity.

Some folks go through life dealing with their aches and pains; how they handle the frustration of chronic muscle and joint distress says a lot about them. Damage to an extremity becomes interesting when the character's existence depends on the use of his hands and feet.

PART III

Unique Traumatic Injuries

BITES: ANIMAL ASSAULTS

Most of the one million bites suffered by Americans each year are inflicted by mad dogs or miffed humans. Other than the terror a dog attack creates or the rage inherent in a human assault, are bites really dangerous? In this chapter, you'll discover the answer is affirmative. To begin with, a lot of human bites aren't bites at all, but rather lacerated knuckles slammed into someone's teeth. Human "bites" can lead to major tissue damage and are contaminated by mouth bacteria, which can lead to serious infections.

Other creepy creatures besides canines may inflict bites with painful, disfiguring results. The damage is created by the ripping or crushing capacity of specific types of teeth and often includes the inoculation (contamination) of the injured tissues with many different types of dangerous bacteria. And there's always the worry about tetanus and rabies.

Biting serves the survival needs of many species. It's not the exclusive attack mode of dogs and dummies. Any creature with a mouth, a moveable jaw or a stinger can inflict a nasty wound. The mechanism of injury varies with the type of teeth—grinding flat molars or slashing canines as well as the style of biting. With some predators, the damage is created by the inoculation of poison. It's called *envenomation*.

Venom is usually associated with snakebites, but unobtrusive little critters that populate hidden niches of your story's environment may be disturbed and retaliate by inflicting a painful poison packet. Every writer knows about the dreadful bites and stings of spiders, wasps, and ants in North America. You may have heard about the bite of the Gila monster, a poisonous lizard of the southwestern U.S. It tears, disrupts tissue, and occasionally breaks bones. But if you've got someone digging around in the Guatemalan jungle, you might consider the havoc wrought by the burrowing little botfly.

What's so bad about a fly? You'll discover the answer later.

Large or small, the biting predator may inflict a terrible wound either by crushing tissue or by injecting poison. And don't think for a moment *Homo sapiens* is excused from this act of aggression. Human bites imply anger and rage and say a lot about the person doing the gnawing. This excerpt from Stephen King's *Rose Madder* says a lot about Norman.

> But in the end, Slowik helped quite a bit. By then they were down cellar, because Norman had begun to bite, and not even the TV turned all the way to top volume would have completely stifled the man's screams . . .
>
> . . .While he waited for the water to run hot, he looked in Thumper's medicine cabinet, found a bottle of Advil and took four. His teeth hurt and his jaws ached. The entire lower half of his face was covered with blood and hair and little tags of skin.

In animals, at least, biting is a primitive response, a matter of self-defense. The animal kingdom evolved a system of feeding and renewal we know as the food chain. It's a nonjudgmental predatory system. As an adjunct to safe survival, animals maintain an order within their ranks by minimizing dangerous fighting among themselves. They ritualize their aggressive behavior. One animal becomes the leader, the alpha male (or female). During the fall rutting season, domination is a matter of short-term conflict, strutting and limited combat.

Occasionally, one of the combatants dies.

As part of Mother Nature's integrated design and despite the efficiency of her ways of orchestrating the animal kingdom, some creatures are bitten in response to a stimulus. In the scheme of things, big animals eat little creatures. Yet in the human world, biting serves no real purpose.

Now let's examine the more common types of nips and chomps. Later in this chapter, we'll talk about the mammal that lost its way. Remember that basic to all bites are the elements of tissue damage (torn, mashed, crushed) resulting in dead flesh (necrotic), the injection of venom, the introduction of bacteria (infection), and the possible disruption of the blood supply to the area (ischemia). Pain, disfigurement, and scarring may be long-term outcomes of bad bites.

Dog Bites

> Buck was beset by three Huskies, and in a trice his head and shoulders were ripped and slashed. The din was frightful . . .
> Dave and Sol-leks, dripping blood from a score of wounds, were fighting bravely side by side . . . Buck got a frothing adversary by the throat, and was sprayed with blood when his teeth sank through the jugular.

No one would have difficulty recognizing this Jack London scene from *The Call of the Wild*. Dramatic use of primeval canine conflict at its best—except the jugular comment, as blood under pressure from the carotid artery next to the jugular was probably responsible for the "sprayed" blood and rapid exsanguination of Buck's adversary. (Forgive me this challenge of one of my literary heroes.)

The terror is no less when a human is attacked by a dog. Typically, a provoked dog attacks the hand, arm, leg, or face. Most breeds have the potential to be provoked, and no attempt will be made to foster the notion that some breeds are worse than others. Some big breeds, like German shepherds, Dobermans, giant schnauzers and pit bulls, are expected to be aggressive. Any animal may be provoked to attack or defend itself or those around it.

Like hair color, the choice of a companion dog will characterize your heroine. Animals add tension to a scene.

Stephen King drops an innocent observation in the beginning of *Gerald's Game* as Jessie lies spread-eagle handcuffed to the bedposts at the lake while her husband crawls onto the bed, his eyes gleaming with erotic interest. Off in the distance, she hears a loon laugh and the whine of a chainsaw, and a dog barks. Pretty much what you'd expect to hear on an evening night in the North Country, it sets a benign if not serene scene for her upcoming terror-driven encounter. Not very much later, Gerald drops off the bed, dead of an apparent heart attack. Later still, the aforementioned dog discovers the cottage and the plump, deceased lawyer. The starving canine sinks his teeth into Gerald's face and tears away a gourmet gob.

ER doctors treat and, where appropriate, suture thousands of dog bites each year. Some bites barely break the skin while others require hours of tedious plastic surgery. Often the victim is an innocent child who unknowingly provokes a dog.

Human Bites

Along came a mammal with the biggest brain of all, complex cerebral circuitry that permitted jealousy, envy, resentment, hatred, and—the species' favorite—revenge. But underneath these sophisticated cognitive functions lies the simple, incalculable rage, the same as what an animal feels when threatened, which reminds us: we are animals.

When that primal rage takes over, humans can and do bite. It's probably the most regressive and repulsive form of human attack. Two things happen when someone takes a chunk out of someone else. As with all well-written fiction, there is an action, then a reaction. Despicable in its intent and style, a human bite provokes physical distress and often a missing part, but more important for the writer, the attack is perceived as indignant, uncivilized and vulgar.

It must be redressed.

So, while the doctor cleans the wound in the ER and sutures together the edges of the bite, or attempts to replace a piece of an ear or a fingertip, the victim seethes with revenge. The trauma prescription is written with the end in sight. You want your character's nose sewn back in place with fifty-eight stitches, each a humiliating marker. Will he leave the ER and chase the black-haired youth who fought him in the bar? Will the youth ever be found? Does the rail-thin kid who bit him have AIDS?

Any injury mentioned in this book where blood or other body fluids are exchanged by direct contact with an open wound may be associated with the transmission of disease. That's what makes a bite so horrible.

The *knuckle* variety of human bite—a striking injury in reality—may involve finger tendons and hand joints, producing complicated hand infections. Each tendon has a sheath, and every joint possesses a cavity. When horrid mouth bacteria enter these sterile spaces through a laceration from a tooth, the resulting infection may require antibiotics, sophisticated hand surgery, and hospitalization.

A *true human bite* may be a crush injury (molar attack) or a laceration (incisors and canines). Tissue loss is possible (use your imagination). Fingers have been chomped off in barroom brawls and these digits are usually not candidates for replantation (even if the deserted digit wasn't lost in someone's mug of pale ale). Soft tissue bites to other anatomic areas are less severe in general and local care, and antibiotics often suffice without a trip to the local HMO.

If you really want to be cruel, remember that any appendage can be bitten off. Any human bite you can imagine has probably been treated by a doctor somewhere.

Snake Bites

Poisonous snakes may be found around the world. They result in 300,000 bites and 30,000 deaths a year worldwide. Chances are your characters will run into one in often traveled and exotic venues. Contact with a snake may be accidental or deviously planned. Although beyond the scope of this book, the locale of your story will dictate the type of poisonous snake encountered.

Of the forty thousand people in the United States bitten by snakes every year, only fifteen die, and these are usually children or the elderly. Approximately seventy percent of venomous snakebites are from rattlesnakes; the remainder involves copperheads, cottonmouths and coral snakes (less than one percent). Maine, Hawaii and Alaska are the only states that do not have a native venomous snake.

Curiously, almost fifty percent of the people bitten by snakes are intoxicated, and up to sixty percent of victims were deliberately handling the reptile! Not every snakebite results in the deposit of venom, and simple puncture wounds are often treated with first aid and observation.

Important questions to be answered after a snake attack:

- Is the snake poisonous?
- Did the snake cause envenomation?
- How far apart are the fang puncture wounds?

Poisonous snakes have fangs, and the distance between the puncture wounds gives a rough estimate of the snake's size. Harmless snakes have teeth rather than fangs and a double row of anal plates.

Clinical Presentation of a Snake Bite Victim

Grade 0   No venom deposit; with pain; fang or tooth marks; an inch or less of redness

Grade 1   Minimal venom deposit; severe pain; fang or tooth marks; one to five inches of redness and swelling

Grade 2   Moderate venom deposit; fang or tooth marks; six to twelve inches of redness and swelling; general symptoms of nausea, light-headedness and shock.

Grade 3   Severe envenomation; fang or tooth marks; more than a foot of swelling and redness; decreased blood pressure; bleeding; bruising; shock

Grade 4   Multiple tooth or fang marks; diffuse swelling and redness beyond local area to other anatomic regions; kidney failure; shock; coma

Pit vipers are poisonous snakes that have the following distinguishing characteristics: The thermoreceptor "pit" lies between the nostril and the snake's eye, the pupil of the eye is a vertical slit and the anal plates on the undersurface of the beast form a single row. Coral snakes vary in color, but the guiding mnemonic is "Red on yellow, kill a fellow; red on black, venom lack." Non-poisonous king snakes have incomplete red and black stripes, while the deadly coral snake of the southern United States possesses completely encircling red-next-to-yellow bands.

Before we finish discussing snakes, two additional questions must be answered: What is it the venom actually does, and how do you treat a snakebite?

When you consider that snake venom is designed to immobilize prey to facilitate swallowing and digestion, it won't come as a surprise that this obnoxious fluid contains enzymes. Enzymes are the active body substances that digest the snake's food, or digest parts of the victim who is bitten. The three main categories of toxins in venom are cardiotoxins (containing enzymes acting on the heart and blood vessels), enzymes acting on the coagulation system resulting in mild bruising to major hemorrhage, and neurotoxins acting on the nervous system, causing mental changes and/or loss of coordination.. Your characters may suffer from any of the following problems afer a snake bite:

- Local tissue damage – redness, swelling, purple-black necrotic (dead) tissue
- Coagulation problems resulting in bruising and/or excessive bleeding
- Blood vessel damage and leakage of body fluid with arm or leg swelling
- Pulmonary edema (body fluids leak out and water floods the lungs), congestive heart failure
- Numbness, paralysis and loss of consciousness
- Kidney failure
- Anemia
- Shock (cardiovascular collapse)

How would a snake bitten victim look?

To begin with there is severe local pain at the bite site, swelling of the tissues and often bruising. Fang wounds are seen. Legs and feet are common sites for folks out in the wilderness. Hands and forearms may be bitten in snake handlers and drunks on a dare. Imagine your character leaning over an immobile pet snake, only to be bitten on the nose or cheek. Imagine if the drunk is naked. Swelling occurs around the bite.

Occasionally, a compartment syndrome occurs. This means the muscles in a tough closed fascial "bag" of the leg or arm swell up and squeeze out the blood supply. Tissues can then die or become necrotic. Shock produces sweating, a fast heart rate, and possible heart rhythm abnormalities. Delerium, seizures, slurred speech, and respiratory muscle failure may occur. Your character may exibit a combination of these signs and symptoms.

The steps for treating a snakebite are outlined on this page.

How to Treat a Snake Bite

- Slow the absorption of venom. Tourniquet above bite site with just enough pressure to block venous flow, not compress the artery. Leave on up to two hours; don't periodically release. This treatment is no longer recommended by experts.

- Immobilize limb with a splint.
- Remove venom from bite site. Make ¼ inch long by ¼ to ½ inch deep incisions over each fang bite. Apply suction—by mouth, if necessary, as long as there are no cuts inside the mouth. This treatment is not often recommended by experts today, but may be used, for example, in remote (delay rescue) areas with bad bites where a large amount of venom was deposited.
- Neutralize the venom. Antivenom is available, which is administered intravenously in successively larger doses depending on the degree of venom deposit, from none for grade 0 to 50cc or more for grades 3 and 4. This is the mainstay of treatment and occurs in a hospital.
- Treat the general side effects. Give IV fluids and blood products for shock, dialysis for kidney failure, special drugs to maintain adequate blood pressure, and antibiotics to prevent infection. This is done in the hospital.
- Surgical treatment may be necessary for dead (necrotic) tissue; any black, bloodless skin, soft tissue or muscles must be completely excised in the operating room. The result may be a huge hole in an arm or leg. *Fasciotomy* refers to cutting open a muscle compartment to release pressure and assisting in restoring perfusion of blood. In the leg, the fasciotomy incision would run between the ankle and the knee laterally (sometimes the fibula is removed); in the forearm, along each side of the forearm between the wrist and elbow; in the hand, along the side of the fingers. If large tissue defects occur, reconstruction with skin grafts, and possibly plastic surgery techniques such as tissue flaps, may be required. Scarring may be significant.

Shark Bites

Before 1968, almost twenty percent of all recorded shark attacks were deadly, but between the mid-1980s and 1994, only five deaths were recorded by the International Shark Attack File. These feared injuries vary from relatively minor lacerations to big bites with extensive tissue and blood loss and the need for complex reconstructive surgery. And, like other animals, the shark's mouth harbors unique bacteria that can cause infection.

The majority of shark attacks occur in the late summer and early fall when bathers are active, and sharks move down the coasts from colder northern waters and inhabit the warm shallows seeking food. With multiple rows of sharp teeth and a torpedo body of awesome proportions, particularly in such species as the great white, the shark plays a central role in humankind's wealth of myth. Anchored in elements of fact, shark lore often outstrips reality, and Peter Benchley's *Jaws* tapped into man's deepest fears. It was disquieting to wade into the ocean for a long time after reading that book and viewing Spielberg's haunting film.

The type of wound depends on the size of the shark, the aggressiveness of the attack, and the body part bitten. The depth and extent of the bite varies from "teeth scrapes," where the shark doesn't bite as much as graze a leg or belly or arm, possibly identifying food, to major amputations or body cavity violations.

A smaller shark may bump, bite, and leave little more than a row of indentations from their teeth. Limb attacks may lacerate large amounts of soft tissue, crush muscle, tear tendons, and expose bone. There are many reports of foot amputations as well as finger and hand amputations. Chest and abdominal bites may result in wounds that enter the thoracic or belly cavity and expose viscera. A lung may be exposed, or loops of intestine. Contrary to myth, sharks have complex brains and can learn behavior patterns. Your character may decide to "seed" the waters near his boat with chum before dumping his girlfriend overboard.

Surgical treatment is needed in most shark attacks. This will vary from cleaning the wound and suturing ("tacking down") down a tissue flap created by the bite, to removing dead tissue and reconstructing the area with plastic surgery techniques. A split thickness skin graft may be taken from another site (often the anterior thigh); rotation flaps refer to "sliding" local tissue over the defect and closing the gap left behind. Major chest wounds may require reconstruction with mesh covered with methyl methacrylate and the placement of chest tube drainage. Abdominal wounds can be closed with sutures, but some will require mesh to bridge a large defect. The latter may be a delayed procedure.

Hospital Treatment of Any Bad Bite
- Give IV fluid replacement and blood products as needed to treat for shock.
- Give intravenous antibiotics.
- Debride, or clean up, the wound. When possible, surgeon attempts to close as much of the defect as possible; if necessary skin grafts or rotation flaps may be needed.

- If a fracture is present, fix the broken bones first, often with internal fixation with metal rods, then repair the soft tissue damage.
- Start rehabilitation immediately.

Horse Bites

Horse bites result in either crush or laceration types of soft tissue injury. Unlike the case when an arm or leg is crushed under a collapsing building when large amounts of tissue debris are released into the bloodstream, a horse bite only causes damage to local tissue. At worst, severe contusions, lacerations and, at times, broken bones occur.

The attack comes when the rider turns her back or when someone approaches a horse that has been mistreated.

Consider that a horse's teeth are designed to tear out grass (the front teeth are tearing, cutting in design) or grind up grass (the back teeth crush). Unless your character was wearing thick clothes over the bite site, some sort of injury will occur. If you must have your concert pianist lose a digit, contrive to have his sponsor's favorite stallion chomp it off just before the fox hunt. Feeding one's mount places the fingers in danger, as the horse may see more food than is being presented and may include part of the hand in its mouth. Palming the apple or sugar cube will keep the fingers away from the horse's muzzle as he maneuvers the delicacy between his impressive pearlies.

Ears are another exposed body part known to be a horse's occasional target. The result may be a mangled or amputated lobe. After disciplining her unruly mount, your character's ear may tempt the ornery steed when her back is turned. Noses have been bitten off by horses. Plastic surgery is needed to reattach any part—assuming it's not too badly mangled.

A shoulder might also tempt the stallion. The result is often a nasty bruise or laceration, depending on the clothing worn. Veterinarians have been known to suffer from serious forearm bites while treating a horse. These injuries range from severe soft tissue damage, including the severing of flexor and extensor tendons of the forearm, to a fracture of either forearm bone or both.

Finally, some horses have the temerity to pick up their owner by the collar. A horse can bite the back of the collar of a riding jacket or the hood of a sweatshirt and half choke the person by lifting him off the ground.

Stings

Unless you live in a bubble, you've undoubtedly been stung by an insect. Mosquitoes, black flies, ants and other smaller insects inflict annoying bites that carry virtually no risk to life or limb. This isn't true of some larger insects and spiders. Depending on where your story takes place, you may wish to give someone a short-term illness — perhaps a sickness that isn't easily diagnosed by the doctors in your scene — that stems from an innocuous insect bite.

Spider Bites

There are at least six genera of spiders in the U.S. Some are harmless. A few are notorious for the damage their bites cause. And the bad actors – the brown recluse and the black widow— have specific geographic homes. They may be found elsewhere by virtue of traveling in the crates of commerce.

Loxoscelism is the medical term for a brown recluse (loxosceles reclusa) spider bite. It is the only medically important spider bite in the U.S. The worst offender (most potent), the brown recluse spider, seldom bites humans even in endemic areas, is virtually never lethal, and only occasionally delivers enough venom to cause tissue damage referred to as necrotic arachnidism. It means a patch of black, dead skin and fat, often requiring surgical debridement (removal). The disease is typically self-limited and self-healing. There are seldom long-term consequences.

You can identify them by their six eyes (most U.S. spiders have eight) and a pigmented violin-shaped pattern on the body. The differential diagnosis a doctor thinks about when she sees a necrotic patch of skin includes a strep or staph infection, herpes infection, diabetic ulcer, fungal infection, syphilis, a chemical burn, anthrax, skin cancer and Lyme disease. In ninety percent of suspected spider bites, the creature isn't available for identification.

Treatment is similar to the management of minor musculoskeletal injuries (Chapter Eleven) including elements of the mnemonic *PRICE*: protection, rest, ice, compression and elevation. Steroids, such as prednisone, hyperbaric oxygen, and antivenom, and excision and skin grafting, have all been used. For most cases, the simple measures work just fine.

Suppose the bite is on the back and results in a patch of dead skin and underlying tissue. A surgeon would take the patient to the operating room. Under general or local anesthesa with sedation, the surgeon would excise the dead tissue by cutting a few millimeters away from the line of demarcation between the necrotic, dead flesh and pink, normal tissue. With a scalpel, she would cut as deeply as necessary to get all of the dead tissue out. Usually this involves only fatty tissue and the overlying skin. The resulting defect may be "pulled together" and closed "primarily" with sutures, or it may require rotating a flap of skin and soft tissue to fill the defect, or the placement of a split thickness skin graft. It's the surgeon's choice – depending on the location and size of the defect.

Other spider bites inflict lesser degrees of injury - with exceptions, of course. The black widow spider is found all over the United States, except in Alaska, and has either two red dots or a red hourglass mark on its belly. The female is larger than the male, whom she will kill if he disturbs her web when she has young. Hence the name. At any rate, this aggressive spider produces a *neurotoxin*, a substance that causes stimulation of the nervous system, producing chest and belly pain. You can imagine how this might mimic either a heart attack or an abdominal catastrophe. The neurotoxin may cause the abdominal wall muscles to become spastic and mimic what doctors call "rebound tenderness." When the doctor pushes on the belly and releases suddenly, severe pain is created. An abdominal crisis doctors call an "acute abdomen" is diagnosed. There can be many causes from a perforated appendix to pancreatitis. Thus, the rigidity of the belly wall secondary to black widow spider venom is similar to the rigidity seen in the face of severe peritonitis. Peritonitis is an indication for immediate surgical exploration. If the spider bite is not seen or the possibility not suspected, the surgeon could be trapped into performing exploratory surgery or a diagnostic laparoscopy for no reason.

Although most scorpions found in the United States cause only painful bites, the kinds of scorpions in other parts of the world are poisonous. Scorpion bites in Brazil carry over a ten percent mortality rate. Israel, North Africa, and Mexico also have poisonous scorpions. Scorpion bites may cause acute inflammation of the pancreas. Pancreatitis, as mentioned above, causes peritonitis, and, once again, may mislead a surgeon into thinking the patient has an intra-abdominal catastrophe. Innapropriate surgery might result.

Also, it is said the venom causes a massive outpouring of the body's own adrenaline. This is referred to as a *sympathetic storm* (the sympathetic part of the autonomic or vegetative nervous system responds to the "fight or flight" impulse). As your character's survival mechanisms get turned on to maximum, the heart is over-stimulated. Blood pressure rises to dangerous levels and the heart pumps out more blood than needed—spinning its wheels, so to speak. The victim may die of cardiac failure because the heart is literally whipped to death. Treatment includes administration of a specific antivenom, admission to the intensive care unit, and systemic support. The latter term refers to special cardiac blocking drugs to control heart rate and elevated blood pressure, intubation and ventilatory support (which breathe for the patient), IV fluids, and sedation. Blood work includes monitoring body chemistries, blood sugar, liver and kidney functions, and oxygenation. Thus, the patient would be in the intensive care unit on a ventilator receiving cardiac drugs and intravenous fluid support. The patient would have a nasogastric tube and a Foley catheter in the bladder to monitor urine output and kidney function.

The *hymenoptera* are a group of well-known arthropods that are responsible for more deaths in the United States than all of the snakebites combined. Wasps, bees, hornets, and fire ants inflict painful wounds, which, if numerous, cause nausea and vomiting and a general sense of illness. Sensitivity to the venom results in an *anaphylactic reaction*, an allergic response to the poison that squeezes off the victim's airway and knocks down the blood pressure, and can cause death if not immediately treated.

Kits are available that contain vials of adrenaline and antihistamines that may be used in an emergency. Local care for most stings includes ice packs, elevation, and rest.

Centipedes, those multisegmented ugly crawlers, can inflict a painful bite, which causes swelling and occasionally an infection.

About that botfly.

In Mexico and Central South America, there are lots of insects to make your character's skin crawl. One such fascinating creature is the botfly, a not-so-little insect I met in the office when a colleague returned from Central America. After vacationing in Costa Rica, the physician developed what looked like boils weeks after returning to the United States. Medical reports describe a variety of clinical findings, which include:

- A crawling sensation in the skin
- A swollen area draining pus like a boil
- A bump with a pore and something white moving inside

The botfly is about the size of a bumblebee and lays its eggs on other insects that then deposit them on the host—that's your character. Larvae hatch from the eggs and crawl into the host's skin, where they form a cavity with a pore through which to breathe. Later, the larvae burrow deeper into the fat and muscle, giving the "crawling" sensation, and mature in six to eight weeks. Remaining in human flesh for as long as three months, the larvae grow until they're over an inch long!

The larvae enter the skin most often on the scalp, face, arms, and legs. But—and here's the good news for the writer—they have also been discovered in the eyelids, genitals, and tongue. How's that for juicy plot possibilities? Treatment employs any method of cutting off the insect's oxygen supply and includes covering the pore with petroleum jelly, beeswax, pork fat, or chloroform in olive oil. When the larvae emerge, you pick them off. They can also be excised under local anesthesia (1% Xylocaine) when the host becomes frantic and screams, "Get them outta me!"

The horror of it all.

Sea Life "Bites"

Ocean critters can raise your character's ire and damage the body just when your scene is serene and breathtaking, say, on a coral reef.

A Portuguese man-of-war is a common jellyfish that consists of a balloon-like sail and dangling tentacles, which are armed and potentially extremely dangerous. Special cysts (nematocyst), or cells, contain a curled hair, which fires out of the cell like a harpoon when the cell is brushed. It deposits venom into the swimmer's skin or any unsuspecting individual who walks a littered beach barefooted after a storm.

The sting may cause mild irritation of the skin or full-thickness skin death and ulceration. Mild nausea may occur or more severe symptoms of vomiting, muscle and joint pain, dizziness, loss of balance, seizures and respiratory failure. Other jellyfish, sea wasps, mollusks, etc., may cause similar symptoms. Treatment varies from local wound care to intensive medical support with special medications in the ICU with cardiac and respiratory support as described above for scorpion bites.

Coral cuts are painful and may progress to tissue loss and ulceration. The wounds should be cleaned with hydrogen peroxide and then protected.

Animal Defenses

Although many animals possess relatively benign self-defense techniques to fend off predators inhabiting their environments, some species have cultivated punishing reprisals. The more sophisticated the animal, the more directed the attack. The less brainy, the less calculated the damage.

Sea urchins and jellyfish don't cogitate much about threats to their welfare, and the indiscriminate volleys of stings from the dangling tentacles know no anger. Reptiles and lower mammals defend themselves when cornered or when a life-threatening attack seems imminent. Humans, wired for thought *and* reflex, often retaliate when threatened and all too often carry out premeditated body trauma. Although humankind didn't invent the ambush, we have certainly refined it.

Bites, particularly human attacks, are despicable precisely because they replace eloquence with a guttural assault. Saliva substitutes for language. Bared fangs replace a smile.

To injure a favorite character or to instantly characterize a despised villain, the bite is as good—or as horrible—as it gets.

Are there other types of bites?

Use your imagination.

Alfred Hitchcock exercised his whimsical inventiveness once with a flock of ravenous birds. But don't forget alligators, grizzly bears, wild boar, rhinos, and bats. They say cougar attacks are up in California.

What animals populate your fictional world?

If it's got a mouth, it can bite.

IMPALEMENT INJURIES AND MUTILATION: FROM FENCING TO FENCES

The youngster in the back seat of the sedan writhed like a speared fish. Moaning and thrashing against the vinyl seat, he seemed unaware that he was pinned down by an oak branch driven through his chest. Moments earlier, the car had slithered off the dirt road, plunged down an embankment, and crunched into the massive oak tree with low-lying limbs. A dead branch had smashed through the windshield, missing the two drunk boys in the front seat and spearing the kid riding in the back.

Less than an hour later, using a chain saw, the paramedics cut the branch off a foot from the terrified boy's blood-soaked denim shirt and loaded him and the branch into the waiting ambulance.

The oak spear missed his heart and great vessels, but collaped one lung. A dramatic injury, it was relatively uncomplicated. The trauma surgeons removed the branch in the operating room with routine surgical instruments and with the OR staff standing by with cardiac bypass equipment ready. They were prepared to charge into action had the boy hemorrhaged when the bloody branch was withdrawn from between his ribs.

He didn't.

The terror of thinking about impalement injuries comes precisely from a disbelief that such a ghastly wound could occur. We visualize the branch with horror, splintered end puncturing the boy's shirt, pushing torn fabric into his pale flesh where it slashed between his ribs, tearing the muscles and cutting off his breath. And as the victim is removed from the field, his rescuers didn't even remove the impaled object! (The paramedics did the right thing.)

OK, it's a far-out example of impalement. It could never actually happen that way. Not even in the bizarre world of fiction, right?

In fact, it's a true story.

Elements of an Impalement Injury

- Sharp object penetrates the body.
  - Full body thickness: impalement object visible at entry and exit wounds
  - Partial body thickness: entry wound only

- Attacking instrument may be in motion.
  - High velocity (arrow)
  - Low velocity (spear, long knife)
- Sharp object may be fixed in place (fence pole).
- Victim usually cannot extricate himself from the impaling agent.
- The resulting injury may be major or trivial even if a major body cavity is penetrated.
- Often the impaling object must be removed surgically in the operating room with general anesthesia.
- Chunks of material (e.g., fence) may have to be cut and transported to the hospital while still stuck in the victim.

Features of an Impalement Injury

Think of impalement as an uncontrolled injury where the victim gets "stuck like a pig," piked by a sharp object because of focused energy with considerable penetrating power. Of importance is whether the body or the weapon is in motion. A sword may be used to impale someone against a wall; a spear may impale someone against the ground. But the body flung from a balcony becomes impaled on the pointed struts of the pristine white picket fence below.

The features of an impaling injury:

- The skin is lacerated at the point of entry and may be punctured at a point of exit.
- The chest, abdomen, extremities, head, and neck may be involved.
- Major blood vessels may be cut, but bleeding is minimal at the time of injury because the object presses against the torn vessels and the direct pressure prevents hemorrhage (tamponade of the bleeding).
- Internal organs may be punctured or lacerated and may leak their contents or bleed.

In a scene from Stephen King's *Rose Madder*, crazy cop Norman Daniels wrestles in a laundry room with a woman named Pam, who struggles to escape his grasp and hits a door:

> There was a noise, a meaty sound that was almost a pop like a champagne cork, and then Pam began to flail wildly, her hands beating at the door, her head back at a strange stiff angle, like someone staring intently at the flag during a patriotic ceremony . . .

... he looked down and saw that Pam's left sneaker was no longer white. Now it was red. Blood was pooling around it; it ran down the door in long drips ...

She looked almost nailed to the door, and as Norman stepped forward, he saw that, in a way, she was. There was a coathook on the back of the damned thing. She'd torn free of his hand, plunged forward, and impaled herself. The coathook was buried in her left eye.

What vital structures in the perforated body part are at risk? How does it feel to get pierced by a cold, steely point? What parts of the body are most sensitive? Let's think up a few impalements to make your story reek with terror:

- A drunk woman falls forward and impales her eyeball on a toothpick protruding from her martini glass.
- A scuba diver misfires his spear gun into his buddy's thigh, abdomen, or scrotum.
- A bow hunter's two year old runs out in front of an animal target to pat the "deer" when his father impales his child on the plastic silhouette while practicing for hunting season.
- A recently released psych patient, now homeless, assaults a jogger and nails her to a wooden fence as if she were on a cross.
- Enraged after losing the national championship to a teammate, a member of the university fencing team files down the end of his rapier and runs the champ through the throat in practice.
- An abusive husband thrusts a freshly sharpened No. 2 pencil into his wife's ear canal.

To assemble a tale of woe, you must let your imagination soar in order to discover what sort of unique injury might serve your purpose. These examples of impalement injuries will get you thinking about sharp objects and soft body parts. The rest is merely a matter of assembly, beginning at the end.

Cross-sectional anatomy of the limbs, trunk, and neck helps you to determine what injuries will occur with a particular impalement. Imagine what structures a sharp object could traverse without actually killing your victim. Here are a few more examples.

There is a famous case of a man who was tamping in a dynamite charge with a metal rod when the charge went off. He was struck somewhere in the forehead, and the rod went into his skull and (presumably) through part of his frontal lobes and the connecting fibers between the two cerebral hemispheres. The man survived to live for years, with no ill effects other than a major personality change.

If your story takes place on a farm, an obvious implement that may be invoked in an impalement injury is a pitchfork. A fall from the hayloft onto a piece of farm equipment is another tragic working injury.

There is a photograph somewhere of a young man hanging from the top of a tall wrought iron fence. The arrowhead-shaped spike had penetrated the fellow's cheek from the outside and was protruding from his open mouth. Did the youngster attempt to scale the fence, slip, and impale himself as he plummeted toward the ground?

Underwater stories flirt with the idea of someone getting impaled by a spear gun. Tales of adventure, where bows and arrows flourish, beg for a scene with someone pinned to a tree by a poisonous arrow. Or in the belly. Or leg. Or neck. A knife driven through a hand into a wooden table might get your character's attention.

Mutilation and Torture

The idea behind mutilation is presumably twofold: first, to play out one's unmanageable rage and inflict revenge; second, to leave a message for those who discover the body. Death and disfigurement each possess a separate horror. But the message is always the same: This could happen to you.

Knit tightly into the psychology of mutilation is the sister terror of torture. Both stimulate the most profound sense of dread, panic, and disgust. Only people who possess a bestial level of perception and appreciation would inflict suffering and unimaginable pain.

Or writers.

So if you're telling a dreadful tale populated by lots of bad guys, you may need to have them torture or disfigure someone. Like it or not, you've got to know how it's done. As before, we'll begin with the information you'll need to build your intimidating scene. But first, ask yourself: What is it about mutilation and torture that we react to?

The answer is twofold:

- We abhor disfigurement of those body parts we view as uniquely human.
- We are repulsed when viewing painful injuries with which we can easily relate, those injuries that we have experienced, that are similar to our past injuries, or close to the kinds of pain we have felt.

What parts of our bodies are unique?

It isn't the sensual aspects of the human form, not the curves, not the tapered legs, or the rippling shoulders, or the thick thighs. These defining anatomic features are sexy. We all respond to an attractive figure according to our sexual orientation. But hormonal intrigue isn't what defines us as special.

It's the human face, hands, and feet.

OK, maybe you'll quibble with me about feet. But we're not searching for hallmarks of human beauty in this discussion. I'm attempting to pursue the idea of a defining structure that makes us so undeniably human in the first place.

Remember Dr. Hannibal Lecter in Thomas Harris's *The Silence of the Lambs*? Officers Pembry and Boyle are feeding the killer in his prison cage in Memphis. Concealing a piece of metal, from which he created a handcuff key, Lecter attacks Pembry as he clears Lecter's supper tray and handcuffs him to the table. Then:

> Lecter grabbed the long end of the baton and lifted. With the leverage twisting Pembry's belt tight around him, he hit Pembry in the throat with his elbow and sank his teeth in Pembry's face. Pembry trying to claw at Lecter, his nose and upper lip caught between the tearing teeth. Lecter shook his head like a rat-killing dog . . .

It's a disgusting scene because it is subhuman. Lecter could have clubbed him to death without the mutilation, but instead he killed Boyle and then left Pembry with a bleeding open face, a reminder to all of Hannibal Lecter's unpredictability. Genius and insanity, separated by an angel's hair.

Consider the intern who evaluates a trauma victim in the ER for the first time, or a medical student who begins the study of anatomy and views the cadaver on that memorable first day. Why are they distressed? Is it because the trauma victim is in shock? Is it because the cadaver is dead?

How do you react to a road kill?

If you'll stop laughing for a moment, it's not such a foolish question. Routinely, we drive past dead raccoons, birds, deer and other carrion and usually don't stop to mourn the passing of one of nature's family. When does the dead animal make you cringe? It's when you see the face—especially the eyes—or you view loops of intestine or something else from "inside", some ugly viscera foreign to your daily experience.

The intern looks at the motorcyle victim on the stretcher and sees his brother. The medical student views the cadaver and sees her grandmother. Both individuals focus on something familiar; they are reminded of something or someone emotionally close to them. Common to both experiences are views of those anatomic parts that we associate with being uniquely human. We are staggered by the dead face, the lifeless hands, and the toe tag.

There's more.

Next you're going to learn why these very human structures are involved in both mutilation and torture. It goes beyond the obvious delight crazed maniacs derive from disfiguring their victims, debasing that which is human, that which is defining about an individual. It is tied to the hard wiring of the human nervous system.

First, consider how body parts are represented on the cerebral (conscious) cortex. One strip of the cortex (sensory cortex) provides sensation while the adjacent strip (motor cortex) provides conscious control of muscles. Pathways, or bundles, of nerves travel from the motor cortex to the muscles and permit you to move your body any way you elect. Other neural highways course up the spinal cord to the brain—specifically to the sensory cortex— from various body parts, returning a kaleidoscope of sensations.

Not all body parts are equally represented on the sensory cortex. Stab someone in the back with an ice pick and he may not know what happened. The impact seems to the victim a mere thump on the shoulder. But push a toothpick under the same person's fingernail and the pain will be unbearable. Why? Because the area on the sensory cortex devoted to the hand is larger. Now you know why it hurts.

All that neural power is supposed to provide you with the ability to feel small objects, improve touch, appreciate pressure changes, and refine and modulate hand and finger movements. It's possible because of the rich pattern of sensory signals the brain receives from the hand. This geographic generosity of the human sensory cortex has produced the Sistine Chapel, Mozart's minuets, concertos and symphonies, and a wealth of literature, sports heroes, and villains. We are unique among mammals because we have an opposable thumb and a supercharged brain to guide it.

The feet are well represented on the sensory cortex as well. So are the genitals.

Imagine that. Thugs with no education, no understanding of microanatomy, actually create anguish true to the nature of the brain.

They know which sensory buttons to push.

Thus, the human nervous system is designed to process a variety of exquisite sensory bulletins, integrating various signals from touching, stroking and prodding to pinching, poking, and stabbing. From pianists to keyboard-crazy adolescents, from artists to inner-city graffiti gurus, humans take for granted the remarkable biological gift provided by their marvelous brains. Receiving signals, sending out motor messages coupled with imagination, humankind has created a culture enriched with a host of expressions of intellect.

But every complex system possesses a potential glitch. Wired for maximum efficiency, the brain also may be overloaded and break down. The sheer volume of sensations received by some people is too much for them to cope with and they decompensate. It's the price humans pay for being smart.

Warthogs don't become depressed.

Sadly, the villains and degenerates of the world also understand the inherent flaws in the wiring of the mind. Both mental and physical torture are possible because of the defenseless nature of our bodies. Few people can distract themselves to the extent that they can completely block out noxious, disagreeable sensations. And although the villain doesn't know his cortex from his elbow, he does know how to take advantage of the sensitive skin envelope.

Mutilation doesn't always result in death. The best advertisement for a subversive individual or group is a walking, talking human signpost with disfiguring scars. Once again, the most effective mutilation is designed to distort those things we hold most precious. An example: How often have you not recognized a friend because she was wearing dark glasses? We are defined by our physical features, and our eyes are truly the windows to our uniqueness. But more to the point, if the eyes are involved in mutilation, the impact is twofold:

- The injured person carries a visible scar (or eye patch).
- The injured person loses a precious gift (sight).

The villain sends a clear message. We will hurt you, and we may change your life permanently without actually killing you. *Reminders.* That's what the bad guys want as they wander about out there among the common folk. A scarlet letter sends a message. A missing ear sends a more virulent message. Fingers may be amputated in the name of torture as well as to leave a visible message.

Scars speak of the horrors experienced when wounds are inflicted.

Torture and Power

To solve a mystery, your detective uses brain power. To obtain answers about who is poking their noses in the bad guy's business, the villain in your story may resort to torture. It's a matter of brute power, not intelligence.

In her book, *The Body In Pain - the making and unmaking of the world,* Elaine Scarry describes the conversion of horrible physical pain into the fiction of power. Her main point is that pain is voiceless, pain produces pre-language, and the shrieks and guttural moans of an otherwise sentient human create an inarticulate animal. Torture takes this private affair and makes it public.

Torture exhibits three differences from other types of pain. Compared, for example, to a dentist's visit or a religious event, Scarry notes that:

- Torture lasts longer and may have no definable boundaries.
- The tortured person does not have control of when the process will begin and end.
- Torture has no purpose beyond the suffering inflicted in the name of a created fiction, a new locus of power.

In order to tell the truth, you need to think about the relationship between torture and power. No matter where in the world your story takes place, there will be someone who wants control over someone else. It may be subtle. But more often it involves inflicting physical pain and emotional suffering. Any of the injuries mentioned in this book from impalement to creature bites may serve the despicable needs of torture.

Before ending this section, it is important to remember that all political regimes, including the American military, have used torture to seek information. Writers must confront the truth wherever it exists. For example, American soldiers took Vietnamese prisoners up for helicopter rides that ended with a push out the door if information was not forthcoming. Regardless of the outcome, in the mind of the victim, torture is a prelude to death.

TWELVE

TRAUMATIC AMPUTATIONS AND REPLANTATION: DON'T LOSE THE MISSING PART!

My springer spaniel galloped across the train trestle a few feet ahead of the charging locomotive, making no attempt to clear the track as he galloped past the bridge abutment. I yelled at the roaring train. Blackie kept running, losing the race with the train by inches with each labored leap, and now his tongue flapped out and soon his tail was within a foot of the huge black machine. As my shouts became lost in the roar of the locomotive, my heart squeezed and Blackie's lean body disappeared beneath the screeching steel wheels. The furry black ball rolled under the locomotive, tumbled for an indeterminable moment, somersaulted beneath the wheels, and bounced off of the wooden ties until at last, a small black mass shot off to the opposite side of the tracks hidden from me, by the train roaring past, and a larger chunk of dog rolled across the snow until it stopped less than twenty feet from where I stood.

I was twelve years old when I saw my first traumatic amputation. Blackie was my first dog and I buried his severed head and his body together beneath the crusted surface of a lonely stretch of Quebec's wilderness not far from my home.

There is something more chilling than it is final about the complete severance of a body part, even when death is not part of the trauma scenario. A head cannot be reattached to the body. But other parts can be and routinely are replanted.

The majority of traumatic amputations are not lethal, and thanks to microscopic surgery, often the severed part may be replaced with the use of special surgical techniques.

The first limb replacement—replantation as doctors call it—of a severed body part didn't occur in a human until 1962, even though surgeons in the U.S. were cutting off and sewing back dogs' limbs in the 1920's. It wasn't until a twelve-year-old boy was rushed to Massachusetts General Hospital in 1962 that successful replantation was accomplished. The unfortunate youngster had been playing beside railroad tracks when a train ran him down, trapping his arm between a train and a bridge support. The arm was completely severed. Dr. Ronald

Malt, a surgical resident at MGH, made medical history when the boy's arm was successfully reattached.

Now the procedure is common all over the world.

First, we need to complete a small housekeeping chore. *Replantation* refers to the reattachment of a completely severed body part. But the whole process is based on the discipline of *microsurgery*, which requires the use of delicate instruments, intense surgeon training, and a special operating microscope. The major focus is on *revascularization* — the correction of cut blood vessels — sewing back together both arteries and veins with delicate sutures. Because of its wide application, microsurgery cuts across all specialty lines, and surgeons have used this technique to transfer tissue as well to as reattach amputated limbs and digits.

To limit the topic, we'll focus on the upper extremity in our discussion. Before we do, it is important to remember that all of the following (and undoubtedly other) tissues have been replanted:

- The lower extremity
- Ear
- Lip
- Lip and chin
- Penis and scrotum
- Scalp

In the scheme of things, when a multiple injured patient arrives in the emergency room, there is little worry that the upper limb injury will threaten the victim's life unless a major hemorrhage occurs. On the other hand, the final disability for the victim, if she survives, will be lost work ability and changes in daily living caused by loss of the severed part. Thus, it is important to consider replantation as an integral part of overall care.

Sharply created traumatic wounds have a better rate of successful replantation than those accompanied by a mangling agent, such as those seen with industrial machines and farm equipment. Machetes, meat cleavers, and knives make reattachment an easier surgical *tour de force*.

Why does an operation for replantation fail?

It fails most often because of excessive total time the amputated part has gone without an adequate blood supply. This period of time is referred to as *warm ischemia time*. It means vital cells in the amputated part have no nourishment, and without cold protection to slow down metabolism, they will begin to die. Experimental studies suggest that the limb ought to be replanted within six to eight hours for optimum function. Cold protection of the amputated part (packing the part in ice) will prolong this time frame; for example, cooled amputated dog legs have been successfully reattached after as long as twenty-five hours.

Though our discussion of replantation issues will focus on the upper extremity, we'll cover the basic principles used in the replantation of other tissues. Any of the following traumatic upper extremity amputations should be considered for replantaion:

- Thumb
- Hand
- One or more fingers
- Arm
- Any ischemic or amputated extremity of a child

There are some trauma victims who should not be evaluated for replantation. And all candidates who are considered must be fully informed about the arduous and prolonged rehabilitation process, loss of work time, discomfort, and possibility of failure. It's possible that some folks just don't think missing a chunk of a finger is a big deal. Prior illness and the severity of the injury itself may exclude otherwise motivated patients from becoming microsurgery candidates.

Who gets rejected during the crucial initial evaluation in the emergency room after the traumatic event? Remember, the first thirty minutes of assessment and resuscitation is when saving the victim's life outweighs saving the limb. At least until the smoke clears.

The following are reasons *not* to consider a trauma victim a candidate for replantation:

- The amputated part is severely crushed.
- The amputated part is extremely contaminated with road dirt, etc., so that it cannot be adequately cleaned.
- The victim has one or more life-threatening injuries that require extensive emergency care including surgery.
- The victim has one or more severe chronic illnesses that are debilitating, such as severe heart disease, poorly controlled diabetes, or extensive crippling arthritis.

Every amputated part should be taken to the hospital with the victim. Only a microsurgeon can determine if the severed part is viable and can be reattached to the victim's body. Even if it can't, some of it (e.g., the skin, blood vessels, and nerves) may be used to repair other injured body areas. If reattachment is to succeed, your characters must know how to handle the severed part out in the field. Here are the steps that must be followed in packaging the amputated part:

- Wrap in moistened sterile gauze. *Don't* attempt to clean the part as vital structures may be damaged.
- Place wet gauze containing the part into a sealed plastic bag or bottle.

- Place the bag/bottle in a basin of water and ice. Don't let the part come in direct contact with the ice.
- Give the package to the ER personnel on arrival.

How A Finger Is Replanted

To demonstrate the steps involved in any type of replantation, we'll examine the replacement of an amputated finger. In a critically injured victim, the severed part may be worked on by a microsurgeon while the patient is being resuscitated and treated for other injuries by the trauma team. The surgical preparation of the part includes:

- Keeping the part as cold as possible
- Shortening the bone to allow repair of nerves and vessels without tension
- Debriding dead tissue
- Labeling nerves and blood vessels
- Flushing out blood vessels with heparin
- Placing rigid wires in injured bones to fix them to the remaining bones in the hand

A second team performs the same procedures on the amputated stump. When both ends are prepared according to the above protocol, the replantation occurs. Each cut structure of the finger is reattached by sutures in a specific order (this varies somewhat from hospital to hospital):

1. Fix bones for stability.
2. Fix extensor tendons. (Flexors are repaired after the extensors because the task is more complicated.)
3. Suture arteries.
4. Reattach veins. (Previously collapsed, but now more easily found because they are flooded with blood.)
5. Delicately reapproximate nerves.
6. Close skin.
7. Apply a bulky loose dressing.

If blood vessels are sewn together with any degree of tension, they will clot and fail to supply blood to the finger. Consider the loss of tissue required to trim ragged skin edges, and you can appreciate the need to shorten the finger bones ever so slightly.

It's all done under an operating microscope.

If the amputation site is at or beyond the last finger joint, some surgeons feel it's not feasible to repair it. You don't get as good a bang for the buck. Of course, it depends on what the victim does for a living.

Replantation of a thumb is usually indicated, and the results have been good. The younger the patient and the cleaner the amputation, the better the surgical outcome.

Replantation at the wrist, hand, or forearm level has produced superb results in some reported studies of patients. However, when you get above the elbow, the results are poor, and fewer of the attempts at elbow or higher replantation are successful. More complications are seen with upper arm replantations.

Ring injuries are caused by traction on a ring that pulls off all or part of the finger. That is, the injury results in the finger being degloved (skin torn back), amputated, or merely lacerated. Varying degrees of successful replantation have been observed, and some surgeons recommend amputation for serious avulsion ("ripped off") trauma.

Are Kids' Injuries Different?

Unlike with adults, replantation of the arm is quite successful in the pediatric age group. The indications for attempting replantation in kids are the same as in adults—if anything, the indications are more liberal. Overall, success rate in all children operated on with various traumatic amputations is eighty-five percent. It's less in avulsion injuries where the tissue ends are ragged and more surgery is needed. In these cases, success rates reach only about seventy-five percent. If the amputation is clean-cut, success of replantation approaches ninety-five percent.

Peripheral nerves regenerate better in youngsters than in adults. Presumably, they are less mature and possess residual "growth ability," for lack of a better term. The sensation kids experience in the reattached part tends to be better than that attained by adults. Of interest is the fact that the replanted part may actually grow with the child as he ages.

A Warning!

Not all replanted body parts function well. The microsurgeon must take into consideration many factors before embarking on the arduous task of sewing a body piece back into position. Worse by far than living with trauma of an amputation is the constant reminder of the horrible event by the presence of a useless limb or digit. Failure can result in some cases with the replanted limb literally hanging off the body.

While replacing two or more amputated fingers seems to provide a superior functional result over multiple amputations, replanting a single digit isn't always clearly an improvement over amputation. The surgeon makes the call using all available information.

Conflict arises when an injury threatens a character's goals. The tension in the story may be escalated at several points along the path to replantation. Some of the following questions may help your creative juices:

- Can the severed part be found?
- Can it be preserved properly for transportation?
- How far away is the appropriate hospital?
- Does someone in an intermediary hospital decide it's not worth the effort to send the victim on to the big-city trauma center?
- What are the other injuries your character suffered?
- Does the HMO think it's economical to save the part?

Your task is to think of what's in your story's unique world that might cause a traumatic amputation. Once again, people in conflict with each other make difficult medical decisions all the more complicated.

Cut off the body part — not the conflict.

THIRTEEN

BURNS AND FROSTBITE:
THE SCARS OF TEMPERATURE EXTREMES

Self-inflicted scrapes, cuts, and bruises are daily events for most of us. Nicks and abrasions go through cycles of healing and reinjury for many hardworking souls who labor throughout their lives with their hands. With time, these minor traumas of daily living heal and leave minimal scarring.

Skin consists of layers. The outermost coating is a mesh of dead cells, and the deeper germinal layer produces the layers above and is protected by the cells above it. As skin is shed, new cells are born in the active germinal layer and the old mantle is replaced. This process goes on with monotonous certainty all the days of our lives.

Unlike amphibians and reptiles, lizards and snakes, we have neither a tough outer protection nor the ability to shed our integument *en masse* and replace it with a new coat. Minor sunburns, scratches, scrapes, and gouges leave us with scabs and enough pain to be reminded we actually wear our feelings on the outside. Scars are the body's way of keeping the protective skin together; in a sense, it's nature's self-suturing. Excessive scarring, as we shall see in a moment, may overwhelm the skin landscape and create both cosmetic and emotional turmoil.

Two of the most devastating injuries known to man occur as a result of extremes of temperature; the worst by far are *big burns*. Local heat, if intense enough, damages all layers of the skin, not just the outer layer as with a sunburn. All sorts of agents of intense heat may damage the skin. And if a burn occurs in a closed space, the airways and lungs may also suffer with a reaction similar to pneumonia.

Cold injury almost always occurs out-of-doors in the harsh winter environment. And just as boiling water, oil, and flame injure in distinct ways, so do the primary agents of cold injury: air, ice, and water. Putting your characters in a polar setting is one way to expose them to the cold. Canadian researcher, explorer, and author Dr. Joe MacInnis described to me the conditions he encountered when he performed the first dives attempted in the Arctic environment. Standing in the dive tent erected over a square opening cut into the deep Arctic ice, air temperature at head level reached almost 80° Fahrenheit while the diver's ankles endured temperatures hovering at ten degrees below zero! But don't think for a moment that cold injuries happen only to Arctic explorers. The potential for cold injury and hypothermia lurks even in temperate regions, not just in the high Arctic.

Common Ground

You might imagine burns and frostbite as distinctly different types of skin damage. In fact, they mimic each other. For both problems, it's an issue of degree of injury. Figure 18 shows the skin layers affected as a burn or frostbite progresses. Regardless of the type of thermal or cold insult, the skin may die partially, in which case it will regenerate itself, or it may succumb completely.

Keep in mind that skin damage is either partial thickness or full thickness. Thus, burns and frostbite injuries are classified according to depth of damage. The outcome of the injury and extent of treatment necessary to clean up the wounds (debridement) depends on whether the deep germinal cells are destroyed or preserved.

In a sense, your skin is a skating rink and life is a frenzied hoard of midget hockey players running over you, etching you with nicks and cuts. Your body has its own built-in Zamboni machine. Surface cells shed like snowflakes; deep cells resurface you daily.

But this surface rejuvenation can't fill in deep gouges. Deep injury means tissue loss with scarring. And scar tissue leaves irregular pits and depressions, an ugly engraving that serves as a reminder of the impact.

Deep injury means trouble.

Burns

While a flame burn of the hand may require extensive reconstructive surgery, it doesn't affect the body's immune system or fluid balance. If small burns are first- or second-degree depth, they may be bandaged with antibiotic ointment and kept protected while new skin resurfaces the area. Small, full-thickness burns on nonessential surfaces (e.g., the back, leg or belly) may also be managed at home, although the pain can be impressive. Thus, the first factor in determining the severity of a burn is the depth.

Minor burns characterize people as smokers, sloppy amateur cooks, or hardworking blue-collar types whose hands reflect a lifetime of toil. Old minor burn scars are white, flat and irregular—something else to read on a character's outward appearance.

Big burns result from home or industrial fires (often caused by careless smokers), forest fires (careless campers), kids playing with matches (careless parents)—you set it up any way you want in the world of your story. The second feature of a burn that determines how sick the patient will become is the percentage of the body burned. Figure 19 gives you a rough idea of what percent of the total body surface is represented by the head, arms, legs and trunk.

Figure 18– Skin Cube

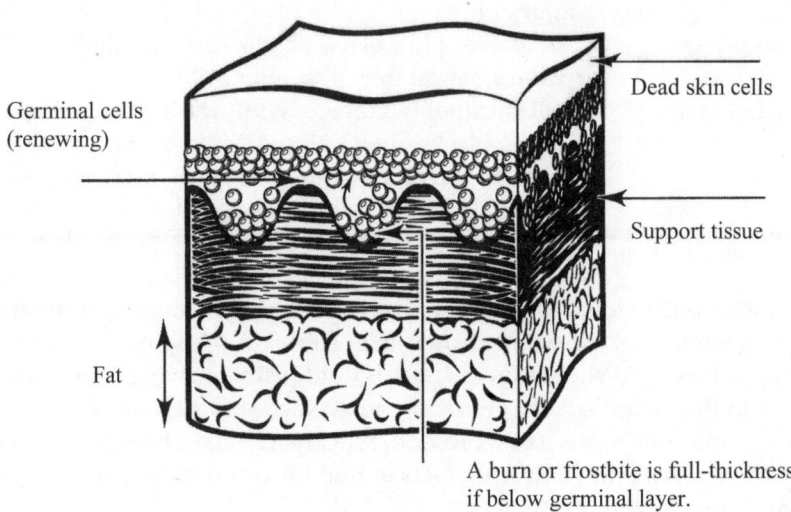

Dead skin cells

Germinal cells (renewing)

Support tissue

Fat

A burn or frostbite is full-thickness if below germinal layer.

The emergency treatment of a big burn begins with replacing the large amounts of body fluid that rapidly leak through the burned skin into the hospital sheets. The victim's "internal sea" is no longer protected by the skin envelope, and body temperature drops swiftly if other treatments such as raising the ambient room temperature aren't started immediately. Antibiotics are given intravenously, and the wounds are smeared with antibiotic ointment. At some point in the future, full-thickness dead skin must be removed surgically and replaced by partial thickness grafts from the victim's remaining patches of intact skin.

One of the first things the doctor will do in the ER is to calculate the burn victim's fluid needs for the first twenty-four hours of care. Interested in *how*? (This is to show you the incredible amount of IV fluid big burns require just to stay even with losses).

Take the percent of surface area burned and multiply it by the victim's body weight in kilograms. If the average person weighs 70 kilograms and suffers a fifty percent burn, you've got 70 x 50 = 3500. Multiply that by 4cc of IV fluid to get the amount to be given over the first day. That's 4cc x 3500 = 14,000cc, or fourteen liters, or fourteen IV bags in twenty-four hours.

The Classification of Burns

First-degree	"Sunburn" type of injury with redness, swelling and moderately severe pain; partial thickness injury only
Second-degree	As above, plus blebs or blisters, containing fluid; painful partial thickness injury
Third-degree	Full-thickness damage with leathery dead skin; white, black, olive colored; little or no sensation; must be surgically removed and replaced; deep germinal layer of cells is destroyed

Your burn victim is going to receive half of this amount in the first eight hours! No, you won't drown her. Her skin's leaking like a fifty-year-old roof, and she needs this much fluid just to survive. The terrible insult to the victim's body occurs because patches of skin are missing in places, and the more gaps present, the greater the changes in body physiology. Keep the following facts in mind if you decide to inflict a big burn on one of your characters:

- Body fluid, or the internal sea, leaks out through the burned skin rapidly.
- Body temperature drops quickly if the room temperature isn't kept artificially elevated (making caring for the burn victim miserable work).
- Protein leaks out with the salt water marking the beginning of potential malnutrition.
- The body's metabolic rate—the speed at which the body burns fuel—soars upward.
- Bacteria find their way into the sterile tissue beneath the burned skin and can establish major infections quite quickly.

Figure 19– Rule of Nines for Determining Percentage of Body Surface Area

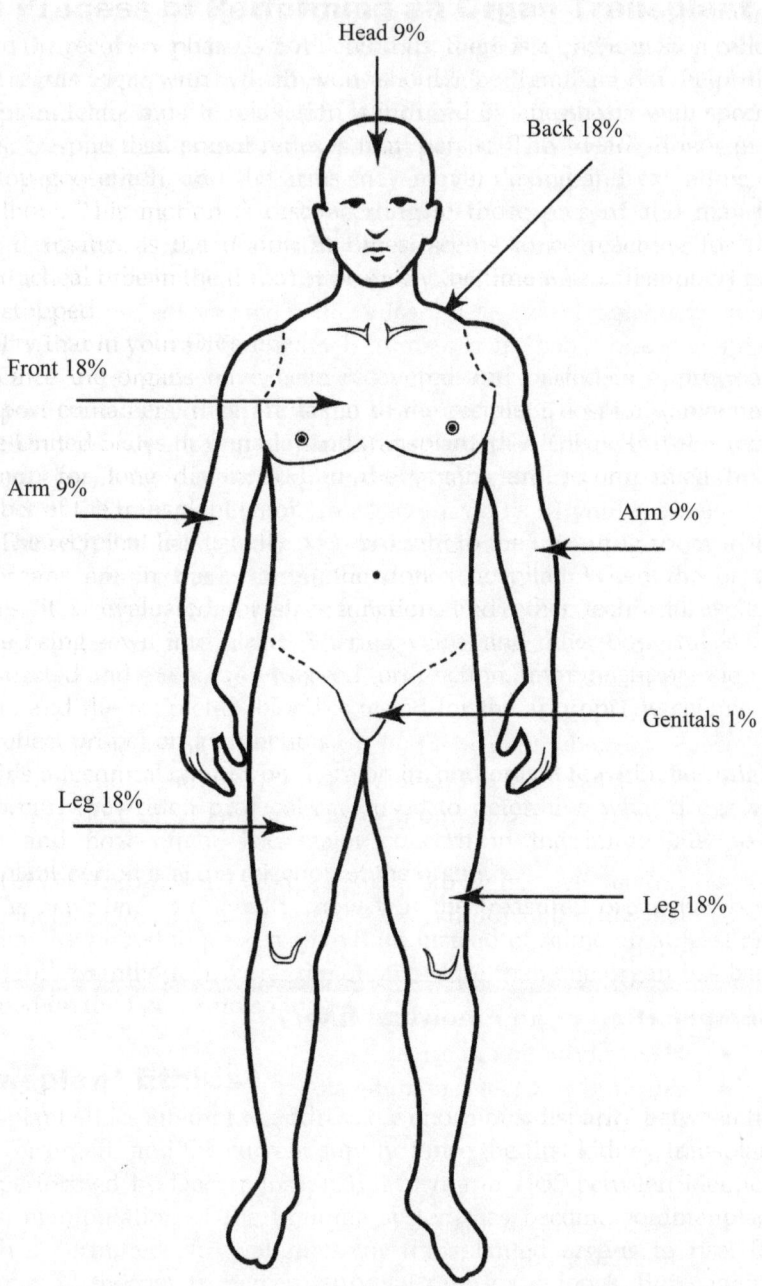

Head 9%

Back 18%

Front 18%

Arm 9%

Arm 9%

Genitals 1%

Leg 18%

Leg 18%

House Fire Smoke Inhalation

More than half of all deaths from house fires occur because the victim inhales smoke, which causes respiratory failure. Various noxious chemicals are found in house fire smoke. These include carbon dioxide, carbon monoxide, nitrogen dioxide, hydrogen cyanide, and others. Burning wood, plastics, fabric, cotton, wallboard and paper create dense smoke that irritates the lining of the windpipe and bronchi, causing the lungs to flood with fluid. Decreased oxygenation occurs, resulting in dizziness and lethargy. It's not the heat, it's the composition of the smoke itself that causes the damage.

The result of smoke inhalation is disorientation, confusion, and, at times, coma. Combine a lung scorch with a big-league body burn and your character becomes critically ill. That means an ICU bed, a ventilator, and a dedicated team of doctors and nurses. In other words, treatment includes intubation, oxygen, mechanical ventilation, pulmonary toilet (suctioning, chest physical therapy), and antibiotics. A slow wean from the ventilator — gradually letting the patient breathe for himself as the number of machine breaths are reduced — permits independent lung function in weeks or, sometimes, months. Prolonged respiratory support (over three weeks) necessitates a tracheotomy to avoid stricture of the vocal cords from the endotracheal tube.

Smoke inhalation may be diagnosed in several ways:

- Suspected if the *history* reveals the fire was in an enclosed space.
- Suspected if the face is burned and the nasal hairs are scorched (singed).
- Suspected if the patient wheezes or has a hoarse voice.
- Suspected if patient has carbon in sputum or inside the mouth.
- Proven by looking into trachea (windpipe) and bronchial tubes - bronchoscopy.
- Proven by testing the patient's blood for carboxyhemoglobin (carbon monoxide has a *240 times* affinity for hemoglobin than oxygen.)

Complication of an Electrical Injury

- Heart fibrillation or arrest
- Respiratory arrest (breathing stops)
- Fractures
- Muscle damage
- Cataracts (delayed)
- Seizures and/or coma
- Internal bleeding
- Loss of arms or legs

- Paralysis
- Kidney failure

Electrical Burns

Over ninety percent of electrical burns occur to men on the job, and although they account for only about five percent of burn injuries overall, these victims have a high death rate. The most severe complications are loss of a limb or long-term neurological symptoms.

The degree of injury depends upon:
- The amount of current passing through tissues
- The amount of heat production with high resistance of tissues
- Total contact time

Electrical energy travels along the course of blood vessels, nerves, and bones, and therefore creates deep tissue injury. Muscle contraction from the electrical current may fracture bones or dislocate joints, and the muscles themselves may be severely damaged, releasing large amounts of the muscle substance *myoglobin* into the circulation. Microscopic fragments of this muscle substance may clog the kidneys and produce kidney failure. Minimal skin wounds may hide major underlying muscle and bone damage.

As a general rule, household current in the 5-milliamp (mA) range only causes pain, while current up to 50 or 60 mA will cause cardiac fibrillation, persistent contraction of the muscles of breathing (diaphragm, intercostals), and a feeling of suffocation. Burns at the site of entrance of the current may be deeper than those produced by flame. Alternating current (AC) is more destructive than direct current (DC).

The doctor's chore in the hospital, when managing a severe electrical burn, is to keep checking the viability of the arms and legs involved in the course of the current to determine if surgical removal of dead tissue is necessary. Also, the surgeon checks blood counts and other lab tests, urine output and kidney function tests, and examines extremity pulses to be assured of adequate blood flow. Severe injury results in edema (swelling), which may squeeze off arterial blood inflow as well as block venous outflow from the limb, resulting in further gross swelling.

Low voltage (household) injuries of less than 1000 volts, such as a hair dryer in a bathtub, may cause fractures from muscle contractions. Cardiac arhythmias may occur. Kids sucking on an electrical cord may sustain mouth burns that require hospital care.

Chemical burns from acids, alkali, or petroleum products may be minor or severe depending on the agent's concentration and the duration of contact. Treatment includes removing the victim's clothing and washing the area for one to two hours with tap water.

As with all major body insults, an electrical burn may have systemic affects and cause grave illness by affecting the heart, lungs, and kidneys.

Lightning

Lightning injuries cause between 150 and 300 deaths per year in the United States. Static electricity in a cloud creates a potential difference, and high voltage of short duration results in lightning striking the ground. Different types occur, which cause various injuries. Depending on whether the lightning is a direct hit, side flash or ground current, different organs are involved. The basic principle is that the current takes the path of least resistance in the body, just as with a man-made electrical current.

A few of the more dramatic lightning injuries include:

- Cardiac standstill (asystole)
- Spasm of blood vessels with cold, pulseless limbs
- Apnea (cessation of breathing) and paralysis of brainstem respiratory centers
- Neurologic symptoms, including paralysis, weakness, vision loss, seizures, brain damage, and hemorrhage into the brain
- Fractures from intense muscle contraction
- Fetal loss in fifty percent of pregnant women struck

Environmental Temperature Damage

A discussion of body damage caused by temperature extremes wouldn't be complete without covering illness that is a direct result of severe environmental temperatures. To complete this chapter, we'll discuss heat stroke, heat prostration, and hypothermia. It's important to understand what happens to people as a result of changes in ambient temperature. In some ways, these problems are fascinating and quite subtle in their effect. These illnesses can play a dominant role in any story that takes place in geographic areas known for their extreme climate.

Before we get to major systemic problems with temperature, it's worthwhile reviewing a few nagging complaints your characters may develop on the ski slopes or at the beach. Referred to as *physical allergies*, these conditions are caused by exposure to less extreme changes in environmental temperature. Various substances in the serum are responsible for these reactions whether induced by heat or cold.

The agents that cause physical allergies are:

- Sunlight
- Moderate cold

- Moderate to severe heat
- Minor skin trauma

The skin reaction and appearance in people with physical allergies is:

- Intense itchiness
- Swelling with patchy areas called wheals (fluid-filled tissue) sitting within large areas of redness

Another fascinating reaction in some people leaves a ridge of swelling wherever the skin is rubbed. Using a blunt instrument (e.g., a spoon or the end of a fork), you may actually write on the person's skin. It's called *dermatographia*. The marks stay raised on the skin for some time. Did your murderer leave a message on his victim's back?

Heat Stroke (Sun Stroke)

This problem is characterized by the inability to rid the body of heat. Instead of sweating to increase surface cooling, sufferers demonstrate hot flushed skin as their core temperature becomes seriously elevated. Often preceded by a sense of fatigue, dizziness, and possibly a severe headache, this condition may progress to convulsions. Death is possible if treatment is delayed.

The elements of this condition that distinguish it from heat exhaustion are:

- The victim feels as if she is "burning up"
- The skin is hot, dry and flushed
- Severe elevation of body core temperature in the range of 104° to 106° Fahrenheit occurs
- Rapid pulse rate is noted with a relatively normal blood pressure

Immediate cooling in the field is mandatory if convulsions and death are to be avoided. Hospital care includes continued cooling, careful monitoring of core temperature, medication to prevent seizures, and large amounts of intravenous saline solution.

Heat Prostration (Heat Exhaustion)

In contrast to heat stroke, heat exhaustion occurs despite appropriate and often severe sweating. Fluid loss may make the victim feel light-headed and weak, but the overall clinical picture with this heat problem looks exactly like shock. The problem is severe fluid loss. These victims are cold and clammy and have a weak, thready pulse; they eventually develop low blood pressure in severe cases—the classic picture of any shock patient. With heat prostration, the body core temperature is normal or sometimes reduced, but never elevated as with heat stroke.

Thus, the appearance of the person suffering from heat prostration includes the following features:

- The victim complains of weakness and light-headedness and describes a history of excessive sweating with little fluid replacement.
- The victim presents with severe sweating, body fluid loss that results in cold, clammy skin, a thready pulse, and low blood pressure symptoms, which could be confused with those of shock due to blood loss.
- If the condition is allowed to progress, the victim may lose consciousness.
- The body temperature is normal or subnormal.

Treatment for heat prostration involves replacing the large body fluid losses with large volumes of liquid by mouth. In severe forms, it may be necessary to hospitalize the victim and give IV fluids. This condition usually responds well to replacing body fluid without a lot of other complicated interventions.

Classification of Frostbite Injury

First-degree	Redness and swelling
Second-degree	Redness, swelling, and the formation of blisters
Third-degree	Death of skin and underlying fat with blood in the blisters
Fourth-degree	Gangrene of skin and underlying fat; full-thickness tissue loss, including muscle and bone

Frostbite

Like burns, frostbite often results from impaired judgment and isn't solely a matter of random exposure to the injuring agent. Just as people who smoke in bed represent a large number of burn victims, so it is that the adventurous soul who doesn't prepare properly for a winter excursion often discovers herself in trouble. Most often, frostbite occurs on exposed areas, such as the nose, cheeks, ears, and poorly insulated fingers and toes.

Before actually suffering from the effects of full-blown frostbite, a lot of outdoors folks experience what is called *frostnip*, a milder cold injury. Characterized by pain and numbness, this condition involves exposed parts, such as the ears, nose, fingers and toes, which become blanched (white). Recovery is complete with adequate rewarming. Frostnip may take your character out of action for hours with pain, while frostbite could sideline someone for days or weeks. Severe cases of frostbite require hospitalization.

The treatment of frostbite is quite different in some respects from the management of burns, and similar in others. After attention to general body rewarming, the partial thickness frostbite wound should be protected and left to heal itself. Sometimes bandages are used; often the part is left exposed. It's a waiting game. The body will replenish spent tissue with new tissue built up from the mother cells deep in the skin, just as with first- and second-degree burns. If full-thickness skin death occurs, skin grafting becomes necessary.

Then there's the matter of fourth-degree frostbite, and that, folks, means the entire body part is lost. Fingers, toes, ears, or nose, the part turns black. Black tissue is dead tissue. In time, if it's a toe or fingertip, it will fall off spontaneously. But often the frostbitten part must be surgically removed.

Amputation.

If your character is isolated in the wilderness away from medical care, and if mummification occurs (the part is shriveled up, black, dry), then he may have to amputate his own dead thing—no matter what it may be. Lubricate that notion and push it through your plot plan.

How to Diagnose Frostbite

Obtain a history of cold exposure with the following features:
- High altitude
- Windy conditions (wind chill factor)
- Wet environment
- Prolonged exposure
- Cigarette smoking
- Chronic illnesses (diabetes, poor circulation)
- Excessive alcohol intake
- Psychiatric history

Perform a physical examination and look for the following:
- White areas (blanching) on exposed skin
- Blebs or "water blisters"
- Black leathery skin fixed to deeper tissue

Hypothermia

Ever wonder why a wolf's paw doesn't freeze while the animal is standing on the windswept Northern tundra? Ever wonder why a sled dog curled up nose to tail in a snow bank beside the Iditarod trail doesn't freeze to death as the windblown snow buries it? Ever wonder how a long-distance swimmer can survive for half a day in water so cold it's supposed to kill you and me in six hours?

Are shaking chills valuable or destructive?

The general effect of cold and a mammal's adaptation to frigid insults are fascinating topics and will complete our discussion of the body's reaction to cold. Imagine a timber wolf portrayed in a Robert Bateman painting, standing in a winterscape with its paws buried in snow. What keeps the pads of the animal's foot from freezing? The tundra and windchill factor surely plunge the temperature at paw level to, what ...twenty, thirty below? Why doesn't the water in the wolf's foot pad cells crystallize and freeze?

In the wolf's leg, the veins returning blood to the heart are wrapped about the main arteries like insulation about a water pipe. Hugging the artery in this fashion, the veins accept heat by direct transfer from the hot arterial blood coming down from the animal's warm core (its chest and abdomen). This transfer of arterial heat warms the frigid venous blood returning from the paws. Thus, the arterial blood that eventually reaches the paw has been cooled by transferring heat to the veins, but is still warm enough to prevent freezing of the paw pad. And the venous blood flows back up to the core conserving the heat it received from the arteries. Body heat is conserved centrally.

Neat, eh?

Our arms and legs act in a similar fashion to conserve some heat, although our thin skin—even with a layer of fat—isn't terribly effective insulation. By contrast, the sled dog doesn't die in winter because he's got a thick pelt, which traps air and remains fluffy and is augmented by that layer of soft snow that buries the animal. It's all insulation. But the system breaks down if the animal becomes wet. And that brings us to the long-distance swimmer. (You see, it's not such a long trip from the Arctic to the English Channel.)

Folklore has it that long-distance swimmers are hefty athletes who sport a generous layer of adipose (fat) tissue to fight off the ravages of cold water. Without a doubt, some swimmers are cherubs, adiposidly unchallenged. The real speedsters are svelte, and they don't use a layer of grease, either.

In 1972, I was Davis Hart's physician when he set a world record swimming the English Channel. There wasn't much information in the medical literature at that time to use to prepare Davis for this endeavor, but we knew Davis's trim physique would leave him at risk for cold-related problems. *Water conducts heat twenty-five times faster than air.* Davis discovered a training program that worked for him. He swam in cold water as often as possible, but he also did a lot of warm pool swimming because of his job. What to do to acclimate to cold water? Davis began to stand in a frigid shower in a plastic garbage can filled with the cold shower water, training his nervous system to acclimate to the harsh effects of mimicked cold water submersion.

It worked. Davis tolerated 62° Channel water for nine hours and forty-four minutes. The first person in the world to swim the English Channel in under ten hours, he set a new world record.

Victims of progressive hypothermia go through three phases of progressive deterioration that blend with each other. The *clinical phases of hypothermia* are:

1. Excitatory. The victim increases activity and shivers to attempt to warm up; blood vessels constrict to conserve heat.
2. Adynamic. Means "without movement." This phase follows the rapid breathing of the excitatory phase; breathing slows as the respiratory center is depressed, reflecting overall metabolic slowdown.
3. Paralytic. The victim becomes almost comatose as the core temperature continues to drop and neurologic signs appear.

These are the kinds of things your character might observe when she drags someone in your story from a glacial stream near Mount McKinley. A character discovered in any of the physical states mentioned above can be successfully resuscitated from extreme hypothermia if proper measures are taken.

What's going on in the victim's "core"?

A lot. And not so much. Things are slowing down. In the extreme case, sudden death may occur if an individual unaccustomed to the cold jumps or falls into frigid water. The explanation may be either that the extreme cold caused sudden cardiac arrest or the cold water produced immediate apnea (stoppage of breathing). You can place your characters at risk by having them jump from bridges, sinking their boats, or having them tumble overboard on an Alaskan cruise.

Of course, they can be saved.

Changes in Body Functions in Hypothermia

- Cardiac system: Blood vessels constrict. Heart rate drops. The amount of blood ejected by the heart is reduced. Blood becomes thick. Ventricular fibrillation finally occurs (the heart quivers uselessly without pumping blood).
- Nervous system: Confusion occurs with prolonged immersion or cold exposure followed by amnesia, delirium, and coma. The reflexes disappear eventually and breathing (the brainstem respiratory center) is depressed and slows.
- Kidneys: Cold exposure and submersion in cold water both produce what doctors call a *diuresis*, meaning excessive

urination. It may cause dehydration and aggravate other cardiovascular problems.

- Muscular system: Discomfort and fatigue occur early on, then loss of muscular power, loss of coordination, and the ability to perform simple motor tasks. Apathy occurs with severe hypothermia.
- Skin reaction: Very much like an allergic reaction, the skin becomes red and the victim may develop wheals or "water" blebs of fluid. Skin becomes cold as blood is shunted into deeper tissues to conserve energy.

Who Becomes Hypothermic?

- The foolish. They go out into hostile cold temperatures unprotected; they do not respect the potential for harm in frigid conditions.
- The unprepared. They consciously or unconsciously take risks by not preparing adequately (this includes misinformed hunters, campers and trekkers); these people believe they are ready for any eventuality when, in fact, they are not knowledgeable about wilderness survival.
- The elderly. They become exposed outdoors by dressing inappropriately or indoors because of inadequate living facilities. Elderly people often don't realize they're becoming hypothermic as their senses are blunted with aging.
- Substance abusers. Alcohol, drugs, or other toxic chemicals blunt the person's level of awareness, and he ignores important symptoms such as shivering, changes in skin color, and temperature changes.
- The homeless.

Shivering is a complicated phenomenon that causes muscles to contract rhythmically and repeatedly for the purpose of generating heat. You don't have to be in subzero temperatures to become hypothermic. Shivering is seen in kids during swimming lessons, in skiers at the end of the day, or in your neighbor walking her dog in November without a coat as if winter wasn't in the air.

There are simple ways to safeguard against cold exposure and avoid hypothermia:

- Dress in layers. Mimic the fur of cold-tolerant animals, and trap air between clothing layers rather than wearing one thick coat.
- Avoid becoming wet. If you do, dry off immediately.

- Carry extra socks and other appropriate clothing if going away from support facilities.
- Wear head covering. At least 20 percent of all body heat loss is via the head and neck.
- Drink adequate fluid—warm when available—to avoid dehydration and to maintain core temperature.
- Avoid use of drugs and alcohol when in a cold environment.
- Plan for unexpected weather changes and formulate a contingency plan to get out of the cold environment.
- Gain fifty pounds!

Other Cold Injuries
Chilblain
This is a type of cold injury characterized by reddish-purple bumps or small, raised areas on exposed surfaces, with swelling and, occasionally, with blistering. Occurring on the face, back of the hands and feet, or any surface chronically exposed to cold but not freezing temperatures, eventually skin ulcers and bleeding may occur. Treatment includes slow rewarming, elevation of the part, and protection from further abrasion.

Trench Foot
Also called cold immersion foot, this injury is seen in wet environments where actual freezing doesn't occur. For example, sailors, deep-sea fishermen, and soldiers are often forced to remain wet for prolonged periods of time. Small blood vessels that supply the exposed part alternately go into spasm, then open up. This produces a cold and, at times, numb limb that then becomes fiery hot with a burning discomfort. Tissue damage progresses from swelling and blisters to ulcers, infection, and, if the condition is severe, gangrene.

Treatment for immersion foot is similar to that for chilblains and includes slow rewarming with protection and elevation. The affected part sometimes demonstrates increased sensitivity to cold long after the injury has healed. Massaging or rubbing a body part affected by chilblains or immersion foot is to be condemned. Friction creates good fiction, but it makes frostbite injury much worse.

Extremes of temperature exist in many areas of the world and some of your characters will have to deal with the threat posed by severe cold as well as sweltering heat. Physical hardship raises the stakes in any story. At times the storm, wind chill, forest fire, or frozen lake becomes another adversarial "character," a source of unpredictable conflict.

Your story's world possesses a climate of its own. Make it work for you.

FOURTEEN

DIVING ACCIDENTS AND ALTITUDE ILLNESS

Innovative technology and immeasurable courage permit humans to venture into the most hostile provinces of the earth. The price of pursuing this peripatetic impulse is measured in novel injuries and spectacular new ways to die. Of course, we're only interested in the non-lethal varieties of damage that severe environmental pressure changes wreak upon worldly adventurers.

Scuba diving and high altitude exposure share a common bond, potential oxygen deprivation. In the underwater environment, the diver carries a life-support system, which contains oxygen (compressed air) as well as other safety devices. Mountain vistas are surrounded by breathtaking views and a breath-racing lack of oxygen. Both locales place the participant at risk.

Diving accidents and high altitude medical problems form a unique and fascinating group of problems. Are any of your characters cocky? Risk takers? Unlucky?

Diving Accidents and Their Consequences

Breath-hold diving goes back to antiquity and served early cultures well in the search for valuable seafood, sponges, and pearls. Over two thousand years ago the Ama, Korean, and Japanese diving women, collected shells and marine plants by breath holding. These practices continue today.

Giovanni Borelli devised one of the first types of diving helmets in the 1600's, and reeds and bamboo tubes were also used near the surface. Edmund Halley, after whom the comet was named, developed the first diving bell with an air supply in 1691, but it wasn't until the 1800's that the world saw the first diving suit. The rigid helmet and waterproof suit design first used by Augustus Siebe in 1837 is still employed, with modifications.

In 1943, Jacques Cousteau and Emile Gagnan invented the scuba (self-contained underwater breathing apparatus) used throughout the world. Virtually flawless at various depths, the scuba unit possesses a special valve that "steps down" compressed air tank pressure and compensates for ambient pressure differences. The valve is triggered by the inhalation effort of the diver.

Deep-diving systems developed in the 1970s and 1980s culminated in single-diver systems that descended to over a thousand feet in the ocean. New illnesses nipped at the heels of the intrepid divers who first used these new submersibles. Mixtures of oxygen and helium were necessary to permit adequate oxygenation without overwhelming problems of super-saturation with inert gases. Research in the field of deep-diving systems continues to improve diver safety and open further fields for commercial exploitation. Although decompression sickness began to appear with "hard hat" divers, it wasn't until large numbers of people began to dive for sport that a multitude of pressure-related illnesses created a new specialty: diving medicine.

Two laws of physics are always mentioned with diving diseases and pressure-related accidents. They explain why the human body so poorly tolerates excessive pressure.

The first is *Boyle's Law,* which states that (assuming the temperature is constant) the volume of a gas is inversely related to the amount of pressure applied to it. So the volume in your lungs as you descend to greater and greater depths becomes smaller and smaller. Then, as you ascend at the end of your dive, the pressure lets up and the gas in your system expands, and if you come up too quickly, the gases in your body fluids will reappear in the form of bubbles.

The second law tells us how much gas actually gets into the tissues during a dive. *Henry's Law* says that the amount of gas that enters a liquid depends directly on the amount of pressure applied. Assuming the temperature is constant, the amount of gas in your tissue at two atmospheres, or thirty-three feet, is half what it is at three atmospheres, or sixty-six feet. The deeper you go, the more gas that enters your body tissues from the tank on your back.

Humans are lousy breath-hold divers compared to whales and dolphins. As oxygen is used up, the diver risks shallow water "blackout" if the dive was preceded by excessive hyperventilation ("over breathing") because the carbon dioxide drive on the brain has been removed. Dolphins can remain submerged for as long as two hours, and most diving mammals have a "diving reflex," in which the pulse rate slows with submersion, permitting more efficient oxygen use.

Three major diving problems are described to give you an idea of what your submerged characters might get into if they don't follow the rules. Each problem is related to what happens to gas under pressure in the diver's tissues.

Decompression Sickness ("The Bends")

The widespread use of compressed air in mining, tunneling, and caisson work resulted in several medical investigators noticing a peculiar illness characterized by the trapping of bubbles in tissue. It wasn't long before Leonard Hill studied animals under pressure and recommended staged decompression for workers coming up from a pressurized work environment. And although a certain degree of resistance to decompression sickness can occur in individuals repeatedly exposed to pressure, the following factors make "the bends" more likely:

- Obesity
- Female gender
- Advanced age
- Alcohol
- Cold environment
- Exertion at pressure
- Fatigue
- Repeated dives

When breathing compressed air at increased pressure, the body utilizes oxygen, but nitrogen, which makes up eighty percent of ambient air, remains in the tissues. The deeper the dive, the higher the content of nitrogen in the tissues. Obese people absorb even more inert (not used by the body) gas because nitrogen is five times more soluble in fat than in water.

As the diver ascends from the depths, gas tension in tissues (particularly of nitrogen) rises because the pressure on the diver decreases. If the pressure is reduced too quickly—that is, if the diver ascends from a long, deep dive without decompression stops—gas bubbles may form in the tissues, and a number of complications may occur:

- Gas bubbles may block arteries and veins and impair the function of organs.
- Gas bubbles may form in cells and rupture tissues.
- Gas bubbles may form in closed spaces with no ability to expand and cause tissue damage from increased compartment pressure.
- Gas bubbles may form in the blood and cause blood elements to coagulate inappropriately and cause a variety of tissue damage.

Decompression sickness is usually divided into two types or patterns according to severity:

1. Type I decompression sickness (pain only)
   - Joint pain (mild or severe)
   - Itchy skin
   - Rash (large flat plaques, sometimes reddish)

- Local swelling
2. Type II decompression sickness (serious)
    - Spinal cord "hit": gas bubbles obstruct arteries to spinal cord, cause ischemia, tissue death, paralysis, incontinence of urine or feces; priapism (uncontrolled erection)
    - Cerebral involvement: headache, blurred or double vision, dizziness, personality changes, convulsions
    - Cardiovascular collapse: air hunger, rapid pulse, blood pressure drop (shock)
    - Type I symptoms that occur while still under pressure

Both types of symptoms begin to appear within fifteen to thirty minutes of surfacing, and the more severe form can progress to death within hours. Fifty percent of all decompression sickness cases appear within the first hour and over ninety percent become manifest within six hours. Professional and avid sports divers may develop hearing loss and vertigo from inner ear decompression sickness, where hemorrhage and repeated attempts at healing affect the semicircular canals and nerves. Divers with extensive experience often have x-rays that show islands of dead bone here and there from previous bubble damage.

Decompression sickness is called the bends because of the prominence of joint pain. Bubbles form in tight joint tissues and create various degrees of pressure. Pain occurs most commonly in the shoulders and elbows with bending and extending the joint. In the severe forms, any tissue may be involved. For example, all parts of the brain may be hit, often simultaneously, resulting in anything from memory loss to no coordination and loss of balance.

Treatment for decompression sickness centers on recompressing the victim. Depending on the location of the accident and support capabilities, this may be done by submerging once more and resurfacing slowly or by transporting the victim to a decompression chamber. Other support measures in treating decompression sickness include steroids to reduce brain swelling, blood thinners to reduce likelihood of blood clot formation, IV fluids for hydration, bladder catheterization for spinal hits, and supplemental oxygen.

Barotrauma

The group of pressure-related problems occurs because gas-filled spaces in the body were not equilibrated with the outside (ambient) pressure during submersion. If we ignore minor problems, such as excessive facemask pressure and cramps from squeezed gut gas, two common forms of barotrauma are seen:
1. Middle ear barotrauma
2. Pulmonary barotrauma

Middle ear barotrauma is the most commonly seen diving problem and must be solved before the diver gets too deep. Between the back of the throat and the middle ear inside the temporal bone lies the connecting Eustachian tube. Its slit-like end in the throat must be opened in order for changing ambient pressure to be transferred to the middle ear cavity where the tube ends. Moving the jaw, yawning, swallowing, or squeezing the nose and blowing gently accomplish this. If not performed properly, symptoms appear. These include ear pressure, and then pain and rupture of the ear membrane with pain relief. This is followed by vertigo (dizziness), if underwater, when cold water stimulates the middle ear.

Conditions that aggravate middle ear problems by making it more difficult to open the Eustachian tube include cigarette smoking, allergies, upper respiratory infections, and, occasionally, throat polyps. If you have a character with the flu that dives, he may blow out his eardrum and resurface in pain, or he may become dizzy and disoriented and nearly drown.

Ear problems in the diver may be simple or complicated. It's the writer's call. Maybe you just want to annoy someone in your story.

On the other hand, *pulmonary barotrauma* is serious business. The lungs contain mostly air, and any failure to exhale on the way up from a dive will result in rupture of lung tissue as the gas expands. There's more. Gas may come out of body fluids in the mediastinum (the space between the lungs) and cause a variety of symptoms. The following list contains most of the symptoms experienced by a diver suffering from mild or severe pulmonary barotrauma:

- Shortness of breath
- Chest fullness
- Coughing up blood
- Chest pain
- Change in the voice

Physical findings in pulmonary barotraumas are variable and depend on what injury has occurred:

- Diminished breathing sounds on one side (as heard through a stethoscope)
- Crepitus in the neck (crepitus is caused by gas bubbles collecting in tissues; the tissue feels squishy, like rolling cellophane)
- Arterial air embolism (bubble in the blood stream); may cause a heart attack or stroke just as a clot would in someone with arteriosclerosis and clot emboli; symptoms are stroke-like paralysis or severe chest pain

In general, lung damage while descending is called *lung squeeze*, while barotrauma during the ascent is termed *burst lung*. Air embolism is the most problematic aspect of burst lung, followed by pneumothorax (collapsed lung) and surgical emphysema a condition where gas fills the chest and travels up into the neck. It can even fill the heart sac.

Treatment of air embolism and surgical emphysema involves recompression or hyperbaric oxygen treatment. A pneumothorax requires the surgical placement of a chest tube, just as with chest trauma.

Nitrogen Narcosis ("Rapture of the Deep")

In the mid-1800s, symptoms were first noted in divers that were variously attributed to claustrophobia, impure air mixtures and high partial pressures of oxygen. It wasn't until 1935 when the great diving researcher A. R. Behnke and his associates properly attributed these peculiar symptoms to the effects of nitrogen excess. As deep diving systems evolved, helium was substituted for nitrogen as the inert gas in the breathing mixture, commonly referred to as *heliox*.

A spectrum of mental aberrations is seen in nitrogen narcosis, all of which rapidly disappear when the victim returns to one atmosphere, or sea level. The picture has often been compared to alcohol intoxication. For each added atmosphere of depth (thirty-three feet), the effect is much like another martini. The aberrations include the following:

- Higher functions are affected first, including judgment, memory, and ability to concentrate and reason.
- Euphoria occurs early, but panic and terror are occasionally seen.
- Cold, alcohol, drugs, and anxiety or fear aggravate symptoms.
- Not all divers react the same.
- Symptoms become worse as the depth increases.
- Symptoms occur within minutes of reaching depth and don't usually progress.

Prevention is the best course of action and requires the diver only to perform non-decompression dives to eighty or one hundred feet for twenty minutes or less. The U.S. Navy Decompression Tables are designed to instruct the diver on how long to remain at specific depths without undergoing decompression. Decompression stops are various depths at which one halts to breathe in order to let the lungs blow off nitrogen now coming out of the body fluids. But the tables aren't perfect. If the diver sticks to shallow dives — say, forty feet or less — she can stay there for extended periods of time.

Other diving problems that can arise are sinus barotrauma, diving suit squeeze, marine animal attacks, coral cuts, and drowning.

It doesn't get much better up on the mountain.

Altitude Sickness

An illness at altitude is altitude illness until proven otherwise.
—Stephen Bezruchka, M.D.

Other than denizens of high altitude, people who periodically go to the mountains fall into two categories:

1. Inexperienced travelers
2. Risk-taking adventurers

Millions of people travel to high altitudes each year, often doing so on rushed schedules as weekend climbers or thrill seekers, or as part of an impromptu outing with little preparation. There meanders in the wake of these thrill seekers a vapor trail of disrespect for the high mountain environment. For some novice climbers, it is a cavalier conviction of immortality; for others, it's just plain ignorance.

A new, belligerent term has wedged itself into the young adventurer's lexicon. The term is *extreme*. People speak of extreme skiing or climbing, and they seek out other extreme experiences, like plunging down a vertical waterfall in a kayak, or plummeting from a bridge with an elastic cord tied to one's body. Somewhere along the path to high-tech, no-boundaries living, we seem to have discarded our senses. Injury or death may be the price one pays when one searches, through risk-taking, for insightful messages in the e-mail of one's soul.

Like scuba diving, mountain climbing demands effort and physical conditioning with a significant additional factor thrown into the risk equation. The world of these activities is unfriendly. Beyond physical exertion and its effect on the person's heart, coronary arteries and general health, the diver and climber find themselves exercising vigorously in a hostile world of oxygen deprivation. And it all takes place at some distance from appropriate medical help.

Altitude conceals, within its magical vistas, a significant threat to anyone who has not undergone acclimation. Before climbing into the rare atmosphere of high altitude medicine, we must organize ourselves and sort out the illnesses to which your characters may fall prey. Twenty-five percent of all folks who ascend to high altitude develop some manifestations of altitude illness.

The major activities that take people to high altitudes include:

- Serious mountain climbing
- Trekking
- Skiing
- Mountain biking
- Sight-seeing

Mountain activities of all sorts have become a growth industry, and peaks in several parts of the world are favorites, including those in the states of Utah, Colorado, Washington, New Mexico, and Wyoming, as well as Central and South America and the traditionally sought-after peaks of the Himalayas. Few casual climbers prepare adequately, and therein lies the dilemma. Your characters may be irresponsible weekend adventurers or serious climbers or trekkers who simply run out of luck.

Either way, you need to know the sorts of feelings and symptoms they might experience.

The illnesses described here are not unique. And although three major illnesses are described separately, they have common features and often appear together in the same victim. All of these diseases are tied together by the same physiological knot: lack of oxygen. Doctors call it *hypoxemia*.

Acute Mountain Sickness (AMS)

Two quick points to remember about AMS: The symptoms are much like a hangover, and they vary in degree from mild to moderate to very severe. (You don't know what a hangover feels like? It's possible, I suppose.)

There's an interesting irony here. Many people travel to extreme mountain heights to experience a "natural high." What do they get for their dollars? A garden-variety hangover! The following is a classification of symptoms of acute mountain sickness.

Symptoms of mild AMS:
- Headache
- Loss of appetite
- Insomnia
- Nausea
- Uneasy feeling of fatigue

Symptoms of moderate AMS:
- Repeated vomiting
- Decreased urine output
- Persistent headache

Symptoms of severe AMS:
- Loss of balance
- Lethargy to unconsciousness
- Cyanosis (blue discoloration) of lips, fingernails

The two other diseases that are seen at altitude are really a part of severe acute mountain sickness rather than isolated problems. The target organs—the lungs and the brain—are affected in the same manner. Each organ becomes wet. This increased tissue fluid, or edema, results from excessively low oxygen levels in the inspired air and the resultant insult to sensitive brain and lung cells.

High Altitude Pulmonary Edema (HAPE)

"Leaky membranes," or a break in the barrier that usually keeps fluid out of the air spaces, causes the lung failure seen at altitude. It's like heart failure in the elderly patient, but instead of pump failure causing excessive pressure buildup in the lung capillaries, it's the capillary membrane that is affected by hypoxemia. Fluid leaks out of the capillary into the air sacs and "internal drowning" begins.

Occurring more often in males, HAPE is seen at moderate altitudes in ski resorts and often doesn't appear until the day after exposure to altitude. Normally, at sea level, the amount of air and blood flow to the lungs is equally matched and blood oxygenation proceeds effectively. With HAPE (as well as with most sick ICU patients on ventilators), there is a mismatch between air exchange and regional blood flow to the lungs. Blood oxygen levels may drop precipitously.

People with early high altitude pulmonary edema become symptomatic in subtle ways. As the following complaints escalate, the victim becomes more aware of the growing discomfort. Findings in early HAPE include:

- Fatigue
- Inability to perform at usual exercise level
- Dry cough
- Increased heart rate

As the illness progresses, symptoms become more bothersome, and severe HAPE mimics lung failure from any cause.

- Shortness of breath at rest (without exercise)
- Productive cough (moderately large amount of sputum)
- Cyanosis of fingernails, lips, etc.
- Severe weakness
- Loss of balance, which may suggest associated cerebral edema
- Sudden death may occur

The profile of that individual who is at highest risk of developing high altitude pulmonary edema is:

- Male
- Overweight
- Poor physical condition
- Rapid ascent to altitude

High Altitude Cerebral Edema (HACE)

Just as lack of oxygen (hypoxemia) is toxic to lung tissue, the same kind of effect occurs with brain cells and, as a consequence, they swell and function poorly. Some experts think HACE is the worst consequence of acute mountain sickness, the end stage of the hypoxemic insult. Whatever the exact cause of the swelling, brain cells are impaired and the person affected demonstrates a variety of symptoms. Because even young people can have small strokes, or TIAs (transient ischemic attacks), at altitude, it's important to pay attention to any of these symptoms:

- Change in behavior—victim does peculiar things
- Inability to make reasonable decisions
- Severe persistent headache
- Vomiting
- Loss of balance
- Lethargy possibly leading to coma

There is interplay between high altitude cerebral edema and pulmonary edema. If you survey the symptoms, it becomes clear that they blend together and may also be confused with other potential issues. A partial list of possible associated problems includes dehydration, alcohol or drug abuse, severe exhaustion, hypothermia, or worsening of a known medical condition.

Treatment of High Altitude Illnesses (HAPE or HACE)
Mild acute mountain sickness may be treated by:
- Remaining at same altitude for a day or two in order to undergo acclimation
- Moderate exercise at same altitude
- Over-the-counter pain medication
- Diamox (acetazolamide) with prior OK by physician; acts like a water pill to cause fluid loss and also acts on the brain to decrease HACE symptoms

Severe acute mountain sickness must be treated by:
- Immediate descent at least 1,500 to 3,000 feet (avoid trap of delaying descent or canceling evacuation plans if victim demonstrates some improvement)
- Administering oxygen
- Physician-directed use of steroids (dexamethasone)
- Use of hyperbaric chamber after descent or portable hyperbaric "bag" at altitude, if available

A less serious altitude problem described by Dr. Michael Weidman is hemorrhage into the retina of the eye. Seldom associated with blindness, it occurs in folks sleeping above 15,000 feet and usually resolves spontaneously after a week or two, regardless of altitude. Sometimes, though, the victim "sees spots" and blindness has occurred.

Prevention of Acute Mountain Sickness

A few basic common sense principles ought to be followed by anyone traveling to high altitude:

- Forget adhering to a tight schedule; make time for a safe ascent!
- Stay warm; dress in layers.
- Practice deep breathing regularly.
- Watch each other for changes in behavior.
- Remain open to suggestions about your own conduct.
- If you can't get up the mountain on your own, don't resort to other means of transportation to get higher; you may get higher—and sicker.

Should older people with medical problems participate in activities at high altitude?

It depends on the individual. Studies have shown that older people with chronic illnesses, such as heart disease and emphysema, can tolerate altitude if they approach their activities slowly and give themselves time to acclimate. It's best to have older folks undergo an exercise stress test before taking on a major trekking, climbing, or skiing trip. The first week or two are the most dangerous when the person's adrenaline rushes with exercise and the exhilaration of pristine alpine surroundings. This added strain might provoke angina or a heart attack.

The world of your story may require a character to plunge the mute, frigid waters of the ocean or scale wind-ripped, jagged peaks in Nepal. In either case, catastrophe shadows the ambivalent availability of oxygen. As you craft your disaster scene, know that danger plays hide-and-seek on every coral reef and lurks behind the innocent beauty of the ice-gilded summit.

FIFTEEN

ASSAULTED ELDERS, BATTERED WOMEN AND INJURED KIDS: THE DEFENSELESS

This chapter will address injuries that occur in the two most common locations where traumatic injuries involve kids, women and the elderly. The first is in the home where injuries are part of a pattern of abuse. The second is outside of the house and most often involves vehicular trauma as an occupant of a car, SUV, van, or truck, or as a pedestrian struck by a vehicle. Each of these three special cases of trauma has unique considerations.

Before going into a discussion of specific injuries, let's take a broad overview and look at the two domains.

Domestic violence is a crime. The occurrence of this outrage has been underestimated for years, may be missed by health care professionals, and tends to escalate and become chronic. Escape for the victim usually requires a support system offering both medical and legal assistance.

All ages and genders are easy prey.

As victims of traumatic injuries, children are no more small adults physically than they are emotionally or intellectually. Kids get hurt a lot. Sometimes it's a consequence of an accident. Often it's intentional.

The demon of domestic violence isn't satiated with harm to children. It sneaks behind the kids and humiliates the mother, the wife. Half of all males who abuse their female partners also abuse their children. Mostly, domestic violence involves males battering defenseless family members. Occasionally, the violence centers on women fighting back.

Consider these facts:

- About three million kids each year are witness to one parent beating the other.
- Physical abuse of pregnant women is the leading cause of birth defects and infant mortality in the United States.
- In the United States, women are at greater risk of being assaulted, injured, raped, or killed by a male known to them than by all unknown assailants combined.

- Abused women make up 25 to 35 percent of injured women seen and treated in emergency rooms.
- Fifty percent of all police calls are for domestic violence.

The elderly are as prone to injury as their younger counterparts. Elderly people, it is true, lose their balance, stumble, and fall as a consequence of failing coordination, strength and eyesight. But some are victims of opportunistic cowards who prey on helpless, debilitated elderly people. Still others are neglected by otherwise reasonable people. Frustration and impatience are common among caregivers for the elderly. Subtle violence can make the elder's life hell. Unable to protect themselves, aged people may suffer at the same hand that attacks a mate or a child.

Despite differences in age, kids and old people are at risk to be hurt for the same reason: they are unable to defend themselves. They are dependent. They are helpless.

In this chapter, we'll discuss accidental wounds as part of the diagnostic dilemma facing the doctor caring for a case of potential abuse inflicted on women, children, and the elderly. Injury pattern recognition has evolved over the last ten years, and diagnostic criteria have been established that apply to the doctor's examination as well as to x-ray evaluation. Specific patterns of common injuries are useful in diagnosing the battered individual.

Batterers leave a recognizable trail of scars.

Not all injured kids, spouses, and elderly people have, as an explanation for their injuries, abuse by an adult. It's important to be sure. And while suspicion may lead to the appropriate unveiling of abuse, it may also, if misguided, destroy a family.

Herein lies fresh fodder for the writer's imagination. You must understand the clues that help to sort out domestic violence from accidental trauma.

Most hospitals have compiled documents that assist caregivers in collecting and documenting data for patient management and the prosecution of criminal acts of violence. The data presented here is modified from several medical and nursing sources.

A hospital's duty to the battered person of any age is threefold:

1. To assess the extent of injury and offer treatment.
2. To provide safety for the battered person.
3. To offer follow-up services for treatment and counseling.

The evaluation of a potential victim of physical abuse should follow several well-defined steps; medical personnel are trained to search for specific clues. In particular, the explanation for an injury must be reasonable and consistent between the victim and the person(s) accompanying the victim to the emergency room or other health care facility.

Health care workers look for the following indicators of domestic violence in the history:

- First contact with the victim reveals the condition of the person's hygiene, clothing and general appearance. Is the clothing ripped, worn, stained, recently washed?
- Is the victim attempting to hide any part of the body? Do you see obvious injuries that have a detectable cause (e.g., obvious cigarette burns, wrist abrasions from restraints, welts around the head and neck, belt buckle marks, tooth or bite marks)?
- Does the explanation given for the injury seem unlikely, or does the victim state she did it to herself (an explanation of self-mutilation)?
- Was there much of a delay between the time the injury allegedly occurred and the health care facility visit?
- Is there a pattern (or cycle) of visits?
- Does the accompanying person insist on remaining in the examining room, answering all of the questions for the victim, seemingly overprotective?
- Are the symptoms vague? Abused women may present for medical care complaining of obscure symptoms, such as fatigue, loss of appetite, or "nerves," or with evidence of alcohol or drug abuse, eating disorders, excessive problems with pregnancy, or frequent return visits to the ER.

These indicators are observed in the physical examination:

- Are the observed injuries symmetrical? For example, are there bruises on both arms or both legs?
- Are there obvious marks the victim tries to conceal?
- Are there several different injuries at various stages of healing (e.g., some black-and-blue bruises, some yellowish, resolving; old as well as new abrasions)?
- Are there lacerations or contusions of the face, breasts, or genitalia, particularly in pregnant women?
- If there are burns, are they on the feet or hands, or on the buttocks?

The only way to identify domestic violence is to ask. These findings should make nurses, doctors, and other health care givers suspicious of major abuse problems in the home. The acute medical emergency that is treated by the ER doctor may not be the real problem. *It may not even be close.*

Children are not little adults. Their small bodies react differently. The elderly are not an older version of young and middle-aged adults.

Their bodies have minimal reserve and little resilience. And women have unique issues not experienced by men.

The child's small body mass produces more force per unit of body area and, therefore, more focusing of destructive energy. The child's head is, relatively speaking, larger, and kids have more blunt (closed) head injuries. A child's bones are less completely calcified and more internal injuries (because of less protection) occur in kids. And kids are less articulate and give poor histories of what happened to them. Children need to be talked into talking.

Because of their reduced physical capacity and lifestyles, the elderly succumb to falls, burns and motor vehicle crashes. With compromised muscular control, diminished vision, and multiple comorbid conditions such as diabetes, hypertension, arthritis, obesity, and multiple medications, the elderly totter between survival and death. A traumatic event may be the final insult. And when the elderly become profoundly ill, a number of ethical issues arise regarding terminating care.

As a general biologic reality, women are smaller and less strong than men. For this reason, women are at risk of being beat up and raped, as well as suffering any of the traumatic injuries that form the core of this book. And although the elderly have more cervical spine injuries, they are often difficult to diagnose on x-ray. This is because of the elderly patient's increased incidence of arthritis and osteoporosis. Degeneration and loss of strength of the large vertebral ligaments, along with narrowing of the spinal canal from bony spurs, makes the likelihood of spinal cord damage (and varying degrees of paralysis) higher than in the younger trauma victim.

Battered, Bruised and Abused Kids

Trust no one—assume nothing.

—Norman Ellerstein

Since employed as cheap labor during the Industrial Revolution, and no doubt before, children have been abused by adults. Reports appeared in the nineteenth century of kids used as chimney sweeps and in coalmines, but it wasn't until the 1960s in the United States that battered and abused children began receiving the attention they deserved. Finally, sexual abuse emerged into the light of day.

Recently, the validity of some allegedly abused children's recall has come into question. But no one challenges the immensity of the problem of battered kids.

Beat-up children get a lot of attention when they arrive at the hospital. The medical team includes a pediatrician, pediatric surgeons, specially trained nurses, social workers, and a host of legal beagles. From unique intravenous solutions to protective custody, battered children receive compassionate care. It's important to get an early court date, involve protective services, and provide the children with new clothes and other creature comforts. A major difficulty is determining which kids are injured innocently and which ones are battered.

What is the definition of a battered child?

It's whatever a particular state's laws say it is. And in America's polyglot society, what may be considered appropriate punishment for a naughty child in one culture may be considered excessive physical trauma in another. There's no easy answer. Usually, child abuse is considered to fall into four categories:

1. Physical abuse
2. Emotional/psychological abuse
3. Sexual abuse
4. Neglect

As a starting point, consider abuse any physical injury or emotional distress to a child that cannot be fully explained by the circumstances of the accident or event described in the history provided by the caregivers. Look for a pattern of physical impairment or serious injury with a confusing explanation. The following are areas of child abuse:

- Injuries that risk the child's life
- Injuries leaving disfiguring marks or those requiring a prolonged convalescence
- Painful, repeated injuries
- Injuries associated with loss of function of a limb or organ

Some parental acts can be considered abusive and may blend imperceptibly into subtle, as well as harsh, emotional and physical assaults on a child. For example, examine the following list of behaviors. Where would you draw the line between acts you consider discipline versus child abuse?

- Scolding
- Yelling
- Shaking
- Slapping
- Strapping/spanking
- Isolating for prolonged period of time
- Hitting with a fist
- Causing multiple bruises and contusions
- Breaking bones
- Causing unconsciousness or other neurological damage
- Depriving of food and water

- Injuring with flame, sharp instruments or weapons

In your story, you must decide whether a family is relatively "normal," a little peculiar, or truly dysfunctional. For example, does the mother feed, love, and provide comfort for her children? Or does she get them most meals but occasionally neglects them while she's out doing for herself? Or is she overly protective? Are the kids overfed and fat? Or are they left to fend for themselves? Latchkey kids? Practically homeless waifs?

Here's the problem: Ninety percent of American parents use some form of physical discipline. Some say it's the only way to get a child's attention; others rely on the Bible for guidance. Not all parents realize their children dislike being hit and embarrassed as much as adults, or that violence begets violence, or that other methods of discipline, such as grounding or losing privileges, make the point and preserve a nonviolent family interaction.

Why does child abuse continue?

- Abused kids become abusing adults; they "pass it on."
- Parents become fatigued and short-tempered raising children.
- Parents may have excessively high expectations for their children and feel the children are not trying to reach their potentials.
- Parents may feel disappointment with a chronically ill or developmentally slow child and seek to discipline the child for being weak and imperfect.
- Child is too small, too big, or the wrong sex.
- The child was unexpected.
- Parents are too young—kids having kids.

All states require that medical professionals report suspected cases of child abuse. The threshold for suspicion and its definition are not standardized, but "cause to suspect" or "cause to believe" that child abuse may have occurred is sufficient to warrant a report to the proper authorities. Some people feel too much parental behavior is being reported. Certainly the initiative is fraught with danger.

Recrimination from falsely reporting a parent as abusive may not be reversible. Is there a way to be sure? Not always. The potential for child abuse can stir conflict into the most seemingly loving domestic nest in your tale.

We'll examine a few examples of difficult diagnosis in cases of potential child abuse. The subject strains beyond the constraints of our coverage here. Useful references are listed at the end of the book for more thorough research.

Abusive Burns

Accounting for ten percent of all types of child abuse, burns may quite often be innocently caused or accidental. When battering is diagnosed, the burns are usually of different stages and could not have been caused by a single event or agent. Some burns have a characteristic appearance, notably small round cigarette burns, often on the buttocks, hands, and feet. And if associated with other types of injury, the flag of suspicion for child abuse should be hoisted. "Branding," or a recognizable pattern of burn, is almost always intentional.

Accidental burns are often from hot water, with scalds in a "splash" configuration, and may have an arrowhead shape as hot fluid flowed down the child's body. Also, accidental hot water burns are of varying depths. But an intended punitive burn, like that on a child held in a tub of hot water, is of uniform depth and degree.

Abusive Brain and Spinal Cord Damage

Infants and toddlers have unique anatomy with relatively large heads, flexible necks, and other anatomic characteristics that subject them to what is called the "shaking impact injury," or the *shaken baby syndrome*. Severe flexion and extension of the neck associated with shaking and, at times, smacking the head against an object (e.g., a wall), causes multiple neck and brain injuries. Occurring most often in infants under the age of fifteen months, the injuries include brain bruises, torn cerebral veins, and the resultant bleeding into the brain or below the membranes. The result is severe pressure on the infant's brain and a mortality rate of about fifteen percent. Even if no impact occurs, half of these kids sustain significant neurologic damage.

A report of a sleepy, irritable infant who "fell off the couch" suggests child abuse. Parents who insist the baby had a seizure before arriving at the hospital must be carefully questioned and the infant evaluated for other impacts. A modified Glasgow Coma Scale will be recorded in the ER. Also, a CT scan of the head will be obtained by the examining doctor if head trauma or bleeding into the brain is suggested on physical examination.

If abuse is suspected, skull x-rays may reveal recent or old skull fractures, and MRI scans add the ability to diagnose very small amounts of blood in and around the brain that otherwise might have been missed. Also, MRI may demonstrate fluid-filled spaces around the brain, which mark a delay between the abusive impact and the time the parents sought medical attention for the child.

Abusive Chest and Abdominal Trauma

Kids get kicked and punched in the trunk in almost twenty percent of reported battered child cases. Children's ribs are pliable and bend with impact, and serious internal injuries are infrequent. Fractured ribs do occur as does disruption of the bone-cartilage joint ("separated ribs") near the breastbone. With a vicious attack, any of the "dirty dozen" adult injuries described in Chapter Seven can be produced in kids with devastating results.

Also, a child's belly isn't like yours or mine. Muscles in the youngster's abdominal wall are thin, and the flexible ribs don't hold their shape and protect abdominal organs very well. This is partly because they don't cover the upper abdominal organs as completely as mature ribs do in adults. In addition, the child's internal organs are relatively large in comparison to the volume of the abdominal cavity and the child's body size in general and are unable to absorb the forces of blunt trauma. Only about five percent of all child abuse damage involves injury to internal organs of the chest and abdomen.

The diagnosis of serious internal damage is not difficult for the pediatric trauma surgeon. The presence of respiratory signs such as gasping for breath, chest pain, or a reluctance to breathe deeply, when coordinated with chest x-ray findings, confirms the diagnosis. Abdominal tenderness and other clinical findings suggest the need for an emergency CT scan of the abdomen, ultrasound, peritoneal lavage, or immediate surgery. Treatment is tailored to the findings. With both chest and abdominal injuries, the question may remain: Was this accidental or abusive?

X-Ray Proof of Child Abuse

Not long ago, a two–year-old was brought to our hospital with a bruised foot after stubbing his toe. The x-ray tech performed the wrong x-ray, and multiple old fractures were noted. After what seemed like endless bickering, the father admitted to abusing the child during the day when the unsuspecting working mother was absent. Only then did the mother recall the child crying whenever she left him alone with his father. Criminal proceedings were pursued.

Some mistakes work out. Wrong x-ray, right diagnosis. The child is now loved and protected by his mother and extended family.

A *bone survey*, a set of x-ray pictures rather than isolated films of the area of clinical concern, displays all of the child's bones. The survey provides proof that there are other injuries highly suggestive of child battering—or may show that the impact presenting to the ER is *not* an obvious repeat performance. Of course, isolated injuries can be the result of abuse. It's hard to be sure.

Here are a few of the diagnostic things a radiologist does in a case of suspected child abuse:

- A "babygram," or multiple x-rays of the entire child, usually done on children under two years of age. May miss injuries.
- Bone scan (radioisotope study). May pinpoint occult fractures not seen on plain x-rays.
- Skull x-rays. May show open sutures (jagged joints between skull plates) from increased pressure secondary to hemorrhage; also may show fractured skull.
- Collarbone x-rays. Used to find a midshaft break, a common abuse fracture.
- Long bone (extremity) x-rays. These show horizontal or spiral fractures from direct blows, as well as disruption of growth plates.

Other x-ray findings in battered kids include broken hand bones, "buckle" (incomplete) breaks in long bones, evidence of torn and healing ligaments, ruptured tendons, and swollen soft tissue. Also, the radiologist can tell approximately when the fracture occurred. Bones with ragged-edged breaks and soft tissue swelling are recent. When bone healing is manifested by the formation of callus (the piling up of new bone around the break), the fracture is over two weeks old—probably more like a month.

Because kids can't always tell their own stories—some parents won't let them—health care providers must be on the lookout for subtle, as well as overt, markers of abuse.

The Pediatric Trauma Patient

The new restraint devices for infants have reduced injuries in small babies and children. As children get older, they begin to sustain adult-like injuries. But there are differences in the patterns of injury and the methods of treatment.

For example, few cervical spine injuries occur in children. However, as adolescents become more aggressive, especially boys, the incidence of broken necks from car crashes and sports events, such as diving and horseback riding, rises. Children's x-rays, unlike adults, may not show fractures or dislocations even if the child has a significant spinal cord injury. For these reasons, immobilization of a child's neck is mandatory until a specialist consult is obtained.

Elsewhere on a child's x-rays, bone growth centers may look like fractures and confuse doctors. And because a kid's bones are soft and pliable, they often sustain so-called "greenstick" or partial fractures.

Simple splinting of pediatric fractures and dislocations is appropriate until an orthopedic consult can be obtained.

Kids have different fluid and blood transfusion requirements than adults. Doctors caring for kids must know the formulas and calculations to properly restore fluid and blood volume losses in traumatized children. And, as with adults (but more so with kids), certain injuries may be observed by the surgeon. Fewer splenic and liver injuries are operated on in the pediatric age group. Post-spleen removal bacterial infection is much higher in kids than in adults.

In your story, a child may sustain suspicious injuries and be left in the ER by irresponsible parents. Your doctor should be suspicious of child abuse if a long interval occurred between the injury and arrival for medical care, if the history of injury can't logically explain a severe injury, or if the history provided by one character differs from that given by another interested party.

Battered Women

Written records about the fate of abused women appeared in the United States sometime in the 1830's. The tragedy escalated through the last decade of the twentieth century and shows no evidence of abating. In the *American Journal of Emergency Medicine* (January 1995), Dr. E.A. deLahunta describes domestic violence as an epidemic. Women now correctly expect their doctors to inquire about potential abuse. Only education can break the vicious cycle of intergenerational learned violence.

While the topic of domestic violence creates images of poverty in the minds of some, it is a classless disease. In the land of the free, we spread battering around—rich, poor, blue-collar workers, blue-bloods, white-collar professionals, tradespeople. A study of forty-two consecutive consenting women seen in a community-based family practice setting revealed the following facts:

- Forty-five percent reported physical, social, or emotional violence in their relationships.
- Thirty percent admitted to being physically battered during their lifetimes.
- Sixty-two percent of the women who reported slapping and hitting also admitted to kicking and punching. Some said sexual violence and weapon use were also involved.
- Twelve percent were currently involved in an abusive relationship.
- None of the women were seen for routine checkups, but for complaints such as migraine headaches and neck stiffness.

Abuse must first be distinguished from the normal bickering and "gnashing of teeth" that periodically explodes within the most benevolent of relationships.

As in every well-written scene in fiction, episodes of domestic violence in real life have an *inciting incident*: Somebody does something to annoy or aggravate the other person in the dyad. It may be innocent questioning or nagging. It may fall on the heels of a job loss, excessive drinking, or other stresses. It may be familiar, repeated or unexpected. The result is often anger. Usually nothing happens. But not infrequently a physical outburst rushes in on the heels of flash rage. Each inciting event enrages a person who usually possesses poor impulse control at best and often a personal history of parents who exchanged abuse.

What happens?

The marginally adjusted individual, with a back story of having been abused, explodes.

We're interested in patterns of injury. As you might anticipate, the batterer's perverted attack is swift, carried out with little imagination. It's a predictable savagery. Here's a partial list of mindless battering methods:

- Slapping to the face, head, and ears. It shocks, hurts, but mostly insults and demeans the victim.
- Smashing attack to the head, chest, or abdomen with fists. Causes bruises, cuts, and larger lacerations; may cause broken bones (e.g., orbit of the eye).
- Strangling of victim with hands, belt, towel, etc. Attacker may time the attack to make victim think she's about to die, stopping just short of asphyxia.
- Kicking attacks to the legs, pelvis, and abdomen. May cause pain, bruising, and lacerations. May cause internal (blunt) damage; for example, a case of liver laceration has been reported.
- Throwing victim down a flight of stairs. May cause abrasions, cuts, or severe internal damage.
- Grabbing victim's clothing or neck and throwing her up against a wall. May involve strangling, head banging, neck snapping; may also include threat of more assaults.
- Using a knife or gun. Weapons may be used to threaten or to actually injure victim. Guns are most often used to threaten unless attacker intends to kill.

There seems to be a pattern to the batterer's attack. Like a Broadway performance, the assault scenario becomes a high-tension three-scene play. Except it's real. Usually, it's repeated. And it's always ugly.

At the heart of domestic violence is a profound lack of communication, beginning usually with males who grew up in paternalistic, disjointed families in which battering was permitted. Like his father, the son quickly learns there's no one to halt his irrational outbursts, which so often end in physical violence. No one talks very much. Wounds heal. Emotional scars remain hidden under a cloak of renewed domestic congeniality, fostered by an ever-hopeful spouse whose physical ailments from repeated assaults are likewise concealed beneath her clothes.

Here's the three-act domestic violence play:

Act 1 is a period of either gradual or exponential tension growth until the batterer (once again) elects to lose control and decides to assault the victim.

Act 2 is the actual outburst or explosion of rage—the attack is on. As more assaults occur, they become more violent and more frequent.

Act 3 is referred to as the loving phase of a battering incident. This final encounter involves reconciliation on both sides. The attacker often truly believes he won't do it again when he acts contrite and tells his victim so. Remarkably, the victim believes the batterer, only to (barely) live through repeated abusive events.

Why do so many women remain in an abusive relationship? Fear leads the list, fear of further abuse to herself as well as fear for her children who may already be part of the abusive pattern. Other feelings oil the slippery slope of violence. They include feelings of guilt for somehow being responsible for the batterer's unhappiness and anger. The victim may feel she somehow provoked him or is inadequate as a wife and mother. Many abused women watched their mothers tolerate abuse and may have grown up with an overwhelming sense of shame.

Violence begets more violence. The abused woman feels she cannot escape, and the beatings become more and more severe. Usually, the woman is financially dependent on the abuser. In the end, she feels desperate, trapped in her violent world, alone, powerless.

The batterer often lives in a disjointed world of rage, with an unshakable personal belief system that includes resentment for others, feelings of insecurity, and, not infrequently, a measure of paranoia. Many males who batter cherish an atavistic view of the interpersonal relationship between men and women. The home is his domain, his castle, and his space to rule as he sees fit. And that rhymes with hit. Which is what happens over and over again.

In a pamphlet entitled "Assaults on Women: Rape and Wife-Beating", Natalie Jaffee states:

Most injuries were to the head and neck and, in addition to bruises, strangle marks, black eyes, and split lips, resulted in eye damage, fractured jaws, broken noses, and permanent hearing loss. Assaults to the trunk of the body were almost as common and produced a broken collarbone, bruised and broken ribs, a fracture tailbone, internal hemorrhaging, and a lacerated liver.

So why do women stay in the abusive relationship?

Besides having no money, no place to go, no place to hide—not to mention fear of the batterer's rage if he discovered she was leaving before she actually escaped—she often hopes he will change. She loves him. Of course, the batterer seldom changes. Or she may believe divorce is wrong. Or she may fear not having adequate skills to rejoin the job market.

What can an abused woman do to escape?

- Secrete away as much money as possible.
- Keep the phone number of the local police nearby.
- Collect and conceal documents needed later.
- Decide where to go (e.g., with a friend or to a shelter).
- Go to ER and have photographs taken of areas of injury. Write down the names of all doctors, nurses, and police officers involved for future reference.
- Seek counseling and support if lack of self-esteem is hindering an escape.

Your battered character may find help through special hotlines, in shelters, in a community mental health care facility, through some women's associations, or through friends. The horror of domestic violence serves as an embarrassing backdrop to modern American life. It belongs in fiction as Stephen King demonstrated in his surreal novel *Rose Madder*.

More information may be obtained from:
Center of Woman Policy Studies
2000 P. St. NW, No. 508
Washington, DC 20036

National Coalition Against Domestic Violence
150 Massachusetts Ave. NW, Suite 35
Washington, DC 20005

The Pregnant Trauma Patient

Pregnancy disrupts the usual known facts of trauma care. First of all, the gravid uterus displaces other organs, interferes with the clinical examination of the abdomen and pelvis, and thus interferes with the doctor's ability to assess the extent and magnitude of the injuries. Instead of one victim, there are two. To save the fetus, you must save the mother. Mother is the baby's life support system. The trauma surgeon and a qualified obstetrician, as well as the hospital and its vital personnel, are the mother's life support system.

Any female trauma victim between the ages of ten and fifty plus may be pregnant. Story ideas spring like magic out of the hysterical milieu a traumatic event involving a pregnant woman produces: a young woman crashes her car in an attempt to abort on her own, a boyfriend or spouse (or other enraged party) may "rig" an accident to induce abortion, a woman may have an accident and not know she's pregnant – use your imagination. Here's more information to authenticate your tale.

The dome of the uterus doesn't begin to rise like a loaf of bread out of the pelvis until after twelve weeks of gestation. Doctors use the level of the belly button (where you can feel the dome of the uterus) to assign a gestational age of twenty weeks to the fetus. So, during the first trimester, the fetus remains huddled inside the thick-walled uterus inside the protection of the bony pelvis. In the second trimester, the uterus has leavened into the belly, but the amniotic fluid cushions the baby. Still, bowel is pushed up under the ribs and is more protected unless a high-riding seat belt crushes the intestine during a crash and forward flexion of the mother's torso. In the third trimester of pregnancy, the baby is large and settled into the pelvis, and the uterine wall is thin and provides little protection to the baby. The placenta is well formed and subject to shear forces, which may disrupt the blood supply from the mother to the baby and result in inadequate oxygenation of the baby. Also, in later pregnancy, a major maternal pelvic fracture may cause a skull fracture, as well as brain damage, in the baby.

Seat belts, steering wheels, dashboards, boots (kicks), and falls may all cause the fetus to indirectly experience compression, deceleration, or torsion forces. The result may injure the fetus directly, or, as mentioned above, indirectly cause harm by disrupting the placenta. In the ER, the doctor must determine how stable the mother is, and whether or not surgery is required to save her and/or her baby.

A few other little information bits about the pregnant trauma patient:

- Lying on her back with a huge uterus may cause pressure on the mother's inferior *vena cava* – the large abdominal vein returning blood to the heart – and dangerously reduces heart blood output.

- Mother and child require more oxygen and the doctor must provide a facemask or intubation to assure adequate oxygenation.
- With penetrating injuries (knife or gunshot), the huge uterus takes the brunt of the insult and the fetus is frequently lost, ironically saving the mother by the uterus displacing other viscera away from the site of abdominal wall violation by the knife or bullet.
- After about ten weeks, a Doppler examination will permit fetal heart sounds to be monitored to help determine fetal viability; fetal heart rates are between 120 and 160.
- The same work-up is used in the pregnant patient as in other victims of abdominal trauma, including CT scanning, Diagnostic Peritoneal Lavage (DLP), and FAST ultrasound – searching for injuries inside and outside of the gravid uterus.
- A qualified obstetrician must assess the traumatized woman and follow her when admitted to the trauma service; pelvic examination looking for signs of labor, leaking amniotic fluid, and especially vaginal bleeding suggesting impending fetal death.
- The fetus may be in trouble even with what may seem to be trivial maternal injuries.
- The trauma surgeon and the obstetrician must decide if cesarean section is indicated.

The ultimate crisis facing a trauma surgeon and obstetrician is the need for a "perimortem" c-section. Mother is crashing. She's having or is about to have a cardiac arrest. The doctors have only four or five minutes to decide to open up the mother and take out the baby.

In your story, they may be out in the wilderness. Remember Hemingway's *Indian Camp*? Nick's physician father performed a c-section with a hunting knife and sewed up the squaw with fishing catgut. Stressful? You will recall her husband in the upper bunk slit his own throat.

Abused Elders

Old folks are easy prey.

In fact, the elderly are a natural setup for abuse for several reasons, not the least of which is their dependency. It seems that whether the caregiver is related to the victim or not, the mere fact of being old, wasted, and invalid reminds young caregivers that aging will eventually trap them as well. Frustration, fatigue, and a sense of futility about their own future years may weigh heavily on the minds of both victim and abuser.

What are the symptoms and signs of abuse of elderly people?

The answer may include any number of complaints, and close observation may suggest an elder abuse problem. Many of these considerations seem normal for an elderly person whose life is nearly over. Without many remaining friends and with well-meaning but preoccupied families, old folks often regress into a clouded acceptance of their inevitable and possibly imminent death. They may express a desire to die, may cry easily, may lose their appetites, and may withdraw socially. These symptoms can progress to a refusal to take medication or to bathe, after which physical deterioration may swiftly ensue. Still, any of these findings should raise suspicion of elder abuse.

Other clues to elder abuse:

- Elder asks to be separated from caretaker who is abusing him.
- Elder seems overly alert when the caregiver is around and watches the caregiver's every move.
- Elderly seems fearful in the presence of the caregiver.
- Elder seems to live in the past, never talking about current activities, particularly those involving the caregiver. As many elderly reminisce, this is a particularly sensitive issue.

The old person in your story may be wearing evidence that points to abuse, such physical ailments that carry suspicion, or odd body marks. A few types of common injuries that may be present with a strange twist include:

- Bruises that remind you of something familiar, such as fingers, rope, or other household objects
- Abrasions on the wrists or legs suggestive of restraints
- Burns with blistering from hot water in unusual places or excessive for the explanation provided
- Bruises on both forearms suggesting self-defense along with bruises elsewhere
- Bruises on both sides of the body, for example, inside the thighs, top of shoulders (pinching "annoyance" bruises)
- Bleeding from nose, mouth, vagina, or anus
- Unexplained chest, abdominal, or pelvic pain

Neglect may be more obvious than abuse. It is insidious, cruel, and reportable. Some of the symptoms may simply seem a little off the mark. For example, the victim may be dehydrated, soiled, apathetic, and improperly clothed for the season. Other evidence of neglect includes over-or under-medication, lack of eyeglasses, walker, or hearing aid. Unpleasant odors or stool or urine stains, unwashed hair, lice, and dirty hands and fingernails all point to a neglected person's inability to care for herself.

What about the caregiver? Any clues there?

The caregiver may light up a torch of his own and send out additional signals of misgivings. Once again, we must approach the caregiver's record cautiously. Look at the situation from his point of view. The elderly patient can be slow moving, combative, resentful, and frequently downright stubborn. Caregivers may be out of the mainstream of health care and nursing. They may return to the work force because of domestic financial problems. Or substance abuse may figure in the equation. Trapped for what may seem like endless hours with elderly clients, even the most well-tempered caregiver becomes irritated.

When does annoyance cross the line to abuse?

Remember, a lot of abuse may be invisible. Threats of withholding medication, ambulation assistance, and creature comforts, or just threatening to carry out physical abuse, can be devastating. And threats can't be seen. The elder may be too frightened to report the abuser. Refusal to touch or to comfort the old person or isolating the person from others also represents an invidious sort of neglectful abuse.

More obvious and inappropriate is the caregiver who:
- Seems agitated or outright hostile
- Won't discuss issues of the elderly person's welfare and is insensitve to the patient's concerns
- Is rough when handling the old person
- Is impulsive or cuts into discussion when elder is talking
- Overreacts to the elder's more minor concerns
- Doesn't seem to be able to communicate effectively with the elder

Any evidence of fondling the elderly or of outright verbal or physical abuse should lead to dismissal of the caregiver, followed by a report to the proper health care association.

Victims of domestic abuse often view themselves as completely dependent on their abusers, and many of them are dependent for economic support. But there is a way out for battered women, abused kids, and mistreated elders. Increasing physician awareness is beginning to help turn the tide as more doctors move past ignoring the problem, or merely offering sympathy, to becoming proactive.

Most states have laws that mandate the reporting of domestic abuses. But the victim and the family must work with the health care team to make appropriate changes in the abused person's environment. It's not easy, but it can be done. No one has to be a victim.

The Elderly Trauma Patient

The frail elderly suffer different patterns of injury when in car accidents and when struck by vehicles. They have a three times higher incidence of sub-dural hematomas, which may be because the elderly are often on anticoagulants (blood thinners) for stroke prevention. And although the elderly have more cervical spine injuries, they are often difficult to diagnose on x-ray. This is because of the elderly patient's increased incidence of arthritis and osteoporosis. Degeneration and loss of strength of the large vertebral ligaments, along with narrowing of the spinal canal from bony spurs, makes the likelihood of spinal cord damage (and varying degrees of paralysis) higher than in the younger trauma victim.

Virtually all systems in the elderly are compromised. Because the body's production of stress hormones is impaired, its ability to be ambulatory because of pre-existing weakness and arthritis only makes rehabilitation more difficult. And they are more susceptible to long bone fractures and hip fractures, which require extensive recovery time and effort by the patient and the ancillary hospital and rehabilitation facility personnel. Often the elderly's nutritional status is marginal or poor and their immune systems are likewise compromised. Wound infection, pneumonia, urinary tract infections, and decubitus ulcers quickly occur.

A special quandary facing elderly trauma patients and their families is the issue of discontinuing care when all efforts seem futile. It is difficult to define futile in exact terms. The essence of the discussion is that care is futile when no improvement occurs, or deterioration continues. These decisions often occur in the intensive care unit. Families may disagree with each other about what their elderly parent would want them to do under the circumstances.

Issues that may arise in the elderly trauma patient include:

- Withholding ventilatory support – "Don't put Mom on a respirator"
- Withholding cardiac drug administration
- Withdrawing the above after they have been tried to no effect
- Giving morphine to the patient to ease labored breathing
- Withhold or withdraw water and food – either by mouth or via a feeding tube
- Agree to or refuse further surgery for a complication

We talk little about death and dying in our youth-oriented society. End of life decisions are difficult often because we most of us have not prepared a family foundation for such discussions. We avoid death talks. We rob the elderly of the conversation they must have with us. It doesn't bother most of them. It bothers us.

Your characters may gain insight and reflect their "deep character" at times like this. Cultural, religious, and secular concerns bubble to the surface of end of life talks. Conflict defines how we deal with our often mutually exclusive philosophies. Our discussions may boil over and scald each other. Spouses, brothers, sisters, sons and daughters, may lose each other in the final days of an elderly loved one's life.

Or, death may be forced into a corner while you, the author, reflect in your prose your elderly character's full, loving life.

SEXUAL ASSAULT: UNSPEAKABLE TRAUMA

A woman is raped in the United States every six minutes, and it is commonly assumed that a significant number of other sexual assaults are never reported. Not all victims are young. Some sixty thousand women over fifty years of age report sexual asault annually. If we include cases of reluctant sexual contact between adults, the number soars.

It has been estimated that thirty percent of all women have been sexually assaulted in childhood or during their adolescent years. One out of every eight males has been sexually assaulted by age eighteen. Sexual assault is the fastest growing crime in America. Unfortunately, not many sex criminals get caught. Too often, the victim possesses a poor self-image, coupled with the perception by many women that theirs is a poor legal position. Thus, many raped women don't seek medical or legal help, and many rapes go unreported. Presently, health care providers are becoming increasingly aware of this horrible dilemma that confronts sexually assaulted women.

What Is Rape?

Rape is defined as the carnal knowledge of a victim without his or her consent that occurs through fear, coercion, fraud, or force. Carnal knowledge is considered any degree of penetration of a body orifice whether or not ejaculation occurs. Lack of consent is integral to a definition of rape, and the threat of harm or death, with or without the use of a weapon, determines the legal degree of criminal sexual assault. Rape may occur in the setting of a drugged, intoxicated, sleeping, or mentally incompetent victim. Any act from fondling to penetration of a body opening with the penis or another object constitutes sexual assault.

Rape is a legal term. The examining doctor's responsibility is to discover and treat traumatic injuries, collect forensic evidence, comfort the victim, and direct her to ongoing therapy.

A useful method of classifying victims of sexual assault is by age. Each age group brings up different issues. The categories are:

- Adults (over eighteen years old)
- Children
- Adolescents
- Elderly

In the interest of space, we'll focus on adults and child sexual assault.

Careful assessment of the rape victim regardless of age is critical, as is gentleness during the vulnerable first examination. It is not the doctor's job to establish whether or not the patient was raped. Rather, the physician must obtain all information germane to the assault, diagnose injuries, collect forensic data, and treat and counsel the victim. The courts determine who is guilty of the crime.

Why Do Men Rape Women?

The answer is complicated, and the following issues have been assessed and a unified theory of criminal sexual behavior has been synthesized by experts in the field. The answer to why men rape women includes data from abnormal behavior, the contribution of genetics, the nature of the male nervous system, and the male's hormonal background. Much of the behavior is learned, of course.

Some contemporary theorists' suggestions on why rape occurs:

- Natural selection probably favored males who learned and indulged in forced copulation while women learned to resist. Men took advantage of their superior strength to sexually subdue women.
- The tendency to use forced copulation as a strategy depends on the size of the sex drive and the person's perception of how successful the aggressive sexual encounter may be. Males learned they can get away with rape. Even today, little legal deterrent exists.
- Two drives predominate to motivate the rapist: the sex drive itself and the urge to dominate and control the victim. The expression of power—hinged on anger—is undoubtedly a major part of the urge to attack and subdue.
- Genes that evolved on the Y (male) chromosome affect the secretion of hormones and the function of the brain, which alters the strength of the sex drive. The rapist's sensitivity to adverse or uncomfortable stimuli is different, which permits him to commit the crime.

Not all rapists are the same. Their backgrounds vary, as do their personalities. As suggested by the list above, the factors that go into stimulating an individual to commit this crime are numerous. Still, in our society, there exist many preconceived ideas about the person who commits what is often considered a crime of base instinct.

Myths About Rape

Myths about forced sex arose because of society's historic view of woman's place in western culture. In the seventeenth century, it was felt that the husband could not rape his wife as she had, through "matrimonial consent," given herself to him in all aspects. During the women's movement in the 1960's, this so-called "spousal exemption" came under attack and the concept of consent was redefined.

Myth: A Woman Should Do What Her Husband Wants

Recognizing that rape is more than sexual assault has perhaps most meaning in the concept of *spousal rape*. Not only is the woman pressed to submit against her will sexually, she is attacked by force, thus confirming that rape is more than a simple sexual attack. It is a violent crime against the victim. And it is all the more repulsive in this instance because the marriage bond is built upon trust. When trust is tossed out, there can be little hope for the preservation of the bond.

Spousal immunity has been eliminated in many but not all states.

Myth: A Man Cannot Force Himself on a Woman

A clear difference now exists between *consent* and *submission*. The meaning of each is elaborated in the points presented below.

- Before the 1970's, the victim was expected to "resist to the utmost" until overwhelmed and the rape consummated. This produced horrible genital and extragenital injuries.
- "Without her consent" implies that all force and energy to resist the assault was *not* used. This strategy avoids serious injury to the victim. Children and the elderly cannot resist anyway.
- "Against her will" implies the victim resisted in vain and was assaulted despite efforts to protect herself.
- Lack of physical injury in a sexually assaulted woman does not imply consent. Intimidation and physical threats cannot always be countered, especially when the attacker has a weapon or the physical size to carry out his threats.

Myth: "She asked for it" —
Rape as a Spur-of-the-Moment Impulse

Rather than a lustful, salivating sex-crazy fool, the rapist is most often an angry man of low self-esteem who hates women. He is incapable of forming solid relationships with women and feels insecure in his activities of daily living. In a word, the rapist is a misfit who feels powerless to control his world.

Rape has been classified by motivation as follows:

- Power rape: 65 percent
- Anger rape: 35 percent

There's actually a difference in attack method between the two. The power rapist thinks out ahead of time who he wants to rape and how he will carry out the attack. Often the victim is about his own age, and, while he uses force in gaining control of his victim, the assaults are not violent. On the other hand, the angry rapist often attacks children and the elderly with little or no premeditation. Nongenital injuries are more common as the angry rapist uses more force than is needed to subdue his prey. At the outer limit of this repugnant behavior is the *sadistic rape* and sexual assault that results in the victim's death.

The rape victim carries her burden of guilt and shame for years. These initial emotions often mushroom into a variety of symptoms and behaviors, many also known as Post-Traumatic Stress Disorder. Included in the chronic illnesses seen in sexually assaulted adult women are:

- Depression
- Low self-esteem
- Development of an addictive personality
- Worry about overall poor physical health
- Development of functional limitations (unable to perform activities of daily living)
- Complaints of multiple chronic diseases

Other problems that may appear in assaulted women include:

- Pelvic infections; sexually transmitted diseases
- Chronic pelvic pain
- Pelvic trauma (e.g., abrasions, bruises, and contusions of the mons and labia, lacerations of vagina or rectum)

The Initial Examination of the Victim

Health care workers are concerned not only with identifying the extent of the victim's injuries, but also with caring for her and with collecting information to convict the suspect. Therapy begins immediately. A rape victim may seek medical care in any of the following sites:

- Emergency room
- Private primary care doctor's office
- Gynecologist's office
- Hospital clinic
- "Doc-in-a-box" neighborhood walk-in clinic
- College or university health center

All victims of sexual assault should have a complete history, physical examination, and evidential evaluation within thirty-six hours of the assault. The examining doctor must complete several duties during the initial evaluation. These include:

- Taking a general medical history as well as asking questions about the rape and what the victim did after the assault (all information documented in writing)
- Performing general and gynecologic examinations
- Collecting appropriate specimens for legal evidence using standard rape kit
- Providing emergency care and proper treatment of injuries
- Providing psychological support for victim at time of exam and arranging for follow-up therapy
- Providing advice regarding options on therapy to prevent pregnancy
- Giving appropriate antibiotics to prevent veneral disease and advising regarding option to be tested for AIDS

The physical examination is not easy for the victim. She feels violated, embarrassed. Her emotional status must be recorded and kept in mind as procedures are carried out in an orderly fashion. Not all injuries to rape victims are genital; four or five percent of these unfortunate victims require emergency surgery to repair lacerations and other bone and soft tissue disruptions.

The examiner must realize she is placing the victim in a situation similar to the rape: The doctor is in a position of control and can make the victim feel helpless. Therefore, the examiner must be objective, nonjudgmental, kind, and gentle. The doctor should ask permission before performing any part of the exam where touching or probing the victim is involved. The vaginal speculum should be warmed (no lubricant other than warm water) and inserted slowly as the examiner talks with the patient. Without a sensitive, caring practitioner, the victim may feel she's being raped all over again.

Evidence of recent sexual intercourse on examination includes:

- Engorgement of labia
- Engorgement of clitoris
- Redness of the posterior vaginal opening (fourchette)
- Presence of semen
- Presence of acid phosphatase

The time of the rape may be determined by the presence of several substances in semen:

- Motile sperm from the victim means the rape occurred within the last three hours.
- Acid phosphatase, an enzyme from the prostate, if present at a certain level in the vaginal washings (specimen), strongly suggests ejaculation occurred within the last twenty-four hours.

- P30, a prostate-specific protein found in semen, indicates ejaculation occurred within the last forty-eight hours.

Examination of the Sexual Assault Victim
History
- Main complaint: What type of assault was it? What body orifices and parts are involved? What hurts? Is there bleeding? Is there evidence of severe injury requiring emergency (resuscitation) care?
- Qualifying questions: Did ejaculation occur? Body penetration? What did the victim do after the assault? Shower? Change clothes? Take an enema? Douche? What is the victim's emotional state? Is she crying? Combative? Screaming? Huddling in fear? Noncommunicative? How many assailants? Did she ingest alcohol? Was the assailant drunk? Did the victim have consensual sex within seventy-two hours of assault? Obtain an explicit account of the sex act.
- Past medical history: Is there a history of chronic illness such as heart disease, lung problems, diabetes, or any other condition that may be worsened by the assault (chest pain, gasping, dizziness because of low blood sugar, etc.)? Are medications in use? Pacemaker? Does the victim think she was pregnant before the attack? Is she using a method of birth control? Did she ever have tetanus prophylaxis?

Physical Examination
Performed with one or more attendants.
- Have the victim disrobe on a clean sheet of paper that gets folded and sent to forensics with other specimens.
- Describe the victim's general appearance.
- Describe the condition of her clothes. Are there stains? Tears in the fabric? Blood?
- What is her emotional state?
- Perform a general examination, and take photographs of any injuries, major or minor.
- Perform gynecological examination and document all injuries and the presence of any fluids or blood. Rarely use colposcope* and photodocumentation.
- Use Wood's Lamp (fluorescent) to identify semen.
- Use Rape Kit to collect: **
    - Semen
    - Pubic hair (with collecting comb)
    - Head hairs (plucked, compared to pubic hair)

— Saline swab of vagina
— Saline swab of perianal skin when indicated
— Blood sample in appropriate tube
— Saliva sample (filter paper inside plastic tube)

*Colposcopy is an examination of the vagina and cervix using a special instrument with magnification and photographic capabilities. It's used infrequently.

**Material collected in the Rape Kit is sent to a forensic crime lab for expert evaluation.

Therapy is aimed at re-establishing a sense of worth and providing strategies to help the rape victim get on with her life. The goal is to assist her in beginning to cope with the trauma and to deal with the flashbacks, the feelings of shame, and of lost self-worth. Frequently, multiple physical complaints arise. These include difficulty in sleeping, lack of concentration, irritability, eating disorders, gastrointestinal complaints, headaches, and others. Studies confirm that these victims use medical care facilities much more frequently *after* the sexual assault than prior to it. Available to the victim are sexual assault response teams, victim assistance programs, rape crisis centers, psychological counseling, and financial aid.

How Is a Rapist Identified?

DNA fingerprinting: The process of analyzing DNA was established by Alec Jeffreys in England in the early 1980s. Appearing like a grocery barcode-like pattern, DNA testing may be used in law enforcement and paternity cases (paternity kits available online for $138.00). With new technology, results are available within hours. Minute samples of blood and other body fluids and tissue such as saliva, semen and skin can be processed with certainty. Many cases of rape have been confirmed, as well as others proven to be wrong, and over sixty imprisoned men have been released because DNA testing proved their innocence.

ABO blood type antigens: They may be identified in saliva, blood, or semen, and many additional antigens may be tested to narrow down the match with those identified in the fluids collected from the victim.

Post-Traumatic Stress Disorder and the Rape Victim

- Victim may have feelings of guilt, powerlessness, shame, fear, embarrassment, anger, stupidity, depression, anxiety, and possible concern for the rapist.
- Stress disorder may be expressed as bad dreams, flashbacks to the attack, difficulty concentrating, avoiding anything that

reminds victim of the assault, loss of ability to relate emotionally to another, becoming easily annoyed.

Sexual Assault Against Children

In children, the definition of sexual abuse includes any sexual activity between a minor child (less than eighteen years old) and a person who holds power and authority over the child. Often sexual abuse of children is classified as either incest or extrafamilial.

Offenders may be under legal age themselves, and the criminal acts may include fondling, pornography, exhibitionism, and/or penetration of the vagina, mouth or anus. No specific profile of a pedophile has been described, but ninety-eight percent of offenders in cases of child sexual molestation are male. Fifty percent of molested children are between ages six and twelve. Forty percent of the criminals are family members, and twenty percent are not known to the child. Almost half of these children are molested more than once. Ironically, children have a greater chance of being sexually assaulted at home.

So much for the myth of the stranger offering candy.

Incest refers to inappropriate sexual contact that involves members of a family with established relationships. It may include anyone in the family whom the child views as a caring, trustworthy adult. Stepparents and significant others, as well as older stepbrothers and sisters, who are acting as surrogate parents may become perpetrators.

The Child Sexual Abuse Scenario

To become abusive, the relationship between the child and the adult (or older child) must possess several features. Above all else, the child must view himself as essentially helpless in the presence of the dominant and powerful adult. Most abusers know the child they select to sexually assault. At times, the assault is purely random.

Minor sexual contact may occur between an adult and a child. But when the true abuse scenario begins, the child feels that it is imperative to submit to the adult's authority. Rather than using threats and force, as in the adult sexual attack, the adult coerces the child with a steady stream of small gifts, compliments, and perhaps extra attention. The adult must have access to the child, particularly when no one else is around.

One can imagine small talk, perhaps offhanded fondling and the first suggestion of exposing each other. Touching would follow as the child becomes drawn into the adult's powerful influence. Suggestions would be repeated that it's all right. They really like each other. No one's around. We enjoy this, don't we? And then the more overt sexual acts follow. Oral sex is often pressed on the child at first. Vaginal or anal sex , or "dry intercourse," where the adult rubs his penis against the child's genitals without penetration, may follow. Some sexual acts may cause the child minor genital irritation that's not easily detected. Others cause serious injury and leave lacerations and other evidence that would be a clear sign of trouble if only the child could reach medical care.

As time goes on, the adult reinforces the relationship's secret nature. At this point, the ever-powerful adult may suggest that the child was the one who actually started the intimate contact. With reinforcement, the child begins to feel guilty. It's her fault. Who can she tell? Threats of physical injury to the child may be made now, and at times, real force is used to make the point.

Will the child reveal the secret? Most experts agree child sexual abuse is grossly underreported and often is revealed only later in life. How does the abusive relationship become known?

- The child confides in someone.
- Someone recognizes abnormal behavior in the child.
- An injury is evaluated by a doctor who suspects abuse and pursues the diagnosis.

Evaluation of the Abused Child

Taking the history of a confused and frightened child is a little different than with adults. Because of the obvious difficulties with communications with a child, special techniques are used. These include the posing of open-ended questions, avoiding leading the child, and employing anatomically correct dolls. The dolls help to clarify something the child has said as well as enabling nonverbal children to communicate.

The physical examination can be performed in a doctor's office by a skilled clinician who is not rushed and who takes time to establish rapport with the victim. A caretaker may have made observations that suggest abuse and may help direct the physician's evaluation. A careful exam of the external genitals, following standard steps and with the use of magnification, permits the identification of small abrasions and cuts that would otherwise be missed. If major vaginal or anal injuries are seen on the initial examination, it is often necessary to take the child to a hospital where operating room facilities permit a thorough examination under anesthesia. If lacerations are discovered, they may be properly repaired at that time. More subtle are changes in the hymen, such as notching, or portions missing because of repetitive penetrating (stretching) trauma.

Several traps await the physician who examines a child for suspected sexual abuse. First, the evidence may have disappeared (small cuts and tears healed) by the time the child is examined. Also, youngsters scratch themselves, causing irritation and inflammation and leaving marks that could be misconstrued as abuse. Many reports on the relationship between the size of the hymenal opening and allegations of sexual abuse have been published and little agreement exists among experts. Overall, an opening of greater than one centimeter in a child is suggestive of abuse, as are recent or healed lacerations of the vagina, or venereal disease. More conclusive is the presence of sperm. Finally, the last trap is to assume that the absence of physical evidence of abuse means it didn't happen. It doesn't mean the child's story is suspect.

Treatment includes timely repair of physical injuries and the provision of emotional support for the victim and the family. Child sexual abuse cases are classified as *acute* when the child is evaluated soon after the assault and when forensic evidence must be collected (following similar guidelines as in adults). Major lacerations are treated surgically. The child may arrive in the ER or doctor's office complaining of genital or anal pain and bleeding. Less acute is the child assessed three or four days after the event. At this juncture, the child's safety is of paramount importance. As suggested above, some evidence may have already disappeared. Also, the children who come to medical evaluation even later are usually not severely hurt and are safe. But, as in the other scenarios, it is imperative that the child's safety be assured, particularly if the perpetrator lives with the child. Child protective services are available in most areas.

Long-term complications are common. Ongoing therapy is an essential part of the multidisciplinary approach to child sexual abuse. Sexually transmitted diseases are unusual in youngsters, but should be treated if present. Girls who are menstruating must undergo pregnancy testing and should be offered medication to prevent pregnancy.

All states require the examining physician to report suspected cases of child sexual assault.

The Sexually Abused Adolescent

As adolescents struggle with an emerging, uncertain self-image, ideas about the role of people around them in their lives become focused, and spiritual values are integrated into the young person's belief system. Interpersonal relationships are important, and communication with adults and other adolescents forms the basis of the adolescent's view of life. At this critical time when values and beliefs are being assessed and accepted as part of the person's self-concept, any disruption may prove to be overwhelming.

Lynn Rew, RN, Ed.D. and Pat Shirejian, MSN, RN, in the *Journal of Psychosocial Nursing* in 1993, describe the feelings, thoughts, and behaviors of sexually abused adolescents that occur in the psychophysiological, social, and spiritual domains of their lives. Because they are not able to cope with the abusive event and the disastrous effect of the loss of trust in adults, these young adults become a setup for *revictimization*. Thus often begins the destructive relationship that leads to thoughts of betrayal, despair and the potential for violence.

What does the adolescent feel after being abused?

- Guilt
- Anger
- Helplessness
- Depression
- Anxiety
- Reduced confidence

These feelings result in confusion and self-blame. This may precipitate flashbacks and a reenactment of the event in the victim's mind. She may regress and become antisocial and, at times, self-mutilation occurs. Alcohol and/or drug abuse may become chronic problems.

Interpersonal relationships suffer because the young person feels betrayed. There is no one to turn to, and he may begin to feel a growing resentment and anger for his parents or other caretakers who can't or refuse to recognize the problem. If the abuse continues and no one helps to extricate the adolescent from the abusive environment, he may begin to experience thoughts of violence and formulate ideas about injuring others, including the perpetrator. Another way a young person may express feelings of being mistreated or ignored is to become inappropriately active sexually and "act out" her frustrations.

Adolescent victims of sexual abuse must be hospitalized if symptoms progress to where regressive behavior is observed, particularly if the youngster entertains destructive thoughts. Regressive behavior includes acting younger than one's age or becoming labile, silly, then withdrawn. The victim needs to sense her own safety in the hospital because nightmares, flashbacks, and fear are common. These terrors may be conquered as therapy progresses. It takes time. Authors Rew and Shirejian emphasize the sense of unworthiness, lack of purpose and feelings of isolation that sexually assaulted adolescents experience, which may lead to anger at God and a profound hopelessness.

Treatment includes giving the young person back some control over his life in a safe environment. The victim is taught to cope with his past feelings and memories and is encouraged to actively learn how to protect himself from further abuse. Finally, the adolescent is encouraged to rediscover his belief system and engage in healthy activities.

Specific messages are passed on to the victim during the initial treatment session. These include reinforcing that she was the victim and the victim is never at fault; that there is no affection or love in the act of incest—it's purely bestial, and if she thought there was any element of pleasure or body response to the sexual act, it was reflexive or instinctual; she had no control over it, and there is nothing about which to feel guilty.

Lastly, the victim is taught she has control over her body and who is allowed to touch her. With time and help, she will hopefully regain control.

SEVENTEEN

ORGAN DONATION: WHO MAKES THE ULTIMATE GIFT?

The gift of a functioning organ requires an unequivocal diagnosis of death, unless the donation is voluntary and the donor is living. Although the study of our victim's demise isn't our prime focus in this book, death occurs with regularity in cases of multiple and severe single organ injury, despite excellent trauma care. The ethical "rope bridge" spanning the uncertain chasm between severe injury and death is narrow and must be constantly guarded.

Insidiously, the discussion of organ donation from a trauma patient arises.

Organ donation spells the end of hope for the horribly injured trauma victim and the beginning of opportunity for a recipient. Before the gift of donating an organ may be pursued, death must be certain. The process of considering a patient as a potential donor may begin at any time, but often commences when the patient's demise seems likely.

The donation discussion begins *before* death occurs.

There is a natural progression from severe brain damage or multiple organ injury without recovery, to the slippery slope of potential death, from the uncertainty of acute coma to the persistent vegetative state. Never are we quite sure about survival. And from the outset, this discussion of body injury has captured a major chunk of our attention *because of the possibility of death*.

Justification for including organ donation in this book falls upon the harsh reality that there is a fine line separating severe head injury, persistent coma, and brain death. Lingering in the minds of everyone involved in the care of a severely injured trauma victim is the issue of recovery, the remote possibility for survival.

Could we be wrong if we give up hope?

High-voltage tension for your tale.

It's important to understand this next heart-lurching step in the management of a trauma victim, even though we're really only interested in the ones who limp away into the sunset. In the real world, and therefore in the world of fiction, the trauma surgeon and the victim's family must be ready to answer the question: Are you prepared to allow your patient/loved one to be an organ or tissue donor?

The results obtained after successful transplantation of these organs have improved over the past several years. Currently, in 2005, the one-year survival rates are:

- Cadaver kidney transplant - living donors 94%, cadaver donors 88%
- Heart transplant, 80 to 90 percent
- Liver transplant, 65 to 70 percent

Before the recent flood of modern medical technology, a patient was dead when heart and lung function ceased. Today, heart and lung support, as well as dialysis for kidney failure, may be carried out by machines almost indefinitely. As technology improved, a new definition of death became necessary.

Above all else, the responsible doctors involved in a potential organ procurement case must assure the victim's family that meaningful survival is not reasonably possible. Before looking at brain death criteria, consider the enormous difficulty posed by the *possibility of recovery*, as reflected in the potential diagnosis of the persistent vegetative state.

The Persistent Vegetative State

To a casual observer, a patient in a persistent vegetative state (PVS) may seem aware and might appear to respond to commands. Parents of young adults mistake unconscious motor activity for willed movement in their loved one. The PVS patient may startle easily, turn away from a visitor, or demonstrate reflex movement. They may grimace, smile, and shed tears. Doctors don't always agree on whether or not a particular patient is in a PVS.

What drives the controversy involving patients in a persistent vegetative state is the need to speak for a person who has lost capacity. This means they cannot speak for themselves. Thus, family members with conflicting agendas often clash at the bedside, or in the media.

Ethicist Doctor Bernard Lo, Professor of Medicine at UCLA San Francisco, describes the persistent vegetative state and its characteristics. Much of Doctor Lo's summation is included here. Several biological facts define the PVS. First, the patient has a beating heart and functioning lungs; the patient is breathing and the kidneys are working (unless renal failure mandates dialysis), but all cortical (higher brain function) activity is gone. Only reflexes from the brainstem, the reptilian brain, remain. It's not a coma.

The diagnosis of the persistent vegetative state requires a careful examination by an experienced neurologist. High tech tests don't help much. A PET scan (positron emission tomography) in a PVS patient shows slow brain metabolism, much like someone under general anesthesia. With a non-traumatic insult such as near-drowning (hypoxia), recovery seldom occurs after three months. After a closed or open head injury, a twelve-month wait is required before doctors can be almost certain of non-recovery. Yes, a few exceptions have been documented. These rare recoveries are associated with moderate to severe neurological deficits.

Total nursing care is required for PVS patients. The mean survival for these patients is two to five years. Death or morbidity often results from severe urinary tract infections, non-healing decubitus ulcers, and pneumonia from aspirating (inhaling) tube feedings and their own secretions.

This condition should be distinguished from *brain death*, which requires an absence of both cortex and brainstem function. In *the locked-in syndrome*, patients are conscious and may communicate by blinking and using computer-assisted message writing, but they demonstrate no conscious muscular function. (B. Lo)

The PVS reminds alert readers of the many cases in the ethics literature that have helped doctors, patients, and their families to deal with victims of brain injury or hypoxic damage who will not regain consciousness. If you are interested, you may wish to look up the cases of Karen Quinlan, Nancy Cruzan, Elizabeth Bouvia, and now, Terri Schiavo. The ethical dilemma raised in all of these cases is whether it is appropriate to withdraw life support. This usually involves a ventilator (Quinlan) or feeding tube (Cruzan, Bouvia, Schiavo). Your characters may take any of the following appropriate positions:

- Stop all treatment as recovery is not possible
- Keep them alive as recovery will happen
- Keep them alive as recovery may happen
- Keep them alive because recovery is only one issue – the person is human and all human life is sacred
- Withdrawing support is murder
- Keeping someone alive without brain function is amoral
- Any or all of the above positions strengthened by personal religious beliefs.

For a writer, character motivation to support a PVS life or take it may hinge on the need to recover national secrets, or to reveal or conceal past murderous behaviors or indiscretions. Judges have ruled to take feeding tubes out, as well as to put them back in. Every one of the above positions has ethical relevance. There is little right and wrong in the PVS arena.

It takes about two weeks to die of dehydration (nutrition isn't the issue). Once a feeding tube comes out, it may not be possible to replace it after seventy-two hours because the opening (and tube tract through the abdominal wall) closes.

Talk about conflict.

Acceptable criteria for brain death include:

- Clinical signs of irreversible brain death as determined by a neurologist or other physician and confirmed by apnea tests (a bedside test that proves the patient cannot breathe spontaneously, that is, without the ventilator)
- Electroencephalogram (EEG) that shows no brain activity
- Special x-ray dye studies (cerebral angiography, CT angiography, MRA) that proves there is either no or inadequate cerebral blood flow

Also, the cause of death must be known. A massive head injury, massive intracerebral hemorrhage, brain anoxia (prolonged exposure to lack of oxygen for whatever reason), or an incurable brain tumor is seldom survived. Organs may be salvaged for transplantation if adequate ventilation and drug support of the heart have been maintained.

Uniformly Accepted Bedside Criteria For Brain Death

Patient must meet all criteria.

- There is no evidence the victim was exposed to toxic substances or suffered from metabolic illness.
- The cause of brain damage is known.
- The condition is considered irreversible (no known treatment is available).
- The victim will not breathe spontaneously with severe artificial elevations in blood carbon dioxide levels to stimulate the brain's breathing centers.
- The victim does not react to painful stimulation.
- The victim does not show any spontaneous movement.
- There are no gag, cough, or corneal reflexes.
- The victim's body temperature is normal.

A previously healthy person who suffers massive brain damage or is brain dead by the above criteria may be an organ or tissue donor if he or she is:

- Between the ages of newborn and seventy.
- Free of systemic infection and transmissible diseases, including cancer (except a primary brain tumor).
- No history of drug abuse or risky behavior that would make HIV infection a possibility.

As compared to organ donation, tissues such as corneas, bone, bone marrow, or skin may be removed and placed into a recipient patient after all vital functions in the donor have ceased. Whole organs require adequate *perfusion*, a continuous supply of oxygenated blood, and will tolerate only twenty or thirty minutes of what doctors call warm ischemia time (diminished oxygen delivery). After that length of time, proper function of the organ cannot be assured.

Tissues, on the other hand, may be used twelve hours after death if the body is not refrigerated, and up to twenty-four hours following death if the body was refrigerated within four hours of the patient's demise. In 1994, seven percent of donated kidneys were discarded. This number increased to ten percent in 1998. And only fifty to fifty-five percent of kidneys were accepted by the first transplant center. The reasons for refusal include organ quality, size, weight, donor's age, and positive serologic (blood) tests for infections.

Since 1992, a new patient in need of an organ has been added to the national waiting list every twenty minutes. In 1999, sixty-five hundred people died in the United States while waiting for an organ transplant. Another 100,000 potential transplant candidates die before they were placed on a waiting list! Only about ten to fifteen thousand organs are donated yearly.

Who Becomes an Organ Donor?

We've talked about patients who have been declared brain dead as appropriate organ and tissue donors. These patients are managed in the ICU with complete vital function support, including ventilation, blood pressure support, and kidney support (including dialysis), as well as intensive nursing care. At times, they are referred to as HBCDs—*heart-beating cadaver donors*. It was long hoped this pool of donors would grow, but instead it shrank and became stable at about ten thousand donors a year.

What other source of organs is available? The following is a source list for organs and tissue:

- Heart-beating cadaver donor
- Non-heart-beating cadaver donor
- Living, related donor
- Anencephalic ("no brain") infant
- Animals

To date, artificial organs (e.g., a mechanical heart) have been used successfully only for temporary support while the patient awaits a donor organ. Kidney dialysis is the obvious exception.

Controversy surrounds the issue of using anencephalic infants as donors, but it is unquestionable that infants and children are dying because of a lack of transplantable organs—just like adults. It's a shame, because anencephalic children cannot have conscious, sentient lives, and their parents can and should make the gift of an organ for other kids in need. This topic will be addressed in the section on transplant ethics.

Non-heart-beating cadaver donors are another matter. This could be a fascinating topic for the clever writer. After a traditional cardiac arrest with the patient's life ending because heart function ceased—our classical definition of death—organs may be salvaged. The problem is warm ischemia time. How long will these organs continue to work after they stop receiving oxygenated blood?

The issue becomes one of redefining terminal care and death itself. If you want someone's kidneys, do you ask the doctor to keep the patient comfortable with morphine? Perhaps a little more comfortable than she is even though she hasn't twitched in a day? Extra morphine that just happens to cut off her life a day or so early making her kidneys available?

The Double Effect

When morphine or other opioids (narcotics) are given to patients in pain or with breathing distress at the end of life, the drug may, in fact, depress the patient's breathing. Thus, morphine has a "double effect." It's unavoidable if you use the drug. The querulous question arises: if you treat the patient's pain, and if you inject enough morphine, aren't you also shortening their life, if not outright killing them?

The ethical resolution of this issue hinges on *intent*. If you give small, incremental doses of morphine that are just enough to assure comfort, *even if you foresee death as a consequence*, as long as your intent is to relieve suffering, the resulting quicker death is acceptable. But if you give a huge morphine dose with the intent of "getting it over with," you are intentionally causing death.

The second treatment is unethical at the least. At the most, it's murder.

This arena lends itself to a fairly narrow interpretation in the world of palliative care. Doctors know their intent and they understand how to alert families to the potential consequences of pain relief in the terminally ill patient. Families may request a compassionate resolution to prolonged suffering.

Or not.

In your story, the family members may disagree. Sis calls her father a murderer for requesting more sedation for Mom. The doctors receive conflicting requests from different family members. Someone sneaks in and . . .

The dilemma is real, topical, and, therefore, in need of ethical exploration through fiction.

The recently dead donors bring up several issues:

- How does the doctor behave in controlling the dying process?
- What does the doctor tell the patient who is considering foregoing life-sustaining care?
- Should doctors insert special catheters to preserve kidneys, for example, *before* asking the family of a victim of near-certain death if they consent to donation? (It's being done.)
- Should doctors immediately take the recently dead body to the operating room for organ removal to decrease warm ischemia time if the patient and family consented before death?

The most commonly transplanted organs are:

- Kidneys
- Liver
- Heart
- Lungs

The most commonly transplanted tissues are:

- Corneas
- Skin
- Heart valves
- Ligaments
- Iliac bone (hipbone pieces)
- Ribs
- Cartilage
- Saphenous veins

What about *legal* considerations?

Many ethical issues surround transplant surgery and the procurement of organs. As was mentioned, the availability of organs doesn't match the actual demand by needy patients. It's a matter of coordinating what's available with the demand. It's all enmeshed in the dilemma of getting past emotional and religious arguments against proceeding with organ donation.

Interestingly, the legal channels for organ donation are wide open.

The Uniform Anatomical Gift Act (UAGA)

Actually, two UAGAs appeared in the medical literature in the latter half of the twentieth century. The last Act confirms the propriety of people over eighteen years of age donating organs or tissue for transplantation in the event of catastrophic illness. The potential donor may make his wishes known by filling out a donor card, having a notation placed on his driver's license, or creating a document such as a living will or advanced directive. Unfortunately, these documents are *frequently* ignored by families.

The Act also allows other famly members to make the donation on behalf of the injured patient. The following family members may grant permission in this order of priority:

1. Spouse
2. Adult son or daughter
3. Either parent
4. Adult brother or sister
5. Legal guardian
6. Person responsible for disposal of the body

In many states, laws exist that require doctors to request organ donation. Of course, the family isn't required to comply, but the request must be made. The mandatory notification of families about a potential donation arose because of the desperate need for organs. Opportunities for organ donation are wasted every day. With improvements in immunosuppression and new drugs becoming available, the missing ingredient in transplantation became opportunity.

The federal government got into the act in 1972 when amendments to the Social Security Act (End-Stage Renal Program) allowed reimbursement by Medicare to needy kidney failure patients for dialysis as well as for kidney transplants. Twelve years later, the National Organ Transplant Act was passed, providing financial assistance to regional organ procurement organizations as well as to a National Organ Procurement and Transplant Network.

Strict standards of care, as well as "required request" protocols, were established by the Omnibus Budget Reconciliation Act. This meant hospitals were obligated to take measures to identify potential donors and inform families of their options in this regard.

So far, pretty interesting. Your "plot brain" should be firing impulses to your cortex with untold possibilities.

There's a lot more to come.

A Short, Short Course on Transplant Biology

Transplant surgeons are experts on (among many other aspects of surgery) anatomy and immunology. For example, kidneys as well as the liver have numerous variations in their structure and blood supply. Organ size, shape (liver), arterial, and venous supply all determine how the organ will be positioned and perhaps where in the body. An *orthotopic* transplant is one placed in the same location as the original. A *heterotopic* kidney, by comparison, is often placed in the pelvis where the renal arteries are sutured to the iliac arteries instead of the aorta. The bony pelvic bowl also provides some protection for the kidney. The surgeon must be prepared to deal with the vagaries of congenital vascular anomalies, as well as potential confounding problems with the donated organ.

The real challenge comes from the immune system. A few pointers will do. When you hear of donors being "matched," it refers primarily to the ABO blood type system and the HLA tissue typing system. The HLA antigens are called Class I. Along with Class II antigens (T-cells, B-cells, monocytes, macrophages, etc.), they serve to differentiate the body as self compared to non-self. Anything not part of the body's own tissues is rejected, hence the need for *immunosuppression*.

A number of drugs make up the transplant surgeons bag of tricks to keep the recipient's immune system from destroying the kidney, liver, lung, heart, or small intestine. To reduce boredom and frustration, I will give you the names of the common drugs and leave it at that. They are (from the most commonly used to the least used) corticosteroids (prednisone), azathioprine, cyclosporine, anti-thymocyte globulin, and OKT3. When they don't work, one of four types of rejection may occur:

- *Hyperacute rejection* – occurs in the operating room as the organ is being transplanted and perfused for the first time with the recipient's blood; it's caused by recipient pre-formed humoral antibodies to ABO and HLA antigen; treatment is immediate removal of the transplant
- *Accelerated acute rejection* – occurs 7-10 days post-transplant; it may be caused by humoral antibodies or T-cell mediated; treatment includes corticosteroids and OKT3
- *Acute rejection* – occurs weeks to months post-transplant; it's caused by cell-mediated antigen; treatment is corticosteroids and OKT3
- *Chronic rejection* – occurs months to years after transplantation; may be humoral and/or cell-mediated; re-transplant or nothing

The Process of Obtaining Organs for Donation

Like a good story, organ transplantation is initiated by a good beginning, possesses a carefully orchestrated middle, and culminates with a flawless end. Each part of the process demands teamwork. Each of the four steps involved is discussed to provide you with "points of entry" for your story; that is, you'll see where conflict may arise in the continuum of organ transplantation.

Identification of a Potential Organ Donor:
The Process of Referral

The process begins at the bedside when a member of the hospital staff—the trauma surgeon, in our case—evaluates a patient, usually in the intensive care unit, and mentions for the first time that survival may not be possible. If the brain death and other criteria mentioned above have been met, or are close to being met, the patient is considered a potential candidate for organ donation. The hospital staff then contacts the regional Organ Procurement Organization (OPO), and this starts the process.

A *procurement coordinator* goes to the hospital and evaluates the potential donor. This individual is usually a physician's assistant or a registered nurse with special training through the American Board of Transplant Coordinators. Depending on the procedures worked out in a particular hospital, the family may be approached either by a physician who is trained as a requestor or by the OPO coordinator. This individual must compassionately and objectively explain to the next of kin the process of donation and be sensitive to their feelings. When the records have been thoroughly reviewed and the appropriateness of a donation confirmed, the next step is taken.

The Process of Obtaining Consent

Once the family accepts the idea that their loved one is dead, only then is mention made of a donation. The procurement coordinator will discuss options. These, the family is informed, include the potential for considering the donation of transplantable organs as a gift. If acceptable to the family, consent forms are filled out. The discussions include what organs and tissues may be donated, as well as the general organization of national recipient waiting lists. If the victim died under questionable conditions or if there are legal questions about the death to be considered, the coroner's office or the local medical examiner must be contacted for clearance.

Evaluation of the Potential Donor and Maintenance of Life (Organ) Support

The procurement coordinator next reviews the chart for specific information about the donor's past medical history, searching particularly for anything that might exclude the patient from making the donation. Indications for donation have recently been expanded, and even some people with diabetes and hypertension may donate organs. Studies show that kidneys from donors between the ages of sixty to seventy-four may be successfully transplanted with a one year graft survival of over ninety percent. Also, once brain death criteria have been met for organ donors, the donor's heart and lung functions are supported and the patient is evaluated for, and must be clear of, metastatic cancer (spread throughout the body) and systemic infection.

Several tests are then performed, including ABO blood typing. CBC (complete blood count), blood chemistries, HIV screening, hepatitis screening, syphilis screening, screening for cytomegalovirus, blood and urine cultures, and special tests to assess adequate function of the organs to be transplanted. The national computer is accessed for a potential recipient, and then the major task shifts to managing the donor until organ and tissue removal occurs.

The *interval problems* seen while waiting for the transplant team include:

- *Hypovolemia*—too little volume or body fluid because patient was "dried out" to improve brain function; must now be corrected and maintained by continuous IV fluid replacement and cardiac drugs such as dopamine. Brain dead patients get *diabetes insipidus*—a loss of a water and salt conserving hormone—which aggravates body fluid losses.
- *Hypothermia*—loss of brainstem centers; may result in a serious drop in body temperature. Warming devices may be used.
- *Clotting problems*—dead brain tissue may release substances into the circulatory system that cause clotting factors to misfire; results in diffuse bleeding.
- *High serum potassium*—results from breakdown of cells; may seriously affect heart function. Easily corrected with medications.

All of these problems must be identified, treated, or prevented by the procurement coordinator until organs and tissue are removed.

The Recovery of Organs and Tissue

When the transplant team arrives at the donor patient's hospital, the donor is transported to the operating room with full monitoring of vital functions (vital signs) carried out on the way. This chore is assumed by the donor hospital staff and includes an anesthesiologist, scrub tech, and circulating nurse. Intravenous fluid and appropriate drugs are given to maintain circulatory function until the aorta is cross-clamped and special organ-preserving solutions are administered by the transplant team. Mechanical ventilation is stopped at this point.

Organ removal occurs first. Then, tissue is recovered after all support has been discontinued. The body is closed just as it would have been if the surgical procedures performed to take organs and tissues had not followed a life-ending pronouncement. The body may then be sent to the funeral home if no autopsy is mandated by local medical authorities. There is no reason not to have an open casket.

The Process of Performing an Organ Transplant

Before the recovery phase is put behind us, there is a phenomenon called the *Lazarus sign* with which you should be familiar. To help the transplant team, muscle relaxation is induced by anesthesia with special drugs. Despite that, spinal reflexes may persist. The "dead" donor may develop gooseflesh, and the arms may move, flexing and extending at the elbow. This motion is disconcerting to those present and may be quite dramatic, as the donor, at times, seems to be reaching for the endotracheal tube in the throat at precisely the time when all support has been stopped.

Try that in your OR scene.

Once the organs have been recovered and placed in appropriate transport containers, they are taken to the recipient hospital (anywhere in the United States or Canada) and transplanted. Airplane travel is most common for long distances, and the organs are accompanied by a member of the transplant team.

The recipient has usually been brought to the operating room while the organs are in transit from the donor hospital. When the organ arrives, it is evaluated for size, function, and other technical aspects before being sewn into place. Arteries, veins, and other body tubes are reconnected and the organ observed for function. Immunosuppression is begun, and the recipient's blood is tested for the appropriate chemicals that reflect proper organ function.

It's a technical chore from here on in, and only a few glitches might still occur. Prewritten protocols are used to determine what drugs are given and how often. The major concern in the immediate post-transplant period is acute rejection of the organ.

As a writer, you should know that the treasured organ has been accidentally placed in preservative fluid instead of saline on at least one occasion, instantly destroying the organ. More than one organ has been dropped on the floor. And so it goes.

Transplant Ethics

Transplant ethics attempt to address the enormous disparity between the need for organs and the current supply. Since the first kidney transplant was performed by Doctor Joseph E. Murray in 1955 between identical twins, manipulation of the immune system has become commonplace and has permitted survival rates for transplanted organs to rise, for example, to the ninety percent survival rate for kidneys. But nagging ethical questions and personal belief systems persist in limiting the availability of transplantable organs. Organ allocations are often made on the basis of how long the candidate has been waiting, prognosis, age, and if the candidate is a parent.

The discussions to follow represent the major areas of concern in transplant ethics. A fundamental shift in the way Americans view death and dying is needed to overcome resistance to organ donation. Our youth-oriented society withdraws in horror whenever death peeks out of its well-crafted cultural cave.

Serious writers ought to explore transplant ethical dilemmas. Fiction may be the best way to get at the truth. As has often been said, non-fiction tells the truth to arrive at deeper truths, while fiction writers lie to get to the truth.

"Presumed Consent"

Cadaveric donors are those we've been discussing whose organs are procured immediately following death. The severely head-injured trauma victim often becomes a donor candidate. The stumbling block that surfaces repeatedly is an uninformed family that does not know the patient's wishes. The most ethically sound policy mandates consent from the family for organ procurement when death seems imminent. The idea of "presumed consent" refers to the approach where the patient is presumed to approve of a donation, unless he or she has explicitly stated a position to the contrary. Other countries such as Spain and Belgium have successfully increased their organ donations with this approach. This process stands on less solid ethical ground.

Living Donors

Ethical concerns abound when surgery is proposed to remove part or all of an organ from a living donor. Medicine's most highly valued ethical principle is "Do No Harm." So the altruistic satisfaction a living related donor may experience must be weighed against the intrinsic risks of major surgery that would otherwise not be performed. Improvements in immunosuppression now make it possible for what Doctor Norman Levinsky calls "emotionally related donors" (spouses, friends) to donate a kidney or part of their liver. Levinsky refers to the University of Minnesota's transplant program, where Matas and his colleagues seek highly motivated donors to make "nondirected donations." These donors are screened for their sanity. It is the ultimate gift, for example, if a liver is transplanted because it is life-saving (whereas kidney transplantation is life-prolonging because dialysis is an alternative treatment choice). The death rate from nephrectomy (kidney removal) is 0.03%, while the mortality rate for partial liver removal is 0.2% (two out of every one thousand partial liver donors will die in the donation process). Thus, organ donations from the living may be related or unrelated, and the motivation may be intensely personal (donating to save one's child) or purely altruistic.

The death rate for children placed on waiting lists for a liver, for whatever diagnosis, is fifty percent. Half of all kids waiting for a liver die. At least two approaches are now used. First, a small segment of a living adult donor's liver is used to compensate for size differences, and second, a cadaver liver is "split" to provide two specimens for two kids.

Should Donors Be Compensated?

The traditional position on compensation for donated organs in the 1980's was a strong stance against any form of payment. The illegal trade in organs has been well publicized since Robin Cook's original medical thriller, *Coma,* raised the issue. Ethical debates now rage over whether or not compensation may be a reasonable consideration. Surely, it says something about shifts in the ethical foundation of our society.

Usually, cultural and religious convictions are the major deterrents in keeping patients and their families from making a donation. It is remarkable that money might very well override one's presumably tightly held moral and ethical beliefs about organ transplantation. One would think the issue of compensation would be less staunchly resisted in a capitalistic society where just about everything (and everybody) is for sale. In a country where hurricane disasters motivate survivors to sell bottled water at exorbitant prices, surely the sale of a life-saving organ ought to at least be entertained. This issue will not go gently into that tumultuous bleak night.

Should Patients With A Rejected Organ Receive A Second (Or Third) Transplant?

As with all surgical specialties, there are bad outcomes with organ transplantation. It may be a matter of a poor match, a compromised organ, or a technical difficulty. Sometimes organs are removed because of a technical error. Both the transplant surgeon and the institution have significant vested interests in downplaying bad results. Large transplant programs compete for valuable, shared organs. Often patients with bad transplant results are aggressively treated. So the question is: How should a failed transplant be pursued?

If a recipient gets another organ – recognizing that each available organ is needed by thousands of people on waiting lists around the country – then someone else is robbed of their chance at improving their life quality or survival. If the first transplanted organ failed, will the second fail as well? Does the surgeon and hospital's reputation get in the way? These are truly bothersome and complex questions of equity and efficiency of organ allocation. The United Network of Organ Sharing uses a point system to designate who will receive newly available organs. But a better evidence-based organ allocation strategy is needed.

What's New and What's Still A Problem In Organ Transplantation?

Thousands of lives are saved yearly around the world by organ transplantation. But too many useable organs are buried each year, healthy organs that could have saved a life or improved the quality of a life. Only a few alternatives to living and cadaver organ donations are possible. Thus, the following ethical dilemmas remain in the public domain and may serve as jump-off issues for writers:

- *Xenotransplantation* – the use of non-human organs, especially primate organs, has been done, and could serve as a renewable supply of organs; to work on a large scale, this would require "animal farms," and would also raise the ethical concern for the proper treatment of animals; recall the past public outcry when a "baboon" heart was placed in an infant.

- *Fetal tissue transplants* – the treatment of Parkinson's disease may include the implantation of fetal tissue in the brain; to achieve neuronal reconstruction, molecular and gene therapy approaches may be more "targeted." Still, is the use of fetal tissue effective and ethical?

- *Fair distribution of organs* – in the U.S., African Americans and other less dominant cultural groups have traditionally received less and poorer medical care (as documented in numerous medical journals); organ transplant is another area of inequity for some cultural groups; on the other hand, these groups donate fewer organs than the more numerous (dominant) cultural groups; also, should destructive behavior (alcoholism, smoking, drug abuse) be a reason to not receive an organ donation? Will an alcoholic who killed his native liver destroy the "new" liver donated by a person or family whose expectation is that it will save a life?

- *The anencephalic newborn* – some babies are born with minimal brain tissue; the cerebral cortex, the conscious part of the brain that makes us human, is missing; these children therefore cannot feel, think, see, hear, or function in any way; these newborns have transplantable organs; they can save the lives of other children destined to die, children with fully formed brains; can there be an ethical objection to this process? There is, but one wonders why.

The end point of body trauma is, hopefully, a survivor with minimal physical and emotional scars. But uncontrolled impact may terminate in death. As you have learned throughout this book, many opportunities present themselves for returning the trauma victim to good health.

Appendix I. A Typical Trauma Case

Coming home in his pick-up from a night in the local bars, E.J., a 56-year-old white male, rams a parked car going about 40 m.p.h. The driver's door is jammed and it takes the paramedics and the police a long time to extricate the victim. There was no windshield "starring" (evidence of direct contact) or steering wheel deformity. When he arrived in the ER, he was complaining of left-sided chest and abdominal pain. He was alert and oriented with a BP of 100/70, pulse of 110, and a respiratory rate of 28. Chest and abdominal abrasions formed a seat-belt sign. He was talking with a cervical collar lying on a backboard.

The paramedics' "run sheet" shows the accident occurring at 1:00 a.m. Extraction was completed by 1:50 a.m. He arrived in the Emergency Room at 2:18 a.m.

The trauma surgeon, Ernesto Ruiz, noted E.J. had no breath sounds on the left (check the "dirty dozen" in Chapter 7), and as part of the primary survey had his resident, Chad Lee, laterally insert a number 36 French chest tube in the fifth intercostal space. Air rushed out, confirming a tension pneumothorax. E.J.'s skin was cool and pale, with palpable pulses. The nurse started two #16 gauge IV lines in his arms and placed a mask on his face with 100% O2. A Foley catheter was inserted into his bladder to monitor urine output. Multiple labs are drawn (blood work), including a blood count, blood sugar, pancreatic enzymes, liver functions, kidney functions, a toxicology screen, and cross and type for eight units of blood. His oxygen saturation was 94% and his Glasgow Coma Score was 15. The nurses removed his clothing and the trauma surgeon completed his primary survey. No bleeding or life-threatening injuries were apparent, although E.J. was in a mild shock state.

Ernesto's secondary survey revealed a distended belly with enlargement of his liver and spleen. The remainder of the physical exam was negative. Further questioning reveals a history of alcohol abuse and depression. He smoked two packs a day and was unemployed. He lives with his mother.

A chest x-ray revealed an expanded left lung. Chad performed a FAST ultrasound exam (Chapter 8). It demonstrated fluid in the abdomen. At this point, his blood pressure dipped into the 90/70 range despite the administration of two liters of saline solution. A CT scan of his abdomen was performed. While getting his CT scan in radiology down the hall from the ER, his blood pressure dropped to 80/60 and his pulse jumped up to 130. Chad notified the operating room. A multiple trauma is coming down.

3:10 a.m.

The operating room buzzes with activity (Chapter 4). A large central venous "triple lumen" IV is placed in the jugular vein for the rapid administration of fluids and blood. Charlie Bricker from anesthesia applies an EKG monitoring leads and inserts an arterial line for direct blood pressure readout. He intubates E.J. and anesthetizes him with a balanced combination of IV drugs and gases. E.J. is prepped with a special iodoform-alcohol solution from nipples to knees, and sterile drapes are applied.

Charlie, the anesthesiologist, says, "Guys, his pressure's in the toilet."

Ernesto Ruiz nods to his chief surgical resident. "Go ahead, Chad."

Chad accepts a scalpel from the scrub tech and makes an incision from the man's breastbone to his pubis. Blood wells up from the belly cavity. They see a liver laceration. The liver is enlarged and nodular – booze signs. They pack the belly and wait.

Charlie Bricker pumps in blood and starts intravenous neosynephrine to bolster the sagging blood pressure. When the pressure gets over a hundred systolic, the anesthesiologist signals for the surgical team to go ahead. "What you got so far?" Charlie asks.

"Blood," says the resident. "A shitload of blood. His liver's cirrhotic like we thought."

"What about his spleen?" Charlie presses.

The trauma surgeon glances over the pinned up drapes separating the anesthesia personnel from the sterile field. "For Christ sakes, Charlie. Give us a chance."

Slowly, they peel away the blood-soaked lap pads. Sequentially, they examine the four abdominal quadrants. There's blood everywhere. In the left upper quadrant the spleen is mush. It's shattered, a grade four injury.

"Bagged his spleen," says the resident. "It's outta here."

The surgeons work in silence, clamping the splenic blood vessels, tying, clipping. After awhile Ernesto hands the scrub tech the specimen. It looks like an eggplant that got run over by a lawn mower. She places the ragged organ in a stainless steel bowl and hands it off to the circulating nurse.

The wall clock reads 4:26 a.m.

"Guys?" There is an edge to the anesthesiologist's voice.

"Spleen's out," says the resident. "Pressure up?"

"Down," Charlie answers. "You got something else going on you missed?"

Ernesto Ruiz takes over. He places a retractor against the right side of the incision and tells the resident to pull. Blood pours out from beneath the liver. It takes only a moment to identify a huge laceration at the entrance to the liver, the portal hepatitis. The trauma surgeon reaches into the belly and squeezes the huge artery, portal vein, and bile duct entering the liver to staunch the hemorrhage.

"You doing a Pringle?" asks the resident.

"Here, you do it." Ernesto Ruiz removes his hand and the resident slides his into the right upper quadrant. He grabs the suction and blood floods the tubing and the glass jars at his feet.

They do this for a long time. The bleeding slows, but does not stop.

Chad Lee squeezes the liver. Ernesto then attempts to place huge chromic sutures mounted on special blunt liver needles. The hemorrhage continues. "Shit," he says softly to no one.

"Give us a bunch of lap pads, please," the resident says. They pack the abdominal cavity again. They wait for twenty minutes as the anesthesiologist administers more IV fluid and hangs two more units of blood.

"Pressures sixty over zip, guys," Charlie says, and points overhead. "I'm starting dopamine and calling for more blood."

"How many units has he received so far?" asks Ernesto Ruiz.

"Eighteen."

"What's your estimated blood loss?"

"Ten liters."

The senior surgeon taps the drapes with the suction tip. "We've replaced the poor bastard's entire blood volume, twice."

Chad scoops up a handful of blood. He says, "No clots."

"You warming the blood, Charlie?" Ernesto asks. They had given a lot of unmatched blood up front. They had pumped it in fast, cold.

"Trying to, Ernie. But we're too far behind to delay giving it."

It's 5:46 a.m.

"We're going to pack and get out," declares Ernesto Ruiz, the trauma surgeon. "We've got to warm him up and try again later. I can't control the bleeder. Probably his IVC."

The circulating nurse enters the room cradling four units of blood. She says, "This is all they've got. Oh, and blood bank says there's an upper GI bleeder in the ER. Same blood type."

The surgeons repack the belly and close only the abdominal skin with towel clamps. E.J. is placed on a stretcher with a huge abdominal dressing, intubated, and ventilated with a bag by Charlie Bricker. They transfer him to the intensive care unit. E.J.'s core temperature is raised with warm IV fluid and warm saline is injected into his bladder through the Foley catheter. He is acidotic, a condition which is corrected with bicarbonate and further fluid resuscitation.

His abdomen swells. His blood counts drop.

In desperation, E.J. is given a radically new treatment for his non-clotting blood: recombinant Factor VIIa. It's an artificially created clotting factor and it's expensive. Factor VIIa has not been used in trauma patients.

E.J. is given Factor VIIa and aggressive standard treatment in the ICU.

The interventional radiologist who performs a study called arteriography – injection of dye into arteries – is notified. He may be able to inject a drug or coils into the hepatic artery and slow the liver's bleeding. Or E.J. may have to return to the OR.

His vital signs slip away from the intensivists. E.J.'s family stays at the bedside as his condition worsens. The intensivists, along with Doctors Ruiz and Lee, hold a family conference. They explain that they have nothing left to offer E.J.

His wife and two sons ask for time. An hour later, they meet with the doctors and ICU nurses at the bedside and request comfort measures only. They are present when E.J. dies.

The family refuses to grant an autopsy. He's already suffered enough, they say.

A beeper goes off. Chad Lee excuses himself.

The family leaves the hospital in tears. Someone mentions getting a lawyer.

When Ernesto Ruiz checks with his resident, Chad explains, "There's a stab wound on the way."

ETA, ten minutes...

Appendix II. Trauma Ethics Rounds

An eighty-seven-year-old woman under your care is dying of lung failure after being struck by a pick-up truck at a pedestrian crossing. She's depressed and wants to die. Recently taken off of a ventilator in the ICU and having been given a feeding tube, she has marginal respiratory reserve on a surgical floor where she was transferred following placement of the feeding tube. The tube is malfunctioning and she is in pain from a broken hip, which is due to be repaired in the near future.

Her husband wants her tube feedings stopped and her opioids increased. Both daughters disagree with Dad and want her feedings pushed in order to get her to orthopedic surgery and out of the hospital. One daughter does not want her mother to receive all the opioids ordered by the doctor, for fear of depressing her breathing. The other daughter and husband can't stand to see her suffer.

You are the covering doctor and have accepted your fellow surgeon's sign-out, at which time your colleague told you she encouraged the family to pursue aggressive nutritional support, insist on having the hip nailed soon, and avoid over-medicating the patient. You disagree, but say nothing.

Points of Discussion:
1. **Withholding** an intervention (refraining)
2. **Withdrawing** an intervention (acting)
3. **Prognosis**
4. **Double effect** – proportionality (euthanasia v. palliation), intentional/foreseen outcome
5. **Voluntary cessation of eating and drinking**
6. **Terminal sedation**

Bibliography

Books

Adams, Brian, *The Medical Implications of Karate Blows*. Canbury, NJ: A.S. Barnes and Company, 1969.

Caras, Rogers, *Venomous Animals of the World*. Englewood Cliffs, NJ: Prentice-Hall, 1974.

Chusid, Joseph G., *Correlative Neuroanatomy and Functional Neurology*, Los Altos, CA: Lange Medical Publications, 1985.

Clemente, C., *Anatomy: A Regional Atlas of the Human Body*. Malvern, PA: Lea and Febiger, 1987.

Advanced Trauma Life Support For Doctors Student Course Manual, Seventh Edition. United states of America, First Impression, 2004.

Resources for the Optimal Care of the Injured. Chicago: American College of Surgeons, 1993.

DePalma, A.F. *The Management of Fractures and Dislocations: an Atlas*. Philadelphia: W.B. Saunders Company, 1963.

Edmonds, C.; C. Lowry; and J. Pennefather. *Diving and Subaquatic Medicine*. Mosman, N.S.W., Australia: Diving Medical Centre Publication, 1976.

Lambertsen, C.J., ed. *Underwater Physiology V*. Bethesda, MD: Federation of American Societies for Experimental Biology, 1976.

Ludwig, S., and A.E. Kornberg, eds. *Child Abuse: A Medical Reference*. 2nd ed. New York: Churchill Livingstone, 1992.

National Safety Council. *Accident Facts*. *Chicago*: National Safety Council, 1994.

Newton, Michael. *Armed and Dangerous: A Writer's Guide to Weapons*. Cincinnati: Writer's Digest Books, 1990.

Northeast Organ Procurement Organization and Tissue Bank, "Protocol for Organ and Tissue Donation." Hartford, CT, 1994.

Sabiston, David C. *Textbook of Surgery: The Biological Basis of Modern Surgical Practice*. Philadelphia: W.B. Saunders, 1977.

Scarry, Elaine. The Body in Pain – the Making and Unmaking of the World. Oxford University Press, New York, 1985.

Shephard, Roy J. *The Yearbook of Sports Medicine*. St. Louis: Mosby Yearbook, 1986-1995.

Greenfield, Lazar J. *Surgery – scientific principles and practice*. Philadelphia. Lippincott Williams and Wilkins, 2001.

Surgical Clinics of North America. Philadelphia: W. B. Saunders Company, 1974-1994.

Thorek, P. *Anatomy in Surgery*. Philadelphia: J.B. Lippincott Company, 1951.

Tintinalli, J.; R. Krome; and E. Ruiz, eds. *Emergency Medicine: A Comprehensive Study Guide*. 3rd ed. New York: McGraw-Hill, 1992.

Wingate, Anne. *Scene of the Crime: A Writer's Guide to Crime Scene Investigations*. Cincinnati: Writer's Digest Books, 1992.

Wilson, Keith. *Cause of Death: A Writer's Guide to Death, Murder and Forensic Medicine*. Cincinnati: Writer's Digest Books, 1992.

Articles

Bezruchka, S. "High Altitude Medicine." *Medical Clinics of North America*, vol. 76, no. 6 (November 1992): 1481-95.

Chen, M.K.; G.H. Burgess; and R.J. Howard. "Surgical Management of Shark Attack Injuries: A Review of Nine Cases." *Contemporary Surgery*, vol. 46 no. 5 (May 1995).

Dupre, A.R., et. al. "Sexual Assault." *Obstetrical and Gynecological* Review 48, no. 9 (1993): 640-48.

Elliot, B.A., and M.M. Johnson. "Domestic Violence in a Primary Care Setting: Patterns and Prevalence." *Archives of Family Medicine* 4, no.2 (February 1995): 113-19.

Guidry, H.M. "Childhood Sexual Abuse: Role of the Family Physician". *American Family Physician* 51, no 2 (February 1, 1995): 407-14.

Murmam, D. "Child Sexual Abuse". *Obstetrics and Gynecology Clinics of North America* 19, no. 1 (1992); 193-207.

Rew, L., and P. Shirejian. "Sexually Abused Adolescents: Conceptualization of Sexual Trauma and Nursing Interventions." *Journal of Psychosocial Nursing* 31, no. 12 (1993): 29-33.

Ruckman, L.M. "Victims of Rape: The Physician's Role in Treatment." *Current Opinion in Obstetrics and Gynecology* 5 (1993): 721-25.

Wiedman, M. "High Altitude Retinal Hemorrhage." *Arch Ophthalmology* 93 (1975): 401.

Glossary

ACCIDENT — The term used by many people when describing an unexpected, injurious event and by those compiling motor vehicle statistics to denote what is also called a crash; implies an uncontrolled adverse event, a concept not universally accepted.

ACCLIMATION — Body changes that occur in response to an environmental or body challenge, such as cold, heat, exercise or low oxygen levels.

CEREBRAL EDEMA — Swelling of brain tissue in response to an insult, such as low oxygen levels or direct trauma. Because of restricted space in the skull, compression of the brain and cranial nerves may produce severe symptoms.

CORTEX — Outer rind of specific organs, such as the brain, bone, kidney and adrenal gland. The cerebral cortex is the conscious part of the brain.

DEAD VICTIMS — Those not addressed in this book, including victims of decapitation, delayed recovery (decomposed body), massive fatal blunt or penetrating trauma or sudden death from any trauma, or victims demonstrating rigor mortis.

DEBRIDEMENT — The surgical process of cleaning up destroyed or dead (necrotic) tissue; usually involves sharply cutting away discolored tissue with a scalpel or scissors and forceps (tweezers).

DISABILITY — Loss of specific body function and ability to perform occupational procedures and tasks of daily living that are considered normal for the average human.

DISLOCATION — The temporary or permanent displacement of a structure from its normal location. Joint dislocation refers to the loss of normal alignment of the joint surfaces and may be partial or complete.

ENVENOMATION — The introduction of poison into tissue from a species that contains venom and a mechanism making this possible upon contact or attack. Snake and insect bites are typical, and degrees of envenomation determine methods of treatment and outcome.

FRACTURE — A break or discontinuity in solid tissue. Usually used in reference to bones, a fracture may be simple, compound (open wound), comminuted (multiple bone pieces), greenstick (partial, often seen in kids), spiral, transverse, or oblique. Solid organs, such as liver, spleen, and kidneys, are often fractured or disrupted with blunt trauma.

ISCHEMIA — Refers to the condition of lack of blood supply and thus inadequate oxygen delivery to a specific tissue or organ; may involve a whole body part such as a leg from blockage of femoral artery with blood clot (embolus or thrombus) or a segment of intestine for similar reasons; may result from excessive pressure on tissue (anterior compartment syndrome of lower leg).

MENINGES — The three membranes of the brain. Dura mater is the tough outer layer attached to the skull, the subarachnoid is the middle layer (space), while the delicate pia mater lines the brain. Gin-clear cerebrospinal fluid circulates in the subarachnoid space, serving as the brain's waterbed.

MULTIORGAN FAILURE — Progressive loss of function of vital organs (heart, lungs, kidneys and brain) as a result of overwhelming infection or shock.

NECROSIS — Refers to dead tissue from any cause (e.g., necrotic liver).

PERITONITIS — Inflammation and/or infection of the abdominal cavity lining as a result of a perforated stomach, intestine, or diseased organ, such as appendicitis or colitis.

PULMONARY EDEMA — A nonspecific lung response characterized by flooding of air sacs with fluid; may be caused by stimulus such as infection (pneumonia), altitude exposure, heart failure, or blunt chest trauma.

REPLANTATION — The surgical process of replacing an amputated body part following an orderly set of guidelines to attach nerves, arteries, veins, and bones using a microscope.

THORAX — Refers to the chest and its contents, as compared to the term "trunk," which includes the abdomen.

TRIAGE — Refers to the sorting out of multiple injuries according to severity. The concept centers on the idea of priority: Who is in the greatest danger of dying quickly?

UNINTENTIONAL INJURY — Used by public health officials to describe accidents without addressing the issue of whether or not accidents or unintentional injuries are preventable (surveys document most people's belief that injuries and/or accidents are preventable).

Index

Other fabulous Writer Tools from Behler Publications:

A personalized tour of the publishing industry; how the various people who comprise this business think, why they make the decisions they do, and how authors can avoid the pitfalls. The four sections cover every aspect of the industry:

- Interviews by industry professionals
- An inclusive "holy Maalox, Batman!" behind-the-scenes tour of the submission process
- Defining the various types of publishers currently populating the industry
- The writer's survival style guide – complete with a four-part manuscript autopsy and punctuation beerfest.

978-1-933016-34-4
Trade Paperback * $19.95 * 6 x 9 * 380 pages
Also available in ebook
www.behlerpublicatsions.com

"You've been served," is one of the single-most frightening sentences. It opens a can of worms to a legal nightmare that few understand. When your fiction calls for a character to sue someone or be sued and survive the ordeal, this book is should be number one on your docket. Donna Ballman will take you and your characters through the grinding wheels of justice so you can sue and litigate your characters to within an inch of their fictional lives.

978-1-933016-53-5
Trade Paperback * $18.95 * 6 x 9 * 283 pages
Also available in ebook

www.behlerpublicatsions.com